The Mental Philosophy of John Henry Newman

Jay Newman

John Henry Newman's writings in theology, apologetics, history, poetry, and educational theory, among other fields, made him one of the most controversial as well as influential modern Christian thinkers. Central to his religious vision was his innovative and complex "mental philosophy," first sketched out at Oxford during his Anglican years and developed in its most detailed form in his celebrated *Grammar of Assent*. In *The Mental Philosophy of John Henry Newman*, Jay Newman (no relation) presents a careful scrutiny of John Henry Newman's phenomenology of belief and epistemology in the context of the nineteenth-century cleric's major work. He departs from traditional historical and theological approaches to Newman's work on belief and critically examines Newman's contribution in this area from the standpoint of contemporary analytical philosophy.

The study examines the sources, aims, and implications of Newman's philosophical project. While it draws attention to the positive value of Newman's original approach, it also explores the weaknesses and dangers of Newman's main phenomenological and epistemological theories. Jay Newman not only makes a significant original contribution to the field of Newman studies but also provides us with a guide to some of the problems and confusions of the *Grammar of Assent*.

Jay Newman is Professor of Philosophy at the University of Guelph. Among his publications are Foundations of Religious Tolerance *and numerous studies of the philosophical and theological writings of John Henry Newman.*

The
Mental Philosophy
of
John Henry Newman

The
Mental Philosophy
of
John Henry Newman

Jay Newman

Wilfrid Laurier University Press

Canadian Cataloguing in Publication Data

Newman, Jay, 1948-
The mental philosophy of John Henry Newman

Includes bibliographical references and index.
ISBN 0-88920-186-2

1. Newman, John Henry, 1801-1890.   An essay in aid
of a grammar of assent.   2. Faith.   3. Theism.
I. Title.

BX4705.N5N48 1986   233   C86-093263-X

Copyright © 1986

WILFRID LAURIER UNIVERSITY PRESS
Waterloo, Ontario, Canada   N2L 3C5

86 87 88 89 4 3 2 1

Cover design by David Antscherl

Printed in Canada

To my parents, Kate and Louis Newman

Contents

Acknowledgments

Earlier versions of some portions of this book have appeared in journal articles, and I am grateful to the editors and publishers of the peri-
odicals in which they appeared for permitting me to make use of
this material: "Cardinal Newman's 'Factory-Girl Argument'," *Proceedings of the American Catholic Philosophical Association* 46
(1972), 71-78; "Cardinal Newman's Phenomenology of Religious Belief," *Religious Studies* 10 (1974), 129-40 (published by Cambridge
University Press); "Cardinal Newman's Attack on Philosophers,"
Proceedings of the American Catholic Philosophical Association 50
(1976), 196-207; "Newman on the Strength of Beliefs," *Thomist* 51
(January 1977), 131-47; "Cardinal Newman on the Indefectibility of
Certitude," *Laval théologique et philosophique* 34 (February 1978),
15-20; "Newman on Love as the Safeguard of Faith," *Scottish Journal
of Theology* 32 (1979), 139-50 (published by Scottish Academic Press
[Journals] Limited). I am also grateful to the following institutions for
facilitating my research and writing during the academic year 1981-
82: the University of Guelph, which granted me sabbatical leave of
absence for the year; the Social Sciences and Humanities Research
Council of Canada, which granted me a Leave Fellowship for the year;
the University of Birmingham, which conferred on me the status of
Honorary Research Fellow for the period of my visit; and the Oratory
of St Philip Neri, Birmingham, which provided me with liberal access
to documents, books, and papers from its Newman Archives. I am
particularly indebted to Gerard Tracey, Archivist of the Birmingham
Oratory Library. It is with great pleasure that I acknowledge the
generosity and hospitality of my colleagues in the Departments of
Philosophy and Theology at the University of Birmingham, and especially of Leon Pompa, Professor of Philosophy, and John H. Hick, then
H. G. Wood Professor of Theology in that university. Earlier versions
of some portions of this book were read as papers at meetings of the
American Catholic Philosophical Association, the Birmingham University Theology Graduate Seminar, the Manchester University
Theological Society, and the Canadian Theological Society, and I
have benefitted from the critical suggestions made by people in attend-
ance at those sessions. Over the years, I have also benefitted from

conversations about J. H. Newman with various philosophers, theologians, and Newmanists: Leslie Armour, Vincent Blehl, Michael Goulder, H. S. Harris, John H. Hick, Ian T. Ker, Nicholas Lash, Harry Nielsen, John Nota, David Pailin, Lionel Rubinoff, James Sandilands, Eric Steinberg, Joyce Sugg, Stewart Sutherland, Edward Synan, and John W. Yolton. Sandra Howlett provided courteous secretarial assistance. Finally, I am grateful to Linda Biesenthal and Sandra Woolfrey of Wilfrid Laurier University Press, and to R. M. Schoeffel of the University of Toronto Press, for their generous attention to the manuscript and their kindness to the author.

This book has been published with the help of a grant from the Canadian Federation for the Humanities, using funds provided by the Social Sciences and Humanities Research Council of Canada.

Chapter One

Newman's Philosophical Project

1 Two claims about how we come to be certain about things

In his *Essay in Aid of a Grammar of Assent*, the Catholic apologist and controversialist, John Henry Newman, makes two claims that, perhaps more than any other in his writings, serve to encapsulate the main themes of his peculiar mental philosophy:

§ It is plain that formal logical sequence is not in fact the method by which we are enabled to become certain of what is concrete; and it is equally plain... what the real and necessary method is. It is the cumulation of probabilities, independent of each other, arising out of the nature and circumstances of the particular case which is under review; probabilities too fine to avail separately, too subtle and circuitous to be convertible into syllogisms, too numerous and various for such conversion, even were they convertible. (230)[1]

§ Every one who reasons, is his own centre; and no expedient for attaining a common measure of minds can reverse this truth;—but then the question follows, is there any *criterion* of the accuracy of an inference, such as may be our warrant that certitude is rightly elicited in favour of the proposition inferred, since our warrant cannot, as I have said, be scientific? I have already said that the sole and final judgment on the validity of an inference in concrete matter is committed to the personal action of the ratiocinative faculty, the perfection or virtue of which I have called the Illative Sense, a use of the word "sense" parallel to our use of it in "good sense," "common sense," a "sense of beauty," &c.;—and I own I do not see any way to go farther than this in answer to the question. (271)

1 John Henry Newman, *An Essay in Aid of a Grammar of Assent* (Garden City, New York: Image Books, Doubleday, 1955; Notre Dame, Indiana: University of Notre Dame Press, 1979 [1870], 230. Page numbers in the text refer to this recent and most accessible edition of the *Grammar*.

1

For over a century, certain readers of the *Grammar* have felt that these claims are laden with epistemological, phenomenological, psychological, and theological significance; but there has been much disagreement among them about precisely what that significance is.

I do not count myself among John Henry Newman's many admirers. Still, the more I study the *Grammar*, the more I am convinced of the importance and originality of the project it embodies. No reflective person can be unconcerned with the questions of what one ought to believe and how beliefs come to be held; and the *Grammar* is, with good reason, one of the most famous of all philosophical approaches to the subject of belief. But the path to an understanding and proper evaluation of Newman's mental philosophy is strewn with obstacles, and we should not be surprised that most philosophers and theologians have sought their intellectual inspiration elsewhere.

2 Two examples: One secular, one religious

Let us be faithful to the spirit of Newman's project and move immediately from the abstract to the concrete. Newman gives many examples of informal inference and illative judgment, and these two are as helpful as any.

The first, offered to an audience of Britons, is not directly relevant to Newman's apologetical interests:

> We are all absolutely certain, beyond the possibility of doubt, that Great Britain is an island. We give to that proposition our deliberate and unconditional adhesion. There is no security on which we should be better content to stake our interests, our property, our welfare, than on the fact that we are living in an island. We have no fear of any geographical discovery which may reverse our belief. We should be amused or angry at the assertion, as a bad jest, did any one say that we were at this time joined to the main-land in Norway or in France, though a canal was cut across the isthmus. We are as little exposed to the misgiving, "Perhaps we are not on an island after all," as to the question, "Is it quite certain that the angle in a semi-circle is a right angle?" It is a simple and primary truth with us, if any truth is such; to believe it is as legitimate an exercise of assent, as there are legitimate exercises of doubt or of opinion. This is the position of our minds towards our insularity; yet are the arguments producible for it (to use the common expression) in black and white commensurate with this overpowering certitude about it?
>
> Our reasons for believing that we are circumnavigable are such as these:—first, we have been so taught in our childhood, and it is so in all the maps; next, we have never heard it contradicted or questioned, on the contrary, every one whom we have heard speak on the subject of Great Britain, every book we have read, invariably took it for granted; our whole national history, the routine transactions and current events of the country, our social and commercial system, our political relations with foreigners, imply it in one way or another. Numberless facts, or what we

consider facts, rest on the truth of it; no received fact rests on its being otherwise. If there is anywhere a junction between us and the continent, where is it? and how do we know it? is it in the north or in the south? There is a manifest *reductio ad absurdum* attached to the notion that we can be deceived on such a point as this.

However, negative arguments and circumstantial evidence are not all, in such a matter, which we have a right to require. They are not the highest kind of proof possible. Those who have circumnavigated the island have a right to be certain: have we ever ourselves even fallen in with any one who has? And as to the common belief, what is the proof that we are not all of us believing it on the credit of each other? And then, when it is said that every one believes it, and everything implies it, how much comes home to me personally of this "every one" and "every-thing"? The question is, Why do I believe it myself? A living statesman is said to have fancied Demerara an island; his belief was an impression; have we personally more than an impression, if we view the matter argumentatively, a lifelong impression about Great Britain, like the belief, so long and so widely entertained, that the earth was immovable, and the sun careered round it? I am not at all insinuating that we are not rational in our certitude; I only mean that we cannot analyze a proof satisfactorily, the result of which good sense actually guarantees to us. (234-35)

This is probably as straightforward an example as Newman could have given. Consider now a more problematic example, one closer to the heart of the religious apologist:

Montaigne was endowed with a good estate, health, leisure, and an easy temper, literary tastes, and a sufficiency of books: he could afford thus to play with life, and the abysses into which it leads us. Let us take a case in contrast.

"I think," says the poor dying factory-girl in the tale, "if this should be the end of all, and if all I have been born for is just to work my heart and life away, and to sicken in this dree place, with those mill-stones in my ears for ever, until I could scream out for them to stop and let me have a little piece of quiet, and with the fluff filling my lungs, until I thirst to death for one long deep breath of the clear air, and my mother gone, and I never able to tell her again how I loved her, and of all my troubles,—I think, if this life is the end, and that there is no God to wipe away all tears from all eyes, I could go mad!"

Here is an argument for the immortality of the soul. As to its force, be it great or small, will it make a figure in a logical disputation, carried on *secundum artem*? Can any scientific common measure compel the intel-lects of Dives and Lazarus to take the same estimate of it? Is there any test of the validity of it better than the *ipse dixit* of private judgment, that is, the judgment of those who have a right to judge, and next, the agreement of many private judgments in one and the same view of it? (247-48)[2]

Having the same streak of sentimentalism that my namesake had, I have always been charmed by this passage, but I am worried about certain implications of the comments with which Newman closes it;

---

2 The quotation is from Elizabeth Gaskell's novel, *North and South* (London: J. M. Dent, 1914 [1854-55]).

and I am also alarmed by the ease with which he moves from examples like the first to examples like the second.

3 Cor ad cor loquitur

The two claims and two examples presented here provide some insight into why Newman is so often associated with *irrationalism*. Like most religious minds, Newman is sensitive to the limits of reason, especially reason as it is understood by intellectuals and deep thinkers. But Newman's concern with the limitations of philosophical argument and analysis is obsessive and one of the pillars of his apologetical strategy. The *Grammar* begins with a motto borrowed from St. Ambrose: "It was not by dialectical discussion that it pleased God to save his people."[3]

Newman has a love-hate relationship with philosophers. He is something of a philosopher in his own right, a commentator on classical problems of ethics, metaphysics, epistemology, and philosophical psychology. He is a professed admirer of such philosophers as Aristotle, Augustine, Aquinas, and Locke. In his *Idea of a University*, Newman offers an eloquent defense of the institution that, according to him, provides philosophical knowledge. But there are places in his writings where he follows the tradition of Tertullian and Peter Damiani in regarding philosophy as a threat to religious orthodoxy; and he frequently indulges in abusive *ad hominem* criticism of specific philosophers and philosophers in general.

Newman's attacks on philosophers often grow out of his view that philosophers have continually attempted to usurp the role of religious teachers. "In a word," he asks, "from the time that Athens was the university of the world, what has philosophy taught men but to promise without practising, and to aspire without attaining? What has the deep and lofty thought of its disciples ended in but eloquent words?" In the same section of *The Idea of a University*, he reminds us that philosophy and reason failed to support Cicero under the disfavour of the fickle populace and could not serve Seneca to oppose an imperial tyrant; they abandoned Brutus in his greatest need and forced Cato into the position of defying heaven.[4] A few pages later, he criticizes a philosopher from whom he had learned a great deal, Francis Bacon:

> Alas, that men in the action of life or in their heart of hearts are not what they seem to be in their moments of excitement, or in their traces or

3 Newman gives the original Latin: "Non in dialectica complacuit Deo Salvum facere populum suum."
4 John Henry Newman, *The Idea of a University*, ed. I. T. Ker (Oxford: Clarendon Press, 1976 [1852, 1889]), 106-107.

intoxications of genius—so good, so noble, so serene! Alas, that Bacon too in his own way should after all be but the fellow of those heathen philosophers who in their disadvantages had some excuse for their inconsistency, and who surprise us rather in what they did say than in what they did not do! Alas, that he too, like Socrates or Seneca, must be stripped of his holy-day coat, which looks so fair . . . .[5]

And in his *Essay on the Development of Christian Doctrine*, he quotes (with cruel delight) St. Justin's observation: "No one has so believed Socrates as to die for the doctrine which he taught."[6]

Newman's resentment and distrust of philosophers carry over to the *Grammar*, into which he incorporates his 1841 protest against "a dangerous doctrine maintained, as I considered, by two very eminent men of that day, now no more—Lord Brougham and Sir Robert Peel" (88).[7] The central theme of this attack is stated quite bluntly: "do not attempt by philosophy what once was done by religion" (88). "I have no confidence, then, in philosophers who cannot help being religious, and are Christians by implication. They sit at home, and reach forward to distances which astonish; but they hit without grasping . . . ." Indeed, they are "like blind men" who, "though they can put a stranger on his way," nevertheless "cannot walk straight themselves, and do not feel it quite their business to walk at all." As for logicians, they "are more set upon concluding rightly, than on right conclusions. They cannot see the end for the process" (90).

Newman's case against the philosophers is not built upon historical observations alone; in his view, philosophy is doomed to fail in its efforts to make men virtuous. "Quarry the granite rock with razors, or moor the vessel with a thread of silk; then may you hope with such keen and delicate instruments as human knowledge and human reason to contend against those giants, the passion and the pride of man."[8] A similar point is made in the *Grammar*, where he warns us: "Life is not long enough for a religion of inferences: we shall never have done beginning, if we determine to begin with proof." We must remember, "Life is for action. If we insist on proofs for every thing, we shall never come to action: to act you must assume, and that assumption is faith" (90-91).

Newman feels that philosophy and science do have their proper place. *The Idea of a University* reminds us that philosophy turns men into gentlemen, that liberal education produces "cultivation of mind"

5 Ibid., 109.
6 John Henry Newman, *An Essay on the Development of Christian Doctrine* (Garden City, New York: Image Books, Doubleday, 1960 [1845]), 340.
7 John Henry Newman, "The Tamworth Reading Room," in *Discussions and Arguments on Various Subjects* (London: Basil Montagu Pickering, 1872), 254-305. This article first appeared in *The Times*, February 1841.
8 Newman, *Idea*, 111.

or "cultivation of intellect," which is its own end.[9] But Newman insists in the *Grammar* that while science does indeed provide us with facts, we have to "take its facts, and give them a meaning, and to draw our own conclusions from them. First comes knowledge, then a view, then reasoning, and then belief" (89). "It is very well as a matter of liberal curiosity and of philosophy to analyze our modes of thought," according to Newman, "but let this come second, and when there is leisure for it, and then our examinations will in many ways even be subservient to action." As for logic, it "makes but a sorry rhetoric with the multitude," for "man is *not* a reasoning animal; he is a seeing, feeling, contemplating, acting animal." "So well has this practically been understood in all ages of the world, that no religion yet has been a religion of physics or philosophy. It has ever been synonymous with revelation" and "No legislator or priest ever dreamed of educating our moral nature by science or by argument" (91-92).

It will be worth our while to reflect later and at some length on Newman's unusual brand of irrationalism, but I have mentioned it here at the outset of our inquiry with a limited purpose in mind—to show how Newman's mental philosophy poses a special challenge to the philosophical expositor-critic. Many admirers of Newman feel that no matter how careless Newman's philosophizing seems to the tough-minded philosophical critic, it is absurd and self-defeating to subject Newman's claims to the same kind of cold, dispassionate scrutiny to which the claims of Aristotle, Spinoza, and Kant are properly subjected. It is almost as if Newman had, by the *style* of his apologetic—with its concomitant disparagement of traditional philosophizing—placed his mental philosophy beyond rational criticism. The hapless philosopher who tries to refute Newman's claims falls into Newman's trap by serving as a model of the heartless, misguided pedant. So we find Frederick Copleston, a Jesuit historian of philosophy, insisting that "those who take an interest in his philosophical reflections tend to look on them as a source of stimulus and inspiration rather than as a rigid, systematic doctrine, which, of course, Newman himself never intended them to be. And in this case detailed criticism of particular points necessarily seems pedantic and appears, to those who value Newman's general approach, as more or less irrelevant."[10] And N. D. O'Donoghue, while disturbed by the fact that "the whole thrust" of Newman's *Grammar* "tends to discredit the way of formal reasoning," warns us that we must not fall into the

9 Ibid., 5-15, 94-105.
10 Frederick Copleston, *A History of Philosophy*, vol. 8, *Modern Philosophy: Bentham to Russell*, pt. 2, *Idealism in America, The Pragmatist Movement, The Revolt against Idealism* (Garden City, New York: Image Books, Doubleday, 1967 [1966]), 288.

"very error which he is exposing right through the *Grammar of Assent*, the error of the cerebral approach to the great problems of existence."[11]

With Blaise Pascal, Søren Kierkegaard, and the humanistic pragmatists and existentialists of our own age, Newman is interested in the "whole" person and is convinced that the great philosophers have overvalued the intellectual dimension of personality. Commenting on the *Grammar*, W. R. Inge observes, "Newman, in this celebrated book, ranges himself with the 'Personalists'; his appeal is to the assent of the *whole* man to religious truth, which cannot be established by the intellect only, still less by the sentiments, which, as a basis for Faith, are 'a dream and a mockery'."[12] So if we probe into Newman's theory of illative judgment using only the logical tools of the analytical philosopher, Newman's many admirers are apt to dismiss our analysis as having completely missed the point.

Newman took as the motto of his cardinal's coat-of-arms the pregnant line "*Cor ad cor loquitur*." If we are to meet Newman at all—as friend or foe—we must do it at least partly on his own ground, the domain of the personal and concrete. We must keep moving back and forth from the logic of the intellect to the logic of the heart, from objective considerations to subjective ones. Most philosophers feel that meeting Newman is not worth the trouble. As J. F. Cronin notes:

> On the one hand non-Catholic philosophers and scientists have treated his work lightly, feeling that it is a work of apologetics, an effort to discover reasons for a faith which is by its very nature irrational. Many Catholics, on the other hand, have not realized the value of his thought. A certain obscurity in its presentation, the difficulty of incorporating it into the traditional scholastic system, have led them to avoid it as another of the bypaths from the broad avenue of thought. They have relegated Newman to the lesser position of the literateur.[13]

4 Newman as a philosopher

If we look beyond Newman's anti-intellectual pronouncements, we find that he is capable and desirous of dialoguing with philosophers. Though he heaps praise on the man of action and the simple man of faith, he cannot conceal the fact that he is himself essentially an intellectual and man of letters. Student and fellow of Oxford colleges, founder of a university, author of countless books, tracts, and articles, avid reader of everything from history and theology to science and

11 N. D. O'Donoghue, "Newman and the Problem of Privileged Access to Truth," *Irish Theological Quarterly* 42 (1975), 247-48.
12 William Ralph Inge, *Faith* (London: Duckworth, 1919), 234.
13 John Francis Cronin, *Cardinal Newman: His Theory of Knowledge* (Washington: Catholic University of America, 1935), ix.

formal logic, he sometimes makes us wonder whether his anti-intellectual diatribes represent just one more of many manifestations of an exaggerated self-distrust. O'Donoghue speaks of "the shattering contradiction whereby this man of notions and images . . . could base his whole approach to truth and certitude on the rejection of notion in the name of a distinction which was itself a notion."[14] This contradiction is a disturbing aspect of his apologetical strategy. "What he is doing is introducing reason surreptitiously in order to show how one can do without reason rather as a man can do without his wife's help once she leaves his meals ready for him, or as A. J. Ayer gets rid of metaphysics by making radical metaphysical assumptions."[15] Here O'Donoghue echoes the statement of Newman's most bitter critic, Charles Kingsley: "Like the sophists of old, he has used reason to destroy reason."[16]

There is a more charitable reading of Newman's statements about philosophical reasoning, one that is eminently plausible if we disregard the nastier side of his polemic. According to this interpretation, Newman is a champion of reason; his aim in the Grammar is to defend reason from attacks by both fideistic irrationalists and rationalistic "liberals" who live by a narrow, truncated concept of reason. Stretching this interpretation to its limits, Cronin suggests, "Rather than being called an irrationalist, Newman might be considered to have pressed the claims of reason too far."[17]

Newman was certainly well read in philosophy. Johannes Artz has provided evidence that Newman's thought was influenced by, among others, Plato, Aristotle, the Stoics, Cicero, Augustine, Aquinas, Suarez, Descartes, Locke, Hume, Butler, Reid, Dugald Stewart, J. S. Mill, and the scholastic philosophers of his own age. Other scholars have provided additional evidence and added important names to the list of influences.[18] And still other scholars have drawn attention to the similarity of Newman's views to those of earlier and later thinkers almost universally regarded as philosophers, for example, Pascal,[19]

14 O'Donoghue, "Privileged Access," 257.
15 Ibid., 255.
16 Charles Kingsley, "What, Then, Does Dr. Newman Mean?" in John Henry Newman, Apologia Pro Vita Sua (Garden City, New York: Image Books, Doubleday, 1956 [1864]), 75.
17 Cronin, Knowledge, 99.
18 Johannes Artz, "Newman as Philosopher," International Philosophical Quarterly 16 (1976), 263-87; Johannes Artz, "Die Eigenständigkeit der Erkenntnistheorie J. H. Newmans," Tübinger Theologischen Quartalschrift (1959), 194-222. See also, for example, Cronin, Knowledge, 1-32; Edward Sillem, ed., The Philosophical Notebook of John Henry Newman, vol. 1, General Introduction to the Study of Newman's Philosophy (New York: Humanities Press, 1969), 149-240.
19 Inge, Faith, 179; Copleston, History, vol. 8, pt. 2, 272; Christopher Hollis, Newman and the Modern World (London: Hollis & Carter, 1967), 181.

Kant,[20] Kierkegaard,[21] Bergson,[22] the humanistic pragmatists,[23] G. E. Moore,[24] and Michael Polanyi.[25]

But can we look upon Newman as a philosopher? Is he a "real" philosopher like Aristotle and Spinoza and Kant? In Copleston's *History of Philosophy*, discussion of Newman's mental philosophy is left for a lengthy appendix, which Copleston begins with this caveat:

> To say that we are concerned here with John Henry Newman (1801-90) simply as a philosopher is perhaps somewhat misleading for it might be understood as suggesting that in addition to his many other interests and activities Newman devoted himself to philosophical problems for their own sake, for their intrinsic interest as theoretical puzzles. And this would be far from the truth. Newman's approach to the philosophical topics which he discussed was that of a Christian apologist.[26]

While "we can pick out for brief consideration here some of the lines of thought which can reasonably be described as philosophical," such selection may involve "a certain mutilation of his thought as a whole."[27] In a similar vein, Thomas J. Norris advises:

> It is important to keep in mind that Newman was never engaged professionally in philosophy. He would not have let himself be considered a philosopher. He resolutely refused to enter at a professional level, the philosophy schools of the day. All Newman's preoccupations lay in another direction, especially that of theology and Christian education. Indirectly, however, Newman did much philosophizing, and this because he was driven to give much time, thought and attention to the perennial problems of the theologian.[28]

"We should never forget that Newman did not want to write a strictly philosophical treatise. He often repeats this,"[29] Dr. Zeno warns, and elsewhere he makes the important observation that Newman actually had many different conceptions of philosophy.[30] Perhaps the best

20 H. P. Owen, *The Moral Argument for Christian Theism* (London: George Allen & Unwin, 1965), 7.

21 O'Donoghue, "Privileged Access," 243; Copleston, *History*, vol. 8, pt. 2, 287.

22 Cronin, *Knowledge*, 129-36; Hollis, *World*, 166-67.

23 Inge, *Faith*, 234-35; Cronin, *Knowledge*, 115-23; Hollis, *World*, 181; Borghild Gundersen, *Cardinal Newman and Apologetics* (Oslo: I Kommisjon Hos Jacob Dybwad, 1952), 131.

24 Jay Newman, "Cardinal Newman's Attack on Philosophers," *Proceedings of the American Catholic Philosophical Association* 50 (1976), 204; M. Jamie Ferreira, *Doubt and Religious Commitment: The Role of the Will in Newman's Thought* (Oxford: Clarendon Press, 1980), 38.

25 Thomas J. Norris, *Newman and His Theological Method* (Leiden: E. J. Brill, 1977), 46; Ferreira, *Doubt*, 38.

26 Copleston, *History*, vol. 8, pt. 2, 270.

27 Ibid., 271.

28 Norris, *Method*, 12.

29 Dr. Zeno, "An Introduction to Newman's Grammar of Assent," *Irish Ecclesiastical Record* 103 (1965), 393-94.

30 Dr. Zeno, "Newman's Psychological Discovery: The Illative Sense," *Franciscan Studies* 10 (1950), 207-208.

answer to our question is Artz's: "Let us consider it as one of our significant tasks to give Newman his place in the history of philosophy. He was not indeed a systematic professional philosopher, but he did give us important philosophical stimuli and also the rudiments of a system. Let us fulfill our task not by a blind enthusiastic adulation, but critically."[31] We can carry out this task without forgetting that Newman was "primarily a preacher" and, in the last analysis, "a deeply ambiguous man."[32]

If Newman's ambiguity makes it harder for us to understand and properly evaluate his mental philosophy, it also lends a certain charm to his philosophical work. Newman is rightly critical of those who tend to divorce philosophy from "life." He himself is more than a philosopher *malgré lui* or a philosophizing apologist. He is, among other things, philosopher, apologist, theologian, preacher, priest, poet, journalist, reformer, educator. More fundamentally, he is a human being with passion and pride, hopes and fears. It is the human condition that gives rise to philosophy and religion, and it is the human situation that philosophy and religion ultimately strive to explain and ameliorate. When we first embarked on our study of philosophy, theology, or psychology, we all did so at least partly because we thought that such inquiry would bring us closer to the practical wisdom needed for coping with the tribulations of life; so when we follow Newman in refusing to separate our deepest rational reflection from our "life"—from our concrete "existential" situation—we return to the spirit of our earliest wonder.

And it will not do to argue that Newman's religious commitment renders his theory of illative judgment unphilosophical. When Socrates, the very embodiment of the philosophical spirit, was charged with impiety by his enemies, he sincerely protested against the accusation. No philosopher, not even a Montaigne or Descartes or Hume, philosophizes in a vacuum. To his credit, Newman has not pretended to be objective and impartial; he has made it clear to us where his moral and religious sympathies lie, and he has invited us to make of this information what we will.

5 The evolving project

Most discussion of Newman's mental philosophy has concentrated on the *Grammar*. Written when Newman was in his late sixties, it is the last major product of an extraordinarily prolific literary career. It would be wrong to infer, however, that Newman only turned to

31 Artz, "Newman as Philosopher," 287.
32 O'Donoghue, "Privileged Access," 242.

philosophy late in life. An early version of Newman's mental philosophy is contained in the celebrated *University Sermons* that Newman preached at his beloved Oxford while still an Anglican. (He made his controversial move to the Roman Catholic church in 1845.) As D. M. MacKinnon notes, "The student of his writings will rightly couple this work of his Anglican period with his later *Essay in Aid of a Grammar of Assent*, and indeed a comparison of the two works would be a fascinating and valuable exercise."[33] That Newman never repudiated his earlier approach to mental philosophy is evidenced by his assistance in the preparation of a third edition of the *University Sermons* in 1871. In his preface to this edition, he comments that at this late date he "is only surprised himself, that, under such circumstances, the errors are not of a more serious character. This remark especially applies to the Discourses upon the Relation of Faith to Reason, which are of the nature of an exploring expedition into an all but unknown country, and do not even venture on a definition of either Faith or Reason on starting."[34] These sermons, especially those preached from 1832 to 1843, introduce many of the concepts and themes around which the *Grammar* was later built. Some scholars feel that "Newman's initial views in the *University Sermons* underwent little alteration, and only minor differences of opinion will be found in both his works on belief."[35] Other scholars feel that the differences are more significant.[36] Newman, of course, would never have written the *Grammar* had he felt that a revised version of the *University Sermons* fulfilled the necessary philosophical task; and in a manuscript of 1860, he remarks on the need to speak with a "distinctness" which the *University Sermons* do not have. Since the Oxford sermons were preached at a time when "I was feeling my way and had not found it . . . I had not the requisite confidence in my own train of thought."[37]

33 D. M. MacKinnon, "Introduction" to John Henry Newman, *University Sermons* (London: S.P.C.K., 1970 [1843, 1871], 9. Cf. Nicholas Lash, "Introduction" to John Henry Newman, *An Essay in Aid of a Grammar of Assent* (Notre Dame, Indiana: University of Notre Dame Press, 1979), 2.

34 John Henry Newman, "Preface to the Third Edition," *University Sermons* (London: S.P.C.K., 1970 [1843, 1871]), x.

35 F. James Kaiser, *The Concept of Conscience According to John Henry Newman* (Washington: Catholic University of America Press, 1958), 89.

36 John D. Horgan, "Newman on Faith and Reason," *Studies: Irish Quarterly Review* (1953), 139-40.

37 John Henry Newman, manuscript of 12 January 1860 on "The Evidences of Religion." This is one of many manuscripts in the Newman archives at the Oratory of St. Philip Neri in Edgbaston, Birmingham, England. I shall refer to such archival material with the symbol O.Ar. and shall give either the number of the packet in which the particular manuscript can be found or the designator Gr.M. for material written after 1864 specifically in preparation for the *Grammar*. The manuscript on "The Evidences of Religion" can be found in O.Ar. A.30.11 and has recently been

It would also be wrong to assume that Newman had little interest in mental philosophy in the long period between the preparation of the two volumes. We learn from his unpublished manuscripts and notes that he was continuously interested in the philosophical issues surrounding belief. In a manuscript written at Easter of 1848, he raises some hitherto unanswered questions:

> Faith involves certainty in the highest degree; it does not admit the faintest shadow of doubt; yet it is the result of reasonings on a contingent subject matter, such as human testimony. How then can reasonings short of demonstration lead to an infallible conclusion?
>
> 1. In this difficulty it is common, especially with rationalizing Protestants, to *deny the certainty* of Faith, and to say that the degree of conviction varies with the premises ....
>
> 2. Others, especially Enthusiasts, have denied the connexion of Reason and Faith, and said that Faith was not the result of proofs logical ....
>
> 3. As to the popular way of speaking, as if the doctrines were to be received because the infallible Church proposed them to us, and the Church was infallible because the revealed doctrine declared it, this is plainly arguing in a circle.
>
> How then is it that faith is *preceded* by reason, yet does not *depend* upon it? And *on what* does it depend? What can give it its *certainty*? What *can* be a ground but sense and reason? Or can it be discursive yet not depend on the reasons, (motiva,) which precede it?
>
> These are the sort of questions which have to be answered.[38]

He returned to these problems again and again during the 1850s,[39] and in January of 1860 he outlined the introduction to a major piece "on the popular, practical, personal evidence for the truth of revelation":

> § I am addressing myself to a question, on which Father Perrone much insists, as demanding a decision in the affirmative, viz. that the motivum credibilitatis is personal to each individual as well as formal, public, and what may be called objective, after the manner of a science.
>
> § The great mass of Catholics know nothing of argument; how then is their faith rational? ... They may have received it by inheritance, they may have embraced it as boys, they have been slowly brought into it by some groove or other which a contracted course of study has formed for them, and then they are told they must take care to be certain it is true, and to force themselves into a sustained pitch of certainty by the action of their will, if they begin to lag ....
>
> § [F]ew persons have submitted to the Catholic Church upon a demonstration of her divinity, but merely on those chance arguments and mere probabilities which came in his way. How then can his belief be

published in *The Theological Papers of John Henry Newman on Faith and Certainty*, ed. Hugo M. de Achaval and J. Derek Holmes (Oxford: Clarendon Press, 1976), one of a series of volumes in which previously unpublished material by Newman has been made readily available to the general public. See p. 84 of this volume.
38 O.Ar. B.9.11.
39 See "List of [Newman's] theological papers, 1846-1886," in *Theological Papers*, xi-xv.

called rational? How can his treatment of his intellect be called honest or dutiful to its great maker and giver?

This is the objection which has given rise to the following Essay.

I propose to draw out the nature of the evidence, or motivum credibilitatis, on which individuals believe, and to inquire what is meant by the prohibition to re-examine the trustworthiness of that motivum.

§ My second chapter shall be an exposition of what is meant by personal proof, giving instances . . . .[40]

Given his unflagging interest in these subjects, why did Newman not write the *Grammar* earlier? The main obstacle was surely Newman's intensely demanding schedule. A classic example of the workaholic, Newman always took on too many commitments. Having founded the Oratory in England in the late 1840s, he was constantly preoccupied with administering its often troublesome affairs. In the following decade, he was involved in unsuccessfully defending himself in a bizarre libel case and in founding a Catholic university in Ireland—to mention just two of the more dramatic of the thousand projects in which he was then involved. Soon after came his famous confrontation with Kingsley and the preparation of his most widely read work, the autobiographical *Apologia Pro Vita Sua*. Only by the late 1860s was he finally able to get back to the philosophical project that had been on the drawing board for so many years.

Since the *Grammar* is Newman's most comprehensive, most systematic, and most interesting contribution to mental philosophy, it is the work on which we shall focus our attention. Commenting on the *Grammar*, Christopher Hollis reminds us that all Newman's books were "books of occasion."[41] Though he had postponed work on the philosophical project in order to deal with more pressing concerns, he always saw the publication of a major work on belief as a rather urgent matter. In a preface which he later dropped, he tells us that he is writing "in the time of an intellectual earthquake, when opinions of men are stirred from their very foundations, and a revolution is passing over the ideas of the civilized world more appalling than any uprooting of thrones, however venerable or upheaving of civil institutions, however ancient . . . ."[42] In putting the *Grammar* in its historical context, we should remember that it was published in the year of the Franco-Prussian War and the first Vatican Council, only three years after Marx's *Capital*, a year before Darwin's *Descent of Man*, and two years before Nietzsche's *Birth of Tragedy*. In reflecting on his philosophical project a decade earlier, he had written: "The reason why I think it of great importance just now is this:—because just now a

40 O.Ar. A.30.11: manuscript dated 5 January 1860. See *Theological Papers*, 81-82.
41 Hollis, *World*, 165.
42 O.Ar. Gr.M.: draft of a preface, "On the nature, modes and grounds of Religious assent," dated 30 December 1868.

scepticism is on foot, which throws on the individual believer the *onus probandi*, in a way never *contemplated*, or at least recognised before—Hitherto a man was allowed to believe till it was logically brought home to him that he ought not to believe ...."[43]

6 The structure of the *Grammar*

Since the *Grammar* is as unusual and ambiguous as its author and does not belong to a single literary or philosophical genre, its structure is apt to baffle those readers who make an initial approach to it without having a reasonable idea of what to expect. As almost all readers of the book have fallen into this category, a consideration of the work's structure is in order, and the most valuable insight into its structure is gained by beginning at the beginning and reflecting on its title.

The *Grammar* is an "Essay," and as David Pailin points out, "In our evaluation we must remember that Newman did not regard his work as a definitive treatise. He called it *An Essay in Aid of a Grammar of Assent* and never claimed that it was comprehensive."[44] The essay is one of the more personal and informal of literary genres, and a piece in the personal style fits both Newman's personality and the subject matter of illative judgment. But some essays are more formal than others, and a good example of a long and rather technical one is the philosophical work to which the *Grammar* pays most attention, Locke's *Essay Concerning Human Understanding*. Given his special interest in this work, the author of the *Grammar* must surely have had it in mind when deciding on a title for his response to it. If the *Grammar* is not a treatise, it is still the most technical of Newman's books, and as O'Donoghue notes, "Even for the professional philosopher the *Grammar* is a difficult book ...."[45] The work is ambiguously semi-technical and semi-personal, making it equally uncongenial to the unphilosophical and professionally philosophical mind.

The book is *in aid of* a grammar of assent, and Newman is well aware that he is not writing the definitive work on the subject. In a draft for a preface, he reflects, "Nay, if I fail in my attempt, I still may solace myself with the belief that my failure is a preliminary condition to the success of others who come after me, and may even contribute to it."[46]

43 O.Ar. A.30.11: "The Evidences of Religion," dated 12 January 1860.
44 David A. Pailin, *The Way to Faith: An Examination of Newman's* Grammar of Assent *as a Response to the Search for Certainty in Faith* (London: Epworth Press, 1969), 187.
45 O'Donoghue, "Privileged Access," 249.
46 O.Ar. Gr.M.: draft of a preface, "On the nature, modes and grounds of Religious assent," dated 30 December 1868.

J.-H. Walgrave sees Newman's reference to "grammar" in the title as a way of drawing our attention to his concern with the structure of thought; he tells us that Newman "intends to confine himself to a description of the structure of thought, to discover its mechanism and movement, using thought itself as his starting-point, in the same way as grammar (hence the title, *Grammar of Assent*) derives the laws of language from current use."[47] But the use of the word "grammar" also signals the book's concern with language, with how we talk and/or *should* talk about assent in its various forms. Although Newman's emphasis on language can hardly be regarded as revolutionary, it makes his philosophical methodology rather more similar to that of contemporary analytical philosophers than most commentators on the *Grammar* have recognized. But Newman's view of language is complex. As J. M. Cameron observes, "Newman is very self-conscious about language and has a severe view of its functions"; he views language as "a set of tools well enough adapted to the furthering of particular practical or even speculative purposes, but compelled to strain itself to breaking point when it attempts to speak of God or the soul or faith. Language is framed to deal with our ordinary commerce with the world of things and persons, not with the subject-matter of theology."[48] The ambiguity of Newman's attitude towards language is reflected in his terminology in the *Grammar*. In Cameron's view:

> His language is that of the ordinary educated persons of his day. He does, of course, employ terms which have a quasi-technical use in philosophy; but these—terms such as "the moral sense," "moral perceptions," "the passions," "nature," "the heart"—are drawn from the tradition of British empiricism. They had become so much a part of educated speech that it is a nice question whether they ought to be considered technical terms at all.[49]

Norris, on the other hand, is convinced that "Newman uses a terminology of his own. Not being a philosopher by profession, he coined his own vocabulary for this work."[50] In one of his drafts for a preface, Newman warns his readers: "I have not recognized the tenets nor used the language of existing schools of thought"; and "Expedience then, not less than my right, leads me to use words in my own technical sense provided that I state what that sense is . . . ."[51] But in a note written in September 1865, he affirms a certain confidence in ordinary language: "I do not wish to attempt definitions of the matters/subjects/things about which I am to write, further than is practi-

---

47 J.-H. Walgrave, *Newman the Theologian*, trans. A. V. Littledale (New York: Sheed & Ward, 1960 [1957]), 62.
48 J. M. Cameron, *The Night Battle* (London: Burns & Oates, 1962), 203-204.
49 Ibid.
50 Norris, *Method*, 30. Cf. Zeno, "Introduction," 393-94.
51 O.Ar. Gr.M.: draft of a preface, "On the nature, modes and grounds of Religious assent," dated 30 December 1868.

cally necessary/useful towards attaining a clear and consistent idea of them." In any case, the *Grammar* is in some sense a book about language, and its consistent emphasis on language provides it with a certain kind of unity.

A more important source of unity is the book's subject matter; the *Grammar* is a book about *assent*. It is important to remember that Newman's main subject is assent, and not apprehension or inference (28, 93). When Newman talks about apprehension or inference, it is always because of his overriding interest in assent. Consider the work's contents:

Part I.   Assent and Apprehension

Chapter 1.   Modes of holding and apprehending Propositions
    1. Modes of holding Propositions
    2. Modes of apprehending Propositions
Chapter 2.   Assent considered as Apprehensive
Chapter 3.   The Apprehension of Propositions
Chapter 4.   Notional and Real Assent
    1. Notional Assents
    2. Real Assents
    3. Notional and Real Assents contrasted
Chapter 5.   Apprehension and Assent in the matter of Religion
    1. Belief in one God
    2. Belief in the Holy Trinity
    3. Belief in Dogmatic Theology

Part II.   Assent and Inference

Chapter 6.   Assent considered as Unconditional
    1. Simple Assent
    2. Complex Assent
Chapter 7.   Certitude
    1. Assent and Certitude contrasted
    2. Indefectibility of Certitude
Chapter 8.   Inference
    1. Formal Inference
    2. Informal Inference
    3. Natural Inference
Chapter 9.   The Illative Sense
    1. The Sanction of the Illative Sense
    2. The Nature of the Illative Sense
    3. The Range of the Illative Sense
Chapter 10.   Inference and Assent in the matter of Religion
    1. Natural Religion
    2. Revealed Religion
Notes

The book begins and ends with discussions of assent and is divided into two main parts, one dealing with assent and apprehension and the other with assent and inference. The symmetry goes further, as each part is divided into five chapters, and the last chapter of each part relates the subject of the four previous chapters to religion.

The symmetry ends here, and while the overall ordering of topics makes sense, it is not exactly rigorous. Norris, though bold enough to lay out the contents of the *Grammar* in a "graphical representation," admits that "Newman does not follow a very rational plan or strict outline." But if Norris is right, then there is a methodological significance to the looseness of the book's structure: "The structure of the work is more pedagogical in tone and spirit than logical in its development. And Newman wished it to be like this. In fidelity to his principles, he felt that a person stumbles across the truth, discovering a point here, a thread there, sometimes by design, but more often accidentally."[52] Still, if the plan of the *Grammar* is not very rational, it is rational enough, as the following rudimentary outline shows.

According to Newman, there are two modes of holding propositions and two modes of apprehending them. When we examine language, we see that propositions take an interrogative, conditional, or categorical form. Corresponding to each of these forms is a specific mental act, an internal act of "holding" a proposition; these three modes of holding propositions are doubt, inference, and assent. In addition to being "held," propositions are "apprehended"; apprehension of a proposition is the imposition of a sense on the terms of which the proposition is composed. The terms, subject and predicate, stand for either notions or realities. Because of its involvement with images, real assent is stronger than notional assent and influences our behaviour to a degree that the latter does not. Real assent is both possible and desirable in religion. Now, assent itself is unconditional and in this sense does not admit of degrees. We can even be certain about things, and we have a right to be certain about many of them. But how do we *arrive* at certitude or any other assent? Assent is normally preceded by inference, and inference in concrete matter is quite different from the formal inference that we associate with philosophers and logicians. Fortunately, human beings possess a power of judging and concluding, which in its perfection can be called the "illative sense." Thanks to this sense, we can arrive at real assent and certitude in many areas, from geography to religion, and we are thus able to lead a rich and active life. Once we understand the nature of assent, inference, and illative judgment, we can also appreciate the kind of personal, implicit reasons that lead even some of the simplest human beings to the rational belief of the Christian faith.

This is a pretty bald outline. (If it all makes complete sense, then there is no point in reading any further.) Still, we can see from it that the *Grammar* is indeed unified and structured in its content.

The *Grammar* has no preface or introduction. It begins with the first line of the first chapter: "Propositions (consisting of a subject and

52 Norris, *Method*, 29.

predicate united by the copula) may take a categorical, conditional, or interrogative form" (25). Students of English literature will notice that this is not exactly one of Newman's liveliest opening lines. It is widely agreed that John Henry Newman is one of the greatest of all English literary stylists: the last passages of the *Apologia Pro Vita Sua* brought tears to the eyes of the unsympathetic George Eliot,[53] and no less talented and imaginative a writer than the equally unsympathetic James Joyce regarded Cardinal Newman as the greatest of all writers of prose.[54] So why does the author of *The Dream of Gerontius* and "The Pillar of the Cloud" ("Lead, Kindly Light . . ."), of *The Idea of a University* and the *Apologia*, open his last major work with so dry and uninspiring a statement? In Norris's view, "The *Grammar* has an abrupt opening, which sets the tone for much of the work."[55] According to this interpretation, Newman is trying to shock us into the realization that an inquiry into the nature of belief must start, as it were, in the "middle." Or is Newman perhaps trying to scare certain kinds of readers away and hold the attention of certain others?

7 The *Grammar* as an attempt at self-vindication

For what kinds of readers, then, was the *Grammar* initially written? Of precisely what were they supposed to become convinced? And why did they *have* to be convinced?

We have seen that the *Grammar* is, among other things, a defense of the simple Christian's right to believe, and all his life Newman clearly retained an "admiration for the *foi de charbonnier*"; but Newman could hardly have expected the *Grammar* to be comprehensible to the *charbonnier*, peasant, or factory-girl, to the "ignorant simple believer."[56] He could hardly have expected the simple Christians of the world to plow through his subtle analyses and finish with their simple faith intact.

Before considering the more obvious answers to our three questions, let us try a somewhat cynical view of the matter. According to Hollis, Newman wrote the *Grammar* in order "to show that his criticism of traditional apologetics did not lead to scepticism,"[57] and this view may be more insightful than Hollis himself realizes. For it is possible that the *primary*—though hidden—aim of the *Grammar* is to defend *Newman himself*, to persuade his Roman Catholic superiors

53 Louis Bouyer, *Newman: His Life and Spirituality*, trans. J. Lewis May (London: Burns, Oates and Washbourne, 1958), 362.
54 Richard Ellmann, *James Joyce* (New York: Oxford University Press, 1959), 40.
55 Norris, *Method*, 29.
56 O'Donoghue, "Privileged Access," 243.
57 Norris, *World*, 165.

that he is not nearly as unorthodox and untrustworthy as many of his Catholic critics have repeatedly insisted.

If one learns anything from the countless biographical studies of Newman, it is that Newman had an uncanny knack for alienating people, often those that he could least afford to offend. Newman was also capable of deep and lasting friendship. But the impartial reader of the biographies cannot help being awed by the number, the range, and (sometimes) the stature of his enemies, critics, and detractors. Newman's more slavish admirers are always quick to remind us that it is not uncommon for great men to be distrusted. For example, according to Dr. Zeno:

> Whereas men of mediocre talents will succeed remarkably and become well-known and esteemed in many circles, genius often stands on a pinnacle, not to be reached by other mortals, and its voice does not reach the ears of the crowd. Its world-wide visions are distrusted, its prophetic warnings are sneered at and scorned, its achievements are neglected and ignored.
>
> In his long, long life John Henry Newman had to pay the debt of genius and suffered from mistrust and contempt, from neglect and misunderstanding.[58]

Such lavish praise is embarrassing enough; but when Newman's more fanatic biographers go further and mechanically impugn the character of everyone with whom Newman came into conflict, we have good reason to be sceptical and irritated.

Having offended his Protestant colleagues by turning traitor to their cause, Newman almost immediately managed to attract the suspicion and distrust of his new co-religionists. In Cameron's words, "Newman was a stumbling-block, an offence, in his lifetime, both to the Anglicans he left and to the Catholics among whom he made his spiritual home; and posterity has found him no less a divisive figure."[59] A controversialist who by temperament could not resist drawing attention to himself, Newman was inevitably drawn into quarrel after quarrel. While being a strong defender of Newman, Thomas Gornall, a Jesuit scholar, admits that Newman's difficulties with his colleagues were partly a result of a flaw in his own personality:

> Newman's misfortune was that over-intensity led at times of severe stress to sudden blackouts in his self-knowledge. The things he did and said at those times have all the same characteristic: excessive self-protectiveness. The positions he then took became knotted and remained so for the rest of his life; even when he looked back he could not see what was wrong. There or thereabouts I believe is the explanation of all the misgivings about him.
>
> As to the hidden cause, it was probably something genetic.[60]

58 Zeno, "Psychological Discovery," 114.
59 Cameron, *Battle*, 223-24.
60 Thomas Gornall, "The Newman Problem," *The Clergy Review* 62 (1977), 138.

Gornall then describes certain actions of Newman that he regards as "bolts of irrationality" that do not cohere with the "rest of the picture" (with Newman's achievement, dedication, etc.). These include Newman's strained relations with the London Oratory and the peculiar "Brother Bernard affair" of 1852. Gornall suggests that Newman's emotional condition deteriorated after the watershed of the Dublin period, and he reminds us of the "darker years" with their "litany of ominous names: Wiseman, Faber, Manning, W. G. Ward, Talbot, Herbert Vaughan, Bishop Grant, Bishop Brown, Barnabò, and Newman in the midst like a baited bear."[61]

Some of Newman's Catholic critics had good reason to distrust him, and not the least of their misgivings was their feeling that Newman had never completely divested himself of the Anglican world-view of his youth. It was bad enough that Newman was an oversensitive nuisance; but if Newman was also unconsciously subverting the church's teaching, he had to be kept in check. The University Sermons belongs to Newman's Anglican period, and while he later expressed his basic satisfaction with the sermons, he was well aware that leading Catholic thinkers had grave doubts about his whole approach to philosophical subjects. Newman could not have expected Catholic scholars to see the University Sermons as a defense of the Catholic position on faith and reason; but this is surely how he had hoped they would view the Grammar. He even took the special precaution of having the sheets of the Grammar critically examined by Charles Meynell, a young scholar with a good knowledge of scholastic philosophy. Newman must have hoped that the Grammar would help to lift the cloud of suspicion hovering over him, much as the Apologia had done a few years earlier. But the Grammar did not have the desired effect: Catholic traditionalists were quick to realize that the Grammar had little in common with reliable, old-fashioned scholastic teaching. As Ian Ramsey points out, "It may be that Catholic critics of Newman sensed more clearly than they could formulate, insights into language, a distrust of traditional logic, an empirical historical approach to 'development' and a concept of a tentative theology which were . . . ill-fitting for their traditional apologetic . . . ."[62] The publication of the Grammar led to Newman's being attacked by new Catholic (and non-Catholic) critics, with Thomas Harper, a Jesuit, being especially prominent among them. And not long after Newman's death, the Grammar came to be widely associated with "modernism," a radical movement that Pope Pius X condemned as the "synthesis of all heresies."[63]

61 Ibid., 138-41.
62 Ian T. Ramsey, On Being Sure in Religion (London: Athlone Press, 1963), 80.
63 In the encyclical letter, Pascendi Dominici Gregis (1907).

In any case, whether or not Newman's primary aim in writing the *Grammar* was to convince the Roman Catholic hierarchy of the orthodoxy of his thirty-year-old mental philosophy, he had other aims and other potential readers in mind. The *Grammar* would not merit our attention here if it were merely an unsuccessful attempt at public relations.

8 Objectives of the project

We have already considered enough passages from Newman's published and unpublished writings to be able to draw up a pretty good list of answers to our three questions. If we had to explain Newman's philosophical project in a very short sentence, the best we could say, I suppose, is that it is an attempt to establish the rationality of faith. But this answer barely scratches the surface and is thus somewhat misleading. For one thing, Newman wants to show that faith is rational *in a positive way*. He wants to establish that the reasoning involved in faith is consistent with commitment and action in a way that abstract reasoning is not. In line with this aim, he wants to show that though faith is preceded by reasonings on a contingent subject matter, it is a matter of genuine certitude. Secondly, Newman seeks to establish that even the simple believer's faith can be sufficiently rational to warrant reflective people's judgment that he has a right to believe. Thirdly, Newman is trying to show that our faith can be regarded as rational even though we cannot explain in detail why we believe. In line with this aim, he tries to explain how certitude in religious matters follows from "personal" proof, from the complex cumulation of probabilities. Fourthly, Newman is trying to lead us, in a very gentle way, to consider the possibility that it is more reasonable to be religious than not to be.

So while the *Grammar* is not, strictly speaking, a theological treatise,[64] Newman is still at his apostolic mission.[65] As the master of the "subjective side of apologetics,"[66] he is the inventor of the apologetical theory "of the harmony between Natural and Revealed Religion as constituting the average man's implicit, and at the same time strongest motive of credibility."[67]

64 O.Ar. Gr.M.: draft of a preface, "Contributions towards a Grammar of Assent," dated 6 November 1869.
65 Sylvester P. Juergens, *Newman on the Psychology of Faith in the Individual* (New York: Macmillan, 1928), 15.
66 Thomas Gerrard, "The 'Grammar of Assent' and the 'Sure Future'," in *Folia Fugitiva*, ed. W. H. Cologan (London: R. & T. Washbourne; New York: Benziger Bros., 1907), 293. This article first appeared in the *Dublin Review*, July 1905.
67 Juergens, *Psychology*, x.

But to whom was he writing? If we accept O'Donoghue's contention that "the *Grammar* belongs in the field of high, relentless, religious controversy,"[68] then we must also accept that he certainly hoped that the book would be read by the fideistic irrationalists and the rationalistic "liberals" that he was so bitterly attacking. The *Grammar* can then be seen as a challenge to these people to mend their ways and to stop browbeating decent religious people. Fideists, being irrationalists, did not have the patience to read through a semi-technical work like the *Grammar*; but a good many rationalistic "liberals" were prepared to take up Newman's challenge. Among them was the eminent Leslie Stephen, who admired Newman for his bluntness: "Dr. Newman is like Mill, a lover of the broad daylight; of clear, definite, tangible statements. There is no danger with him of losing ourselves in that mystical haze which the ordinary common-sense of mankind irritates and bewilders."[69] But there was little else in the *Grammar* that Stephen admired: "Dr. Newman has a scepticism of his own, which sometimes coincides with and sometimes sanctions that dangerous mode of apology which would destroy the validity of the reasoning process itself in order to evade reasonable conclusions."[70]

In S. P. Juergens's view, "the *Grammar* was addressed not to controversialists but to inquirers."[71] We are all inquirers; all men by nature desire to know.[72] But Juergens has a certain type of inquirer in mind—intelligent, relatively educated persons who seek guidance because they are deeply troubled by the apparent conflict between faith and reason, between the traditional teaching of the church of their fathers and the contemporary teaching of philosophers, scientists, and social reformers. One such person was William Froude, Newman's very dear friend, and we know from Newman's correspondence that the plight of Froude and others like him weighed heavily on Newman's mind.[73]

Edward Sillem makes the shrewd observation that, throughout the section of the *Grammar* entitled "Belief in one God," Newman "uses the personal pronoun 'I' *au sens fort du mot*, to mean himself. His question is, 'Can I, J. H. N., attain to any more vivid assent to the Being of God, than that which is given merely to notions of the intellect?

68 O'Donoghue, "Privileged Access," 250.
69 Leslie Stephen, "Dr. Newman's Theory of Belief," *Fortnightly Review* 131 (1877), 685.
70 Ibid.
71 Juergens, *Psychology*, 15.
72 Aristotle *Metaphysics* 980a.
73 See Gordon Huntington Harper, *Cardinal Newman and William Froude, F.R.S., A Correspondence* (Baltimore: Johns Hopkins Press, 1933); Walgrave, *Theologian*, 60-64; Lash, "Introduction," 3-7; A. J. Boekraad, *The Personal Conquest of Truth According to J. H. Newman* (Louvain: Editions Nauwelaerts, 1955), 163-69.

etc.'."[74] And Artz is speaking almost euphemistically when he observes that "the *Grammar* could only be written by one who had a strong tendency to self-analysis."[75] Newman, after all, was obsessed with himself, and a good case could be made for the position that Newman's chief objective in writing the *Grammar* was to persuade *himself* of the compatibility of his Roman Catholic faith and his Oxford-cultivated reason.

But times change, and nowadays the *Grammar* is mainly of interest to academic scholars. It is hard to know whether Newman would have been more disappointed than amused to learn that the *Grammar's* readers are now usually epistemologists, philosophers of religion, or philosophizing theologians. However, we should not be surprised that the book has received much attention from people who have little or no interest in the religious issues that were of central importance to Newman himself. For Newman's strategy in the *Grammar* is such that secular assents must receive as much attention as those of religious faith. While Newman has no intention of playing down the important role of Divine Grace,[76] he feels it is imperative to show that when considered with regard to *rationality*, assents and inferences concerning religious matters are not remarkably different from other assents and inferences in concrete matter. The rationalistic "liberals" tended to assume that the fundamental religious assents are quite extraordinary. Newman aims at undermining this assumption by showing that illative judgment in the domain of religion is rather similar to illative judgment in the arts and sciences and even to the illative judgment involved in the cognitive processes of everyday life. In order to achieve this end, Newman has to give examples involving all sorts of subject matter. He has to talk about assent as such, not just the assent of religious faith. He has to talk about apprehension as such and inference as such and illation as such. So he ends up not with an essay in aid of grammar of *religious* assent, but with an essay in aid of a grammar of assent. And that is how the *Grammar* has come to be taken seriously by many readers who have not the slightest interest in Newman's "apostolic mission."

9 The *Grammar* as phenomenology of belief

One way of looking at the *Grammar* is to see it as involved in two large philosophical undertakings, one phenomenological and the other epistemological. Newman himself never uses these terms in describ-

74 Edward A. Sillem, "Cardinal Newman's *Grammar of Assent* on Conscience as a Way to God," *Heythrop Journal* 5 (1965), 382-83.
75 Artz, "Newman as Philosopher," 269.
76 Cameron, *Battle*, 206.

ing his philosophical project; and he is not always aware that he is actually engaged in the Grammar in two distinct (though related) tasks. We shall see later that his failure to distinguish between the two tasks sometimes leads him into confusions and errors.

The terms "phenomenology" and "phenomenological" are used nowadays to refer to various philosophical approaches that share a central concern with description of the contents and structures of consciousness. Many scholars feel that the terms are used according to their strict and proper sense only when they refer to the philosophical approach of Edmund Husserl and his followers. When Newman wrote the Grammar, Husserlian phenomenology had not yet been invented; but much of what Newman is doing in the Grammar bears a striking resemblance to the kind of analysis that we find in the writings of such phenomenologists as Husserl, Sartre, Merleau-Ponty, and Marcel. According to Dr. Zeno, Newman wants to give "a phenomenological description of human thinking . . . ."[77] For Walgrave, "Newman is the greatest master of description of mental phenomena."[78] Many Newmanists seem to feel, and with some justification, that by characterizing Newman's approach as phenomenological, they promote both appreciation of his originality and interest in his work. This spirit surely underlies Artz's observation that "Newman has anticipated the phenomenological method, founded by Edmund Husserl, without accepting Husserl's limitation to the intentional or formal object (where existence remains out of consideration) but including the real material object as existing, like Max Scheler."[79]

Philosophy books have traditionally been filled with claims about objective reality and arguments in defense of those claims. In sharp contrast, phenomenological studies are made up mainly of rigorous descriptions of things subjective. The Grammar consists largely of such descriptions and contains remarkably little in the way of metaphysical speculation and formal argument. Newman knew that what he was doing in the Grammar was quite different from what the classical and scholastic philosophers had done in their metaphysical and theological treatises, and in a draft of the section of the Grammar on belief in God, he writes, "I wish it to be understood then that, in the pages which follow, I am not directly showing why we believe in God, but how we believe in Him . . . ."[80] According to John Hick, the central aim of the Grammar is "to describe the informal ways in which our convictions are in fact arrived at,"[81] and O'Donoghue echoes this

77 Zeno, "Introduction," 390.
78 J.-H. Walgrave, "Religious Experience through Conscience," Louvain Studies 4 (1972), 110.
79 Artz, "Newman as Philosopher," 283. Cf. Pailin, Way to Faith, 172; Boekraad, Conquest, 135-40.
80 O.Ar. Gr.M.: draft on ch. 5, dated 15 July 1868 (transcribed 22 September 1868).
81 John Hick, Faith and Knowledge, 2nd ed. (London: Macmillan, 1967), 69.

claim when he argues that the *Grammar* is first and foremost "an account of how people come to a religious certitude."[82]

Some commentators have characterized this aspect of Newman's work as "psychological" rather than "phenomenological."[83] But while there are times when it is useful to think of the *Grammar* as a contribution to the psychology of belief and faith, treating the book as psychology can be very misleading. For one thing, the term "psychological" has a much wider extension than the more technical term "phenomenological," and not much is to be gained from comparing Newman's approach to religious belief with, say, Freud's. Secondly, while Newman lived before the heyday of depth psychology, he had remarkable foresight when he made what is, in effect, a distinction between phenomenological and psychological approaches to mental phenomena:

> It is more reasonable to say that we had no intelligent mind at all, than to say that the various qualities of beautifulness, greatness, rectitude, and truth are not present to it as distinct things and affect us with distinct sentiments. Putting aside all the psychological questions of their origin and mode of subsistence, which are psychological or logical questions, and beside our purpose, we contemplate them by means of powers natural to the mind . . . .[84]

Thirdly, as we shall see later, one of the great weaknesses of the *Grammar* is its *failure* to give proper consideration to relevant psychological questions.

It is hardly surprising that Newman, influenced as he was by so many British empiricist philosophers, had a great interest in "phenomena." We get a good insight into his conception of and interest in phenomena from an unpublished manuscript written in or around 1860:

> *Phenomena.* When I speak of phenomena, I mean those impressions upon the mind which it is usual to call sensible. I use the word *impressions*, because the mind seems to itself passive as to their coming or going.
> *Sensations.* By sensations I mean those impressions upon the mind, which are not sensible, yet are passive. Such is the coming and going of pure memory, of sense of right and wrong, of the sense of beauty, of shame; of the passions, as anger and fear.
> *Regard.* The mind actively contemplates these phenomena of sense (as well as a multitude of subjects besides, which are not to our present purpose). It remembers them when absent; it recognizes them when they come again; it observes when they come in the same order. It forms them into separate wholes; it traces that wholeness to a unity beyond themselves or external to itself, and gives names to these assumed entities.[85]

82 O'Donoghue, "Privileged Access," 249.
83 Juergens, *Psychology*, 2.
84 O.Ar. Gr.M.: manuscript on certitude as a constituent state of mind, dated 28 January 1867 (transcribed 30 August 1868).
85 O.Ar. A.18.11: material for an introduction, n.d.

What did Newman expect to accomplish by merely *describing* how the mind works? Very much indeed. First, Newman thought that his phenomenological distinction between real and notional assent would serve to explain why the religious assent of the simple believer is more efficacious than, and hence superior to, the weaker religious assent of the liberal intellectual. Moreover, he thought that by establishing that certitude is natural and inevitably has a place among our mental acts, he would be showing how pointless it is for the liberals to argue that certitude is rarely if ever warranted. And he also thought that by establishing the existence of informal inference and illative judgment, he would be showing that the philosopher's concept of rationality is hopelessly narrow and inadequate.

Newman, then, was not simply concerned with the phenomenological question of *how* we believe. He was ultimately concerned with what we have a *right* to believe and what we *ought* to believe. He realized, as many philosophers before him had not, that we cannot give informed answers to the more interesting questions until we have arrived at a sensible answer to the phenomenological question. Unfortunately, he himself did not always distinguish clearly between the phenomenological and epistemological questions.

10 The *Grammar* as epistemology

Most questions about the general kinds of propositions that we have a right or obligation to believe belong to the branch of philosophy known as epistemology or theory of knowledge. The classical aim of epistemology has been to shed light on the difference between knowledge and mere opinion, but in recent years the scope of epistemology has been broadened to include all inquiries into the nature of evidence and the intellectual justification of belief. (I contrast "intellectual" justification here with "moral," for perhaps some beliefs ought to be held even though there is little or no evidence to support them.) When Newman confines himself to a description of the believing mind, he is engaged in phenomenology; but when he goes on to consider the nature of evidence and the intellectual warrantableness of certain kinds of belief, he is engaged in epistemology.

So much attention has been paid to Newman's phenomenology that it is sometimes easy to forget that the *Grammar* is also an epistemological study. While Pailin feels that Newman's primary concern in the *Grammar* is with the phenomenology of religious belief, he reminds us that "to limit his work to phenomenological description is an inadequate appraisal"; the *Grammar* also deals with "the possibility of our subjective certitude corresponding to objective truth."[86] Wil-

86 Pailin, *Way to Faith*, 187.

liam Fey adds, "In the *Grammar of Assent* Newman attempted to distinguish some of the intellectual activities which combine in our objective (certain) knowledge in such a way that we are given an opening to reality."[87]

Pailin recognizes, however, that Newman's use of the term "certitude" is riddled with confusion because of his failure to make a "constant and clear distinction" between epistemological and phenomenological issues.[88] In his discussion of assent and certitude, Newman moves from the epistemological to the phenomenological reference "without any indication that he is committing a logical type-jump."[89] In a recent study, M. J. Ferreira also acknowledges that Newman makes conflicting claims in regard to the indefectibility of certitude: "His zeal carried him at times into two false equations: (1) the equation of justified certitude with correct certitude, and (2) the equation of the state of an individual's mind with the normative object, truth." Ferreira immediately adds, "In the very same chapters that he makes these claims, however, he denies them as well."[90]

Newman was probably quite fascinated with his phenomenological project, but he could hardly have allowed the *Grammar* to remain suspended at the level of phenomenology. Newman knew that he had to go beyond phenomenology if he was to establish the *rationality* of faith, the *reasonableness* of religious belief. He knew that he had to move from the descriptive to the normative, and while sometimes he carelessly makes a "logical type-jump," there are places in the *Grammar* where he follows a sensible epistemological strategy. This strategy is quite different from the one that underlies the epistemic logic of such contemporary epistemologists as Jaakko Hintikka and R. M. Chisholm,[91] and it is more akin to that of such recent British philosophers as G. E. Moore and Wittgenstein. Newman is a strong believer in common sense and is quite amazed at the sceptical doubts that many great philosophers think we ought to share with them. Newman starts with the assumption that there is something terribly wrong with any epistemological theory that dictates that we do not have a right to be certain that, say, Britain is an island. Then, by *comparative analysis*, he goes on to show that the kind of evidence that supports such a belief is not remarkably different from the kind that supports religious belief.

---

87 William R. Fey, *Faith and Doubt: The Unfolding of Newman's Thought on Certainty* (Shepherdstown, West Virginia: Patmos Press, 1976), 145.

88 Pailin, *Way to Faith*, 179.

89 Ibid., 184-85.

90 Ferreira, *Doubt*, 105.

91 See, for example, Jaakko Hintikka, *Knowledge and Belief* (Ithaca, New York: Cornell University Press, 1962); Roderick M. Chisholm, *Theory of Knowledge*, 2nd ed. (Englewood Cliffs, New Jersey: Prentice-Hall, 1977 [1966]).

However sensible it may seem to most of us, Newman's initial assumption is apt to strike some philosophers as being intolerably presumptuous, and Newman himself feels obliged to come to its defense. His defense comes in two parts. In the first, he exploits his phenomenological observation that certitude is "natural"; he reasons that if certitude is a universal phenomenon, it is absurd for philosophers to insist that certitude is rarely if ever warranted. This line of argument gets him into all sorts of trouble. The second, more powerful part of his defense is pragmatic. We *need* to believe that Britain is an island; we need to feel *certain* that it is an island. The belief "works," and life is for action; thought must be subservient to action. Can we afford to go through life worrying about the obscure possibility that Britain may not be an island? When we make plans for travel or some other practical matter, must we allow for such a possibility? In Cronin's view, the central thesis of the *Grammar* is "that thought is intimately related to life; that the mind, far from sitting apart in cold judgment upon syllogisms, is a living power influenced by feeling, habit, heredity and environment, one with the entire conscious life of the subject, bound by the necessity of reaching decisions for a life of action . . . ."[92]

Similarities between the *Grammar* and certain works by philosophical pragmatists have long been recognized.[93] In Hollis's view, "Newman agreed very largely with the pragmatists that action is the only real test of belief."[94] For John Passmore, Newman's mental philosophy is essentially one of the European "analogues" of pragmatism.[95] Being associated with pragmatism has not always made Newman's mental philosophy more attractive. As Horgan notes, "Such affinities and comparisons with unorthodox systems have had the effect of making Catholic philosophers and theologians steer clear of Newman."[96] But affinities there are, especially with the humanistic brand of pragmatism preached by William James and F. C. S. Schiller. The pragmatists themselves have not been blind to those affinities. For example, in his essay "Faith, Reason, and Religion," Schiller attaches great importance to the personal character of faith and places himself in an intellectual line with Newman as a philosopher who refuses to "depersonalize knowledge." He then tells us that James's pragmatism is a wider application of principles that Newman and others had already successfully applied in the field of religion, and he adds that Newman's "illative sense" has explanatory value in philo-

92 Cronin, *Knowledge*, xv.
93 Cf. note 23 above.
94 Hollis, *World*, 181.
95 John Passmore, *A Hundred Years of Philosophy* (London: Duckworth, 1957), 100-101.
96 Horgan, "Faith and Reason," 149-50.

sophical realms other than that of religion.[97] Borghild Gundersen rightly points out that Newman would have regarded humanistic pragmatism as an ally of immanentism and would have rejected many of its central doctrines;[98] but even Gundersen admits that Newman's philosophy "contains immanentist and pragmatist elements, by being more concerned with action than with metaphysics, by preferring empirical methods to abstractions, and by emphasizing the subjective elements of religion, as conscience, the illative sense, and personal experience."[99]

Newman, of course, did not see himself as engaged in phenomenology or epistemology. He did see himself as working "in the province of mental philosophy,"[100] but he never bothered to break this territory down into subdivisions.

11 The politics of the *Grammar*: Newman against the "liberals"

Newman's philosophical apologetic is an important part of his life-work, but still only a part, one battle in a war that lasted for sixty years. His admirer, Father Sillem, tells us that "Newman's life-work was one long, unrelenting and at times bitter struggle, carried on single-handed and without assistance of any kind from contemporary theologians or philosophers, against Liberal Rationalism, that is to say, against the doctrine, inherited from the philosophers of the Age of Enlightenment, that truth is accessible to 'the Reason,' and to 'the Reason' alone."[101] From 1828 on, "liberalism" was Newman's bête noire, and all of his major works, literary or otherwise, are animated by his deep antipathy to it.[102] The *Grammar* is no exception; indeed, in a way it is Newman's most effective attack on "liberalism," as it attempts to meet the enemy on its own terms. "The remote but very influential cause of the book," Zeno writes, "seems to me his lifelong energetic desire to make men religious, to preach the truths of revelation, to save men from the dangers of liberalism in religion, of indifferentism and of atheism."[103] And Newman was not just committed to saving individuals; he was out to save society itself from the insidious

97 F. C. S. Schiller, "Faith, Reason, and Religion," in *Studies in Humanism* (London: Macmillan, 1907), 351-53.
98 Gundersen, *Newman and Apologetics*, 125-36.
99 Ibid., 131.
100 O.Ar. Gr.M.: draft of a preface, "On the nature, modes and grounds of Religious assent," dated 30 December 1868.
101 Sillem, "Way to God," 377. Cf. Sillem, *Notebook*, vol. 1, 23-66; Boekraad, *Conquest*, 67-114.
102 Horgan, "Faith and Reason," 133.
103 Zeno, "Introduction," 391.

scourge of "liberalism." In spite of its rather dignified, semi-technical style, the *Grammar* is an angry political document, an attempt to stem the tide of anti-ecclesiastical progressivism. Newman realized, as most of his fellow ecclesiastics did not, that there was a very good chance that ecclesiastical religion was about to be deprived of the central role it had long played in the social life of the more civilized regions of Christendom. He saw himself as having to keep his finger in the dike, holding back the flood-waters of secular humanism.[104]

The terms "liberal" and "liberalism" are notoriously ambiguous and were already so in Newman's day. Newman himself did not have a completely clear idea of what he was attacking. We learn from the *Apologia* that he first associated liberalism with "the anti-dogmatic principle and its development."[105] And he never abandoned his view that the liberal is, at bottom, a pseudo-Christian reason-worshipper who is endeavouring to rob decent human beings, like the factory-girl, of their confidence in revelation as a source of wisdom. What dismayed him most was the success with which such "liberals" had infiltrated ecclesiastical ranks. In the last verse of his 1833 poem, "Liberalism," he sounds the keynote of his crusade:

> And so ye halve the Truth; for ye in heart,
> At best, are doubters whether it be true,
> The theme discarding, as unmeet for you,
> Statesmen or Sages. O new-compass'd art
> Of the ancient Foe!—but what, if it extend
> O'er our own camp, and rules amid our friends?[106]

As the years passed, and he became more bitter and frustrated, Newman's concept of liberalism became increasingly fuzzier. He began to view as liberals all progressive Christians whose interpretation of scripture and attitude towards the church differed even slightly from his own. He came to associate liberalism with rationalism, latitudinarianism, indifferentism, Manicheism,[107] atheism, and Protestantism. By the time he wrote the *Grammar*, he had gotten into the habit of using "liberalism" as a general term of disapprobation and abuse, much as others have used terms like "heretic" and "communist."

Contemporary Newmanists never tire of warning us that we must not identify the master's hostility to *religious* liberalism with hostility to the kind of *political* liberalism that many decent human beings

---

104 See Sebastian Karotemprel, *God and Secular Man* (Calcutta: Kirma KLM [Private], 1977).
105 Newman, *Apologia*, 163.
106 John Henry Newman, "Liberalism," in *Verses on Various Occasions* (London: Burns, Oates, 1880 [1868]), 140-41.
107 Gulielmo G. Topmoeller, *The Problem of Dogmatic Indifferentism according to John Henry Cardinal Newman* (Rome: Sfera, 1956), 17.

now find so attractive. There is much value in this warning; but Newmanists tend to draw too sharp a line between religious liberalism and political liberalism. In an interesting study of Newman's political thought, Terence Kenny rightly observes: "It is a measure of the flexibility or vagueness of political terms that Newman can as easily and as truthfully be called either a liberal or an anti-liberal."[108] But Newman's liberalism and anti-liberalism have both a political and religious dimension, and the two dimensions are not wholly unrelated. Moreover, "Newman can criticize liberalism, when thinking of its spirit and motives, while at the same time approving of its particular concrete results."[109]

Consider first Newman's liberalism. The mature Newman cannot be regarded as anti-democratic; his attitude towards democracy evolved from being very negative to moderately positive.[110] His progressive attitudes towards secular education and the role of the laity in the Catholic church annoyed prominent Catholic reactionaries. He came to the defense of the progressive Catholic periodical, *The Rambler*. And while he professed his personal belief in papal infallibility, he made known his worries about its being defined as a dogma and his objection to "a sweeping application of infallibility to all the pronouncements of any Pope and the way in which the proponents of such views anathematized everyone else as unorthodox."[111]

But while such flashes of liberalism were frequent and profound enough to constitute a pattern, Newman's mind was largely conservative, politically and religiously. In the course of both his Anglican and Roman Catholic careers, he argued time and time again against specific extensions of the fundamental freedoms of thought and speech. Two aspects of his conservatism merit special attention here, his lack of social conscience and his bigotry.

Kenny, who finds much to admire in Newman's personality, regretfully concludes from his investigations that Newman did not have much in the way of a social conscience.[112] "It is indeed curious," Kenny remarks, "that a man who can preach the need for the individual Christian to take a stand on social matters should himself fail to go far in this direction in practice."[113] The only explanation Kenny can offer is that Newman must have been "absolutely engrossed" in his apologetical project. "It never seems to have occurred to him that there was any possibility of intellectual development among some of

---

108 Terence Kenny, *The Political Thought of John Henry Newman* (London: Longmans, Green, 1957), 127.
109 Ibid., 147.
110 Ibid., 173-87.
111 Meriol Trevor, *Newman's Journey* (Glasgow: Collins, 1974), 235.
112 Kenny, *Political Thought*, 166-73.
113 Ibid., 168.

the poor and uneducated, and consequently he was hostile to Manning's plans to educate the Catholic poor and to Manning's apparent lack of concern for the education of the rich."[114] Although he probably had a genuine sympathy for the factory-girls of Birmingham and actually did some social work in the Edgbaston area, he simply could not understand why people like Cardinal Manning, Marx, and Bentham spent so much time worrying about the economic condition of the poor. Like Luther at the time of the peasant uprisings, he was far more concerned with souls than bodies. Perhaps his intense hatred of Benthamism had made him somewhat callous; or maybe he was just too much of an Oxford-trained élitist to be able to relate well to the ungentlemanly masses.

As for his bigotry, it was something that he freely admitted. In one of his Anglican sermons, he rails against "the religion of the day," telling us, "In every age of Christianity, since it was first preached, there has been what may be called a *religion of the world*, which so far imitates the one true religion, as to deceive the unstable and unwary."[115] This "religion of the day" is "especially adapted to please men of sceptical minds,"[116] for it is "pleasant and easy" and teaches that "benevolence is the chief virtue; intolerance, bigotry, excess of zeal, are the first of sins. Austerity is an absurdity;—even firmness is looked on with an unfriendly, suspicious eye."[117] In an Anglican sermon called "Tolerance of Religious Error," he advocates aggressive proselytizing, warning that "those who think themselves and others in risk of an eternal curse, dare not be thus indulgent."[118] Newman had no difficulty whatsoever in making the transition from anti-Catholic bigotry to anti-Protestant bigotry. The younger Newman had been so viciously anti-Catholic that in later years he had to eat large portions of humble pie. In his 1877 preface to the third edition of his Anglican work *The Via Media*, he writes, with much embarrassment, "The third and fourth Lectures are anti-catholic from beginning to end,"[119] and adds that they contain "the coarse rhetoric of hard names and sweeping imputations in advance of proof, proof not only not adduced, but not even promised."[120] "I wish these Lectures did not furnish instances of this reprehensible polemic. There was a great deal of calling of names all through them, (I do not mean as regards individuals but as against 'Romanism',) of which the Author has

114 Ibid., 169.
115 John Henry Newman, "The Religion of the Day," in *Parochial and Plain Sermons*, 8 vols. (London: Rivingtons, 1868 [1834-43]), vol. 1, 309.
116 Ibid., 316.
117 Ibid., 312.
118 John Henry Newman, "Tolerance of Religious Error," ibid., vol. 2, 289.
119 John Henry Newman, *The Via Media of the Anglican Church*, 2 vols., 3rd ed. (London: Longmans, Green, 1899 [1877]), vol. 1, xviii.
120 Ibid., xxvii.

cause to be ashamed."[121] But what had Newman learned? In his first work published as a father of the Oratory, he writes:

> § When we consider the beauty, the majesty, the completeness, the resources, the consolations, of the Catholic Religion, it may strike us with wonder, my brethren, that it does not convert the multitude of those who come in its way. Perhaps you have felt this surprise yourselves; especially those of you who have been recently converted, and can compare it, from experience, with those religions which the millions of this country choose instead of it. You know from experience how barren, unmeaning, and baseless those religions are; what poor attractions they have, and how little they have to say for themselves.[122]

> § They [Protestants] have the same obstruction in their hearts to entering the Catholic Church, which Pharisees and Sophists had before them; it goes against them to believe her doctrine, not so much for want of evidence that she is from God, as because, if so, they shall have to submit their minds to living men, who have not their own cultivation or depth of intellect, and because they must receive a number of doctrines, whether they will or no, which are strange to their imagination and difficult to their reason.[123]

That Newman had even less respect for non-Christians almost goes without saying. We shall be reconsidering Newman's bigotry when we examine the last two chapters of the *Grammar*, and at that time we shall pay special attention to his theological anti-Semitism.

Expressing his resentment of some of the harsher attacks on Newman, John Elbert remarks, "To dismiss the author of 'The Development of Christian Doctrine' by attributing to him the brain of a rabbit, may be characteristic of the manner of Carlyle but it hardly makes a claim worthy of consideration; or, to tax the writer of the 'Apologia' with exercising the deliberate fascination of the serpent, after the fashion of J. H. Hutton, is an exhibition of mind that must strike the average student as grotesque."[124] Fair enough. But a good many of us have reason to believe that Newman was not the saintly figure that his more fanatic admirers would have us believe. And more to the point, we should not forget that the *Grammar* is an attack on the spirit of a philosophical and political movement that, for all its weaknesses, embodies some of our highest ideals.

What indeed did the classical liberalism of Newman's age advocate? The following analysis by two historians is not wholly satisfactory, but it gives us a more realistic and more balanced view of nineteenth-century European liberalism than Newman does:

121 Ibid., xxviii.
122 John Henry Newman, *Discourses Addressed to Mixed Congregations* (London: Longmans, 1849), 192.
123 Ibid., 204.
124 John A. Elbert, *Evolution of Newman's Conception of Faith* (Philadelphia: Dolphin Press, 1932), 9.

Liberals were generally men of the business and professional classes, together with enterprising landowners wishing to improve their estates. They believed in what was modern, enlightened, efficient, reasonable, and fair. They had confidence in man's powers of self-government and self-control. They set a high value on parliamentary or representative government, working through reasonable discussion and legislation, with responsible ministries and an impartial and law-abiding administration. They demanded full publicity for all actions of government, and to assure such publicity they insisted on freedom of the press and free rights of assembly. All these political advantages they thought most likely to be realized under a good constitutional monarchy. Outside of England they favored explicit written constitutions. They were not democrats; they opposed giving every man the vote, fearing the excesses of mob rule or of irrational political action. Only as the nineteenth century progressed did liberals gradually and reluctantly come to accept the idea of universal manhood suffrage. They subscribed to the doctrines of the rights of man as set forth in the American and French Revolutions, but with a clear emphasis on the right of property, and in their economic views they followed the British Manchester school or the French economist J. B. Say. They favored *laissez-faire*, were suspicious of the ability of government to regulate business, wanted to get rid of the gild system where it still existed, and disapproved of attempts on the part of the new industrial laborers to organize unions. Internationally they advocated freedom of trade, to be accomplished by the lowering or abolition of tariffs, so that all countries might exchange their products easily with each other and with industrial England. In this way, they thought, each country would produce what it was most fitted for, and so best increase its wealth and standards of living. From the growth of wealth, production, invention, and scientific progress they believed that the general progress of humanity would ensue. They generally frowned upon the established churches and landed aristocracies as obstacles to advancement. They believed in the spread of tolerance and education. They were also profoundly civilian in attitude, disliking wars, conquerors, army officers, standing armies, and military expenditures. They wanted orderly change by processes of legislation. They shrank before the idea of revolution. Liberals on the Continent were usually admirers of Great Britain.[125]

We saw earlier that Newman incorporates into the *Grammar* his 1841 attack on the liberalism of such men as Brougham and Peel. By the time of the publication of the *Grammar*, Brougham and Peel were dead, but liberalism continued to be advocated by many men of great moral and intellectual stature, and most impressively by John Stuart Mill. Leslie Stephen admired both Newman and Mill for their clarity, but he also saw them as the outstanding exemplars of two competing world-views.[126]

125 R. R. Palmer and Joel Colton, *A History of the Modern World*, 3rd ed. (New York: Alfred A. Knopf, 1965), 432-33.
126 Stephen, "Theory of Belief," 680-81.

Chapter Two

Modes of Apprehension and Belief

1 The "holding" of propositions

When one reads a philosophy book, one should pay special attention to its opening pages, for to accept uncritically the author's first few ideas is to prepare the way for one's complete seduction. So, for example, to accept the definitions and axioms with which Spinoza begins his *Ethics* is to have already committed oneself to accepting the grandiose positions he advocates later in the book. Newman's style of philosophizing is starkly different from Spinoza's, but in the early pages of the *Grammar* he proves to be no less accomplished a seducer. We saw earlier that the *Grammar* begins "abruptly"; but Newman begins where he does because he knows precisely where he wants his readers to end up.

The first chapter of the *Grammar* is a discussion entitled "Modes of holding and apprehending Propositions." Newman would like us to believe that his opening discussion of modes of *holding* propositions is necessary simply because, first, the *Grammar* is a book about assent; and, second, assent is primarily a mode of holding a proposition. But one of Newman's main objectives is to establish the "unconditionality" of assent, to show that doubts need not (and cannot) enter into assent; so he begins the *Grammar* by *contrasting* unconditional assent with conditional "inference." A second main objective is to show that the "real" assent of genuine Christians is somehow superior to the mere "notional" assent of liberal Christians; so he must also talk about modes of *apprehending* propositions.

The *Grammar* begins with some classifying:

1. Propositions (consisting of a subject and predicate united by the copula) may take a categorical, conditional, or interrogative form.

(1) An interrogative, when they ask a Question (e.g. Does Free-trade benefit the poorer classes?) and imply the possibility of an affirmative or negative resolution of it.

(2) A conditional, when they express a Conclusion (e.g. Free-trade therefore benefits the poorer classes), and at once imply, and imply their dependence on, other propositions.

(3) A categorical, when they simply make an Assertion (e.g. Free-trade does benefit), and imply the absence of any condition or reservation of any kind, looking neither before nor behind, as resting in themselves and being intrinsically complete. (25)[1]

Newman goes on to say that these three modes of "shaping" a proposition "follow each other in natural sequence": "A proposition, which starts with being a Question, may become a Conclusion, and then be changed into an Assertion; but it has of course ceased to be a question, so far forth as it has become a conclusion, and has rid itself of its argumentative form—that is, has ceased to be a conclusion,—so far forth as it has become an assertion" (25). And since, Newman continues, "The internal [mental] act of holding propositions is for the most part analogous to the external act of enunciating them," there are three ways of holding them—Doubt, Inference, and Assent— corresponding to the three ways of enunciating them (26).

These opening moves by Newman merit careful scrutiny, for they lay the foundation of his entire philosophical apologetic; and bland though they may seem, they have far-reaching implications. We should begin by taking note of the importance that Newman attaches to propositions. As Fey notes, "He began by surveying the field of knowledge keeping the proposition at the center of his discussion. He was interested in the mental act by which we grasp and affirm the significance of a judgment expressed in a proposition."[2] Newman tells us that propositions consist of a subject and predicate united by the copula, but he does not bother to define the term "proposition," a term being used here in a rather different way than it is used by the factory-girl and the charbonnier. In warning us about the dangers of misinterpreting Newman's statements, Dr. Zeno writes:

> When he uses philosophical terms he does not do so as a philosopher and he attaches his own particular meaning, his personal sense, to those terms. Hence we need to find out what exactly Newman means by them. If we give them always the received meaning, the book becomes a hopeless chaos, irritating and misleading. This explains why there are so many adverse criticisms of the Grammar of Assent.[3]

While there is some truth in these observations, we have a right to assume that Newman usually means what he says. Newman's aim, after all, is to communicate with the reader, not to mystify him; and if

1 In the Doubleday and Notre Dame editions of the Grammar, Newman's text begins at p. 25 because the opening pages are devoted to introductions by contemporary scholars.
2 Fey, Faith and Doubt, 145.
3 Zeno, "Introduction," 393-94.

Newman does not bother to define "proposition," it is because he expects the fairly educated reader to understand what he is talking about. And what Newman has in mind here is a form of words in which something is affirmed or denied of something else.

Newman rightly believes that to assent is to have a certain attitude towards a proposition; it is to *accept* or *affirm* or *agree to* a proposition in a way that cannot adequately be described but is easily and naturally grasped by simple introspection. Newman does not deny that assent has emotional and behavioural aspects, but he recognizes that assent is essentially the acceptance of a proposition, a matter of "holding" that x is y. He does not have to argue for this point; anyone who understands this particular use of the English word "assent" will spontaneously agree with him here.

This use of the term "assent" is rather dated, and nowadays we use the term "belief" to denote the mental act of accepting a proposition. Sometimes Newman associates the term "belief" only with "real" assent (in contrast with "notional" assent) (87), but he does not do so consistently. And since our term "belief" means the same as Newman's term "assent," we will, where possible, replace his dated term with our own.

While we must agree with Newman that belief or "assent" is essentially the acceptance of a proposition, we would be unwise to accept his entire classificatory scheme. Newman pretends that there is something obvious and natural about this scheme, but it has been carefully cooked by Newman to further his objective of establishing that belief is unconditional. In fact, Newman's scheme *assumes* what Newman later attempts to prove. Newman realizes that one need not and cannot offer a proper definition of "assent," and so the purpose of his classificatory scheme is not to enable us to understand what belief is but rather to give us a preliminary insight into his view that belief is fundamentally different from the mental act of "inference" or conclusion.

Newman begins the *Grammar* by considering the verbal forms that a proposition can take, and the list he gives is short and arbitrary. The following are some of the more serious objections that a contemporary logician or epistemologist is apt to raise. (1) It is not clear that a question is a proposition. What does a question affirm or deny? (2) If a question qualifies as a proposition, then why doesn't a command or exclamation? Newman does not make it clear what *principle* of classification he is following. (3) It is not at all obvious that conclusion and assertion represent two different *forms* of a proposition. "Free-trade benefits the poorer classes" can be a conclusion as well as an assertion. (4) There are all sorts of verbal "forms" that a proposition can take. Propositions can be written or spoken, clear or obscure, simple or compound, descriptive or normative, analytic or synthetic.

They can be enunciated in English or Spanish or Urdu. They affirm or deny and are expressed with or without reservation. They can refer to the past, present, or future. Why does Newman think that his list of verbal "forms" is so much more interesting than other possible lists?

Newman's list of ways of "holding" propositions is equally short and arbitrary. Here are two of the more serious objections that the phenomenologist will want to raise. First, it is hard to understand why Newman regards inference as a mental act, as a mode of holding a proposition. Inference is a way of arriving at an assertion or belief, but is it also an attitude towards a proposition? Second, is it judicious for Newman to lump together under one label—whether that label be Doubt, Inference, or Assent—such apparently different propositional attitudes as being certain, being reasonably certain, regarding as beyond reasonable doubt, being inclined to believe, and regarding as plausible?

Newman also makes two gratuitous assumptions while setting up his classificatory scheme. The first is that the modes of "shaping" or "putting" a proposition follow each other in the "natural sequence" he describes (question to conclusion to assertion). Sometimes we do begin with a question and move on via reasoning to an assertion. But often we begin with assertion and only ask ourselves questions later. (Similarly, sometimes we begin with belief and only have doubts later, doubts that are not always resolved.) Moreover, the reasoning that results in conclusion and assertion is not always initiated by a question or doubt. A second gratuitous assumption is that the internal, mental act of holding propositions is "for the most part analogous" to the external act of enunciating them. The relationship between thought and language is more complex than Newman here pretends. For example, when I make the assertion "Free-trade benefits the poorer classes," I may be holding the belief in any of a hundred significantly different ways; I may think this proposition reasonable, highly reasonable, beyond reasonable doubt, certain, and so forth. In fact, I may not even hold the belief at all; I may be lying or involved in some complicated form of self-deception.

Newman, of course, is not interested in classification per se; he is interested in convincing us that belief is unconditional. In the first paragraph of the *Grammar*, he boldly announces that assertion involves "the absence of any condition or reservation of any kind." He later adds that "if we rest our affirmation on arguments, this shows that we are not asserting; and, when we assert, we do not argue. An assertion is as distinct from a conclusion, as a word of command is from a persuasion or recommendation" (26). And just as conclusion and assertion are "distinct," so are the mental acts that "correspond" to them, inference and assent. He writes: "Doubt, Inference, and Assent, are with reference to one and the same proposition, distinct from each other; else, why should their several enunciations be distinct? And indeed it is very evident, that, so far forth as we infer, we do not doubt, and that, when we assent, we are not inferring, and, when we doubt, we cannot assent" (27). Newman realizes that these points are not "very evident," for he returns to the subject of belief and inference in the second part of the *Grammar.* In light of the questions that we have raised, the most that we can say for the opening pages of the book is that they announce one of the *Grammar*'s main themes.

Before moving on to a preliminary discussion of apprehension, Newman makes two general observations. First, "in this Essay I treat of propositions only in their bearing upon concrete matter, and I am mainly concerned with Assent; with Inference, in its relation to Assent, and only such inference as is not demonstrative; with Doubt hardly at all" (28). Newman dismisses Doubt because whether it is understood as "a suspense of mind" or the "deliberate recognition of a thesis as being uncertain," it is equivalent to one or other of the two remaining mental acts (28). Second, assent to a proposition requires some intelligent apprehension of it in a way that inference does not; "we can infer, 'if x is y, and y is z, that x is z,'" whether we know the meaning of x and z or no" (28-29).

2 The apprehension of propositions

Newman adds a new dimension to his classificatory scheme by telling us that in addition to *holding* propositions in different ways, we also *apprehend* them in different ways. "By our apprehension of propositions I mean our imposition of a sense on the terms of which they are composed." Sometimes the terms, subject and predicate, "stand for certain ideas existing in our own minds, and for nothing outside of them," while at other times they stand for "things simply external to us, brought home to us through the experiences and informations we have of them." Newman now introduces his famous distinction between "real" and "notional." He gives the name "real propositions" to those propositions "which are composed of singular nouns, and of which the terms stand for things external to us, unit and individual." Apprehension of real propositions can be called "real apprehension," and examples of such propositions are "Philip was the father of Alexander" and "The earth goes round the sun." Newman gives the name "notional propositions" to those propositions "in which one or both of the terms are common nouns, as standing for what is abstract, general, and non-existing." Apprehension of notional propositions can be called "notional apprehension," and examples of such propositions are "Man is an animal" and "To err is human, to forgive divine" (29).

When he tells us that common nouns stand for what is non-existing and speaks of the mind's gift "of bringing before it abstractions and generalizations, which have no existence, no counterpart, out of it," Newman is letting us know that he has rejected the metaphysical "realism" of the scholastics in favour of the "nominalism" of the British empiricist school. As O'Donoghue observes, "in his attitude to notions he is an extreme nominalist."[4] Newman's rejection of one of the central doctrines of traditional Catholic philosophy did not win him friends in the Catholic church and contributed to his reputation for unorthodoxy; even some of his admirers have expressed deep regret at his adoption of the nominalist position.[5] This is not the place for an analysis of one of the oldest and most complicated of metaphysical debates, but it is worth our while to note how naïve and uncritical Newman has been in his *manner* of embracing nominalism. In the *Grammar*, he does not bother to defend the doctrine or even to allude to the classical objections to it. Yet, he knows that it has been considered false and dangerous by many philosophers, including the leading philosophers of his own church, and he even has some insight into *why* they have regarded it as pernicious. Sometimes he is inclined to regard the whole issue as above his head. We learn of his bewilderment from an unpublished note:

> If abstract truths, (or what nominalists call "generalizations" from experience) are objective, (as realists would hold,) therefore they are objects—what *is* the *object*? Beautifulness, for instance—*What* does the mind see when it contemplates this abstraction?—is it God? if not, is it one of the Platonic everlasting ideas external to God? if not, can it be any thing at all, and are we not driven to agreement with the school of Locke and of sensible experiences.
> I dare say there is some simple refutation at once to the following answer, which has this only recommendation, that I have held it these forty years strenuously—on the other hand I am so little versed in the controversy....
> I do not allow the existence of these abstract ideas corresponding to objective realities with Locke—but then, I do not pass over the experiences gained from the phenomena of mind so lightly, as I fancy the school of Locke is apt to do....
> . . . .
> I have a clear idea of what I mean by anxiety. It is an abstract word—it denotes a *mode* of mind. It does not denote a generalization or universal on the one hand, or an intuition of some extra-mental object on the other. I contemplate anxiety, not as a thing, yet it has its *root* in that which is a thing.[6]

The *Grammar* itself, however, does not give us the slightest intimation of Newman's perplexity and uneasiness. Banishing his doubts,

4 O'Donoghue, "Privileged Access," 257.
5 Horgan, "Faith and Reason," 143.
6 O.Ar. A.30.11: "On apprehension and assent through the imagination....," dated 26 April, 5 May, and 7 September, 1868. See *Theological Papers*, 135-36.

he moves to assertion: notions, abstractions, "have no existence, no counterpart" in the real world beyond the mind. This ontological downgrading of notions is to play a key role in his philosophical apologetic, which is all the more reason for us to regret that he never bothers to offer a precise definition of "notion" in any of his philosophical works.[7]

Newman closes chapter 1 with some informal remarks about the two modes of apprehension. He tells us that "the same proposition may admit of both of these interpretations at once, having a notional sense as used by one man, and a real as used by another"; that "the multitude of common nouns have originally been singular" and "many of them . . . remain still in the apprehension of particular individuals"; that "in the same mind and at the same time, the same proposition may express both what is notional and what is real"; that "[o]f these two modes of apprehending propositions, notional and real, real is the stronger; I mean by stronger the more vivid and forcible"; and that "inferences, which are conditional acts, are especially cognate to notional apprehension, and assents, which are unconditional, to real" (30-31). These points are not developed here at any great length, but Newman returns to them in later chapters. Accordingly, we shall save our consideration of them for later.

The next two chapters of the *Grammar*, "Assent Considered as Apprehensive" and "The Apprehension of Propositions," attempt to clarify the concept of apprehension. Chapter 2, the shortest of the book, is devoted exclusively to defending the false thesis that "I apprehend a proposition, when I apprehend its predicate" (32). Newman had pointed out in chapter 1 that apprehension is a necessary condition of belief, i.e., that we cannot accept a proposition that makes no sense to us. He now sets out to consider "what measure of apprehension is sufficient" (32). But while common sense suggests that some apprehension of both of the terms of a proposition is requisite for belief, Newman argues that "[t]he subject itself need not be apprehended *per se*. . . .":

> The subject . . . is the very thing which the predicate has to elucidate, and therefore by its formal place in the proposition, so far as it is the subject, it is something unknown, something which the predicate makes known; but the predicate cannot make it known, unless it is known itself. . . . The very drift of the proposition is to tell us something about the subject; but there is no reason why our knowledge of the subject, whatever it is, should go beyond what the predicate tells us about it. (32-33)

He offers the following example:

> If a child asks, "What is Lucern?" and is answered, "Lucern is medicago sativa, of the class Diadelphia and order Decandria;" and henceforth says

7 Zeno, "Psychological Discovery," 214.

obediently, "Lucern is medicago sativa, &c.," he makes no act of assent to the proposition which he enunciates, but speaks like a parrot. But, if he is told, "Lucern is food for cattle," and is shown cows grazing in a meadow, then, though he never saw lucern, and knows nothing at all about it, besides what he has learned from the predicate, he is in a position to make as genuine an assent to the proposition "Lucern is food for cattle," on the word of his informant, as if he knew ever so much more about lucern. (33)

Now, suppose that having confused lucern with Lucite, I mistakenly inform the child that "Lucern is a plastic compound used for airplane windows," and take him to the airport. Or suppose that he asks "What is epistemology?" and I mischievously answer "Epistemology is food for cattle," and take him to see cows grazing in the meadow. In saying obediently that "Lucern is a plastic compound used for airplane windows" or "Epistemology is food for cattle," is the child doing much more than speaking like a parrot? And even if Newman's claim makes *some* sense for analytic propositions (which questions like "What is Lucern?" elicit), how much sense does it make for propositions like "Epistemology ran down the street"? Can a child believe this in a more "genuine" way than he can believe that food for cattle is medicago sativa?[8] Does apprehension of the predicate make a difference here?

Not only has Newman advanced a false thesis; he has failed to answer his question about "what measure of apprehension is sufficient." It would be nice if Newman could tell us how far the separate terms of a proposition must be grasped in order for us to be able to apprehend the proposition that they form.[9] Newman wisely declines to attempt an answer to this question, and we shall soon see why.

But let us return for the moment to Newman's strange view that "I apprehend a proposition, when I apprehend its predicate." One may be tempted to wonder why Newman rushes—in just a few pages—to offer such a half-baked theory. We see why when we consider the second half of chapter 2; and, as usual, there is an apologetical motive lurking in the background. Newman writes of a way in which "the child can give an indirect assent even to a proposition, in which he understood neither subject nor predicate":

> He cannot indeed in that case assent to the proposition itself, but he can assent to its truth. He cannot do more than assent that "Lucern is medicago sativa," but he can assent to the proposition, "That lucern is medicago sativa is true." For here is a predicate which he sufficiently apprehends, what is inapprehensible in the proposition being confined to the subject. Thus the child's mother might teach him to repeat a passage of Shakespeare, and when he asked the meaning of a particular line, such as "The quality of mercy is not strained," or "Virtue itself turns vice, being misapplied," she might answer him, that he was too young to

8 Cf. Pailin, *Way to Faith*, 105-106.
9 Ibid.

understand it yet, but that it had a beautiful meaning, as he would one day know: and he, in faith on her word, might give his assent to such a proposition,—not, that is, to the line itself which he had got by heart, and which would be beyond him, but to its being true, beautiful, and good. (34)

It does not take much imagination to realize that the "child" Newman has in mind is the Roman Catholic layman and the "mother" of whom he is thinking is the Roman Catholic hierarchy. Newman is trying to deal with the following problem: if apprehension is a necessary condition of belief, how can simple (or even learned) Christians believe some of the complex and obscure teachings of the church that Roman Catholics are obliged to believe? The church teaches that "God is pure act," but how can the factory-girl be expected to apprehend this proposition clearly enough to be able to believe it? Newman's answer is that she, putting faith in the priest's word, might give her assent to such a proposition—not, that is, to the proposition itself, but to its being true and profound. Even if the factory-girl cannot believe the proposition per se, she can believe it in the sense of believing it to be true.

Some readers have felt that it is actually the main aim of the entire first part of the *Grammar* to show "that you can believe what you cannot understand"[10]; and this is certainly the aim of chapter 2. Does Newman succeed here? Some philosophers would argue that the concept of *truth* is itself more obscure than Newman's analysis leads us to believe; after all, some philosophers have spent entire academic careers reflecting on the nature of truth. Newman would regard such an objection as academic silliness; and he is right in believing that the factory-girl sufficiently apprehends the predicate "true" to be able to assent to ordinary propositions of which it is a term. But it is still not clear that the pious factory-girl is doing much more than speaking like a parrot when she enunciates the proposition " 'God is pure act' is true." For if Newman's analysis is correct, then it is possible to believe that " 'Epistemology ran down the street' is true." Not much is to be gained from such an analysis, and the Catholic epistemologist is being more reasonable when he admits that most Roman Catholics are not in the position to believe the more recondite teachings of the church.

Newman has not adequately answered his question about what measure of apprehension is sufficient for belief. The question is itself rather ambiguous, and it is noteworthy that Newman is prepared to settle for the rather bland answer that apprehension of the predicate is sufficient. This false answer does not go very far in the way of *measur-*

10 This view goes back to Caswall (1877). See C. S. Dessain, *John Henry Newman*, 3rd ed. (Oxford: Oxford University Press, 1980), 148. Cf. Lash, "Introduction," 12; I. T. Ker, "Newman on Truth," *Irish Theological Quarterly* 44 (1977), 67.

ing; it says, in effect, that *some* apprehension of *one term* is sufficient. Newman realizes that he cannot tell us *how far* the predicate (itself) must be grasped. There is no standard of measurement that will enable us to give a simple answer to *this* question.

In chapter 3, however, Newman brings us as close as we can ever get to the measuring of apprehension. Contrasting *examples* of real apprehension with *examples* of notional apprehension, he concludes that real apprehension is, in general, stronger than notional. It is stronger by two criteria, and corresponding to the two criteria are two types of data. The first criterion is phenomenological. By introspection we realize that real apprehension is accompanied by vivid imagery. When we perceive, remember what we perceive, or imagine, our mind has before it impressions and sensations that do not accompany apprehension of notional propositions. When experiences about the concrete are "in fact presented to us," then "we can actually point out the objects which they indicate" (38-39). But, in addition, "I can bring before me the music of the *Adeste Fideles*, as if I were actually hearing it" (40), and "The picture, which historians are able to bring before us, of Caesar's death, derives its vividness and effect from its virtual appeal to the various images of our memory" (42).

The second criterion is behavioural. Real apprehension influences our behaviour to a degree that notional cannot. Newman develops this point in chapter 4 when he contrasts real and notional *assents*. But he prepares us for his later discussion when he observes:

> Each use of propositions has its own excellence and serviceableness, and each has its own imperfection. To apprehend notionally is to have breadth of mind, but to be shallow; to apprehend really is to be deep, but to be narrow-minded. The latter is the conservative principle of knowledge, and the former the principle of its advancement. Without the apprehension of notions, we should for ever pace round one small circle of knowledge; without a firm hold upon things, we shall waste ourselves in vague speculations. However, real apprehension has the precedence, as being the scope and end and the test of notional; and the fuller is the mind's hold upon things or what it considers such, the more fertile is it in its aspects of them, and the more practical in its definitions. (47)

And providing us with a bridge to the next chapter, he writes:

> As notions come of abstractions, so images come of experiences; the more fully the mind is occupied by an experience, the keener will be its assent to it, if it assents, and on the other hand, the duller will be its assent and the less operative, the more it is engaged with an abstraction; and thus a scale of assents is conceivable ... varying from an assent which looks like mere inference up to a belief both intense and practical .... (47)

So while there is no simple answer to the question of how much apprehension is requisite for belief, apprehension can be "measured" in terms of its vividness and its influence on our behaviour. By examining a person's behaviour, we are sometimes in the position to determine that a person does not actually apprehend a proposition that he claims he apprehends; and similarly, examining his behaviour may lead us to conclude that his belief is not as strong as it could be—or as strong as he thinks it is. For though belief is unconditional, there is still a sense or two (i.e., phenomenologico-behavioural or phenomenological *and* behavioural) in which some beliefs are stronger than others.

By placing before us a few carefully selected examples, Newman has gone some way, though not far, in defending his claim in chapter 1 that "[o]f these two modes of apprehending propositions, notional and real, real is the stronger" (31). The examples of chapter 3 support his earlier claim that real apprehension, unlike notional, "excites and stimulates the affections and passions, by bringing facts home to them as motive causes. Thus it indirectly brings about what the apprehension of large principles, of general laws, or of moral obligations, never could effect" (31). If Newman is right, phenomenological insight into the difference between real and notional apprehension—into the way in which imagery plays a role in one that it does not in the other—even enables us to understand *why* one influences behaviour to a degree that the other cannot.

Newman's little story has some disquieting features. One is that in spite of his examples, Newman has not been able to hide the fact that "apprehension" is itself a concept, a "notion," and a fuzzy, imprecise one at that. In chapter 1, he defines "apprehension"—a semi-technical term—as "imposition of a sense" on a proposition's terms; but he knew then that such a definition is not very revealing. His examples, phenomenological observations, and remarks about behaviour have all helped to clarify the concept, but the concept is still not as clear as Newman would like it to be. This is brought home to us by the distinction between apprehension and understanding with which he begins chapter 3. In chapter 2 he is not careful to distinguish the two; he writes of a way "in which the child can give an indirect assent even to a proposition, in which he *understood* [my emphasis] neither subject nor predicate" (33). But a few pages later, he writes:

> I have used the word *apprehension*, and not *understanding*. . . . It is possible to apprehend without understanding. I apprehend what is meant by saying that John is Richard's wife's father's aunt's husband, but, if I am unable so to take in these successive relationships as to understand the upshot of the whole, viz. that John is great-uncle-in-law to Richard, I cannot be said to understand the proposition. In like manner, I may take a just view of a man's conduct, and therefore apprehend it, and yet may profess that I cannot understand it; that is, I have not the key

to it, and do not see its consistency in detail; I have no just conception of it. Apprehension then is simply an intelligent acceptance of the idea, or of the fact which a proposition enunciates. (36)

These comments are not very helpful, and they draw our attention to some disturbing features of Newman's treatment of apprehension. For one thing, Newman is abandoning a term from ordinary language, "understanding," in favour of a semi-technical one that he is not finding it easy to analyze for us. Moreover, Newman is trying to get us to accept the view that we can believe what we cannot understand; his position is that apprehension, not understanding, is a necessary condition of belief. But many of us find it hard to accept the view that one can believe what one does not understand, especially when the difference between the ordinary concept of understanding and the semi-technical concept of apprehension is not entirely clear. We are more naturally inclined to think of understanding as something that admits of kinds and degrees, to think that a child, a carpenter, and a chemist have a different *kind* or *degree* of understanding of what wood is, for example. When we ask a child "Do you understand (or know) what I mean by 'wood'?," he can truthfully answer "Yes," or "I'm pretty sure that I do," even if he does not have the same understanding of wood that the carpenter or chemist has. If a child cannot tell us *anything* about wood, then in what sense can he be regarded as having "apprehended" it? If a child sees or perceives wood without having *any* understanding of what is before him, we can hardly say that he "apprehends" *wood*; he has merely had sensory experience.

Another disturbing feature of Newman's analysis is that it presents examples that seem to have been specifically chosen because they support Newman's position that real apprehension is stronger than notional. We shall develop this criticism when we examine Newman's analysis of real and notional *assents*. But even at this stage we must challenge Newman's analysis on two levels. First, on the phenomenological level, we should note that some "notions" seem to have a *clarity*, in kind and degree, that most images do not. A. J. Boekraad and others attach great importance to Newman's "Platonism,"[11] but one of the central themes of Platonic teaching is that the sophistic empiricists are naïve in believing that Ideas and mathematical objects are not as real *or as clear to the mind* as physical objects and their images are. Secondly, on the behavioural level, we must express grave doubts about Newman's assumption that notional apprehension has relatively little influence on behaviour.

Still another disquieting feature of Newman's analysis is the sharp line it draws between things and notions. Whatever value such a distinction has as a piece of ontology, its phenomenological value is

11 Boekraad, *Conquest*, 50-60. Cf. Gundersen, *Newman and Apologetics*, 140.

questionable. Newman himself is prepared to admit that both modes of apprehension "may co-exist in the same mind" (47; cf. 30-31). "When a lecturer in mechanics or chemistry shows to his class by experiment some physical fact, he and his hearers at once enunciate it as an individual thing before their eyes, and also as generalized by their minds into a law of nature" (30-31). It may well be that people often (or even usually) have before their mind something that is not simply a "thing" or a "notion." Moreover, Newman has not explained why vivid imagery cannot easily attach itself to notional apprehension.

If Newman has indeed selected examples that *fit* his view about the relative strength of the modes of apprehension, then his examples hardly constitute a defense of that view. But then how did he arrive at such a view? For one thing, Newman seems to have accepted uncritically the view of his British empiricist teachers that perception is the paradigm of knowing (and the related view that the perceptible object is the paradigm of a real object); starting with such an assumption, he was naturally led to the conclusion that all other modes of knowing are *based on* perception and therefore must fall short of it in terms of quality and influence. Secondly, as an apologist, Newman wants to believe, and wants *us* to believe, that being a good Christian depends more on having religious images in one's head than having philosophical concepts in one's head; if real apprehension is stronger than notional, then intellectual "liberals" are doomed to be inferior to factory-girls in terms of Christian commitment. Newman's will to believe may have made it easier for him to ignore counterexamples. Finally, we cannot rule out the possibility that Newman does not believe what he has written.

This last point calls for elaboration. Throughout his long career, Newman was frequently accused of being a liar and deceiver. It was such an accusation by Kingsley that had led Newman to write the *Apologia*. Kingsley had bluntly expressed what many of Newman's detractors had long felt: "Truth, for its own sake, had never been a virtue with the Roman clergy. Father Newman informs us that it need not, and on the whole ought not to be; that cunning is the weapon which Heaven has given to the saints wherewith to withstand the brute male force of the wicked world which marries and is given in marriage."[12] Newman answers in the *Apologia* that he has always acted on the principles of St. Philip Neri, who could not endure liars.[13] Kingsley, of course, was a bigot, as were many of Newman's detractors. But we must remember that Newman was an apologist and a

12 Charles Kingsley, Review of Froude's *History of England*, in *Macmillan's Magazine* (1864), 217.
13 Newman, *Apologia*, 352-53.

controversialist and was more concerned with saving souls than with leading men to philosophical wisdom. It is instructive to consider some observations by an admirer and defender of Newman, E. D. Benard, who warns: "We must beware of mistaking for a positive opinion of Newman a mere concession made for the sake of narrowing down a discussion to a precise controversial apex"[14]; ". . . Newman wrote as he did because of the readers for whom his work was intended."[15] Referring to a famous statement by Newman about conscience and the pope, Benard admits that "to the Catholic reader even now this sentence is somewhat of a shock"[16]; but he comforts his co-religionists by observing that Newman here "was not writing to convince loyal Catholics. His purpose was to assure Protestant Englishmen . . . ."[17] Newman is a controversialist, a propagandist, a proselytizer; his work is largely polemical and aims at persuasion. He is not the pathological liar that his ruder critics have claimed; but he is usually adept at doing those deceptive things that all controversialists at least occasionally do, such as exaggerating, ignoring obvious counterexamples, employing fallacious arguments, and pretending. So while we have a right to assume that Newman usually means what he says, we cannot always be so confident that he is saying what he believes.

3 "Profession"

Chapter 4, entitled "Notional and Real Assent," begins by reiterating that real apprehension is stronger than notional and quickly moves on to consider certain relations between modes of apprehension and modes of "holding" propositions. Newman warns us that it is the "variation in the mind's apprehension of an object to which it assents, and not any incompleteness in the assent itself, that leads us to speak of strong and weak assents, as if Assent itself admitted of degrees" (50). He then speaks of the resemblance between notional beliefs and inferences (the latter being considered as acts of "holding" various propositions): "notional Assent seems like Inference, because the apprehension which accompanies acts of Inference is notional also,—because Inference is engaged for the most part on notional propositions, both premiss and conclusion. . . . Only propositions about individuals are not notional, and these are seldom the matter of inference" (51). Not only is this claim false, but Newman himself will

14 Edmond Darvil Benard, *A Preface to Newman's Theology* (St. Louis: B. Herder Book Co., 1946), 56-57.
15 Ibid., 61.
16 Ibid., 59.
17 Ibid., 61.

devote the second half of the *Grammar* to *proving* it false. However, even if we assume that Newman is thinking here only of what he will later call "formal" inference (as opposed to "informal inference in concrete matter"), his claim is still false, although we can understand why he makes this mistake. A nineteenth-century thinker, Newman did not view formal logic in the way that contemporary philosophers do; following his teacher, Whately, and others, he associates formal inference with *syllogism*. A syllogism is far more likely to have a "notional" conclusion than an argument of the form *modus ponens* is. We shall come back to this point when we examine the chapters of the *Grammar* on inference.

Newman now returns to the business of classifying and discusses five types of notional belief: "I shall consider Assent made to propositions which express abstractions or notions under five heads; which I shall call Profession, Credence, Opinion, Presumption, and Speculation" (52). I think that Newman realizes that his way of classifying notional beliefs reflects his own special interests; for consider his cautionary use of "I"-phrases in these representative statements:

§ "I shall consider Assent made to propositions ... under five heads; which I shall call ...." (52)

§ "There are assents so feeble and superficial, as to be little more than assertions. I class them all together under the head of ...." (52-53)

§ "I shall here use the word ["opinion"] to denote ...." (64)

§ "By presumption I mean ...." (66)

Before one dismisses this use of "I"-phrases as purely stylistic, one should consider Newman's sensitivity to the fact that an adequate classification of notional beliefs cannot be derived simply by examining ordinary, everyday language. When listing the various kinds of notional belief, Newman does not consider such everyday locutions as "I think that," "I hold that," "I feel that," "I am inclined to believe that," and "I suspect that." The terms that he has chosen for designating the various notional beliefs—"profession," "credence," etc.—are not technical terms but are used by Newman in a special way. Speaking of "opinion," he warns us that it "is a word of various significations, and I prefer to use it in my own" (64). "Speculation is one of those words which, in the vernacular, have so different a sense from what they bear in philosophy" (75); Newman elects to use it in its "philosophical" sense. Newman, of course, is not blind to the importance of everyday locutions; he never is, and his analyses of profession, credence, etc. indicate that he sees everyday locutions as giving the listener *some* insight into what kind of assent the speaker has made. But Newman has made a fair point: *if* his own distinction between, say , profession and credence is a valuable one, then it may well be relatively unimportant for us to worry about the force of an everyday locution like "I feel that" insofar as this particular locution is used by those whose belief is credence or opinion as well as by those whose belief is profession. Some contemporary epistemologists will want to argue that such everyday locutions as "I feel that" must be more important than Newman recognizes, and though they may be right, they are making a value judgment, and perhaps they are being less sensitive than Newman to the fact that a philosopher's way of classifying beliefs reflects his own special interests. Newman's use of "I"-phrases may simply indicate his recognition of the limited value of ordinary language in characterizing the various forms of belief; but perhaps Newman is also acknowledging the subjective dimension of descriptions of propositional attitudes. An earlier Newman list of "mental postures," that of 1853, is significantly different from the one in the *Grammar* and includes such items as "surmise" and "suspicion,"[18] so Newman must have recognized that there are alternative ways of handling the classification of notional beliefs.

Newman says many interesting things in his analyses of the various kinds of notional belief, but for our purposes it is best to concentrate on one of his analyses, that of profession. What he says about this weakest kind of belief tells us all we need to know about his method of analysis in chapter 4. He writes: "There are assents so feeble and superficial, as to be little more than assertions. I class them together under the head of Profession" (52-53). What we want to know now is how a mental posture can be little more than a locution, an enunciation, "assertion"; whether assents of profession are really so similar in degree of weakness as to warrant their being classed together under a single head; and whether it is appropriate to designate the most feeble belief by the label "profession." Having announced the existence of beliefs of profession, Newman gives examples and does some more classifying. As always, his examples are not ordinary examples; they are the sort of examples that we are accustomed nowadays to getting from phenomenologists and existentialists. They are not given simply for the purpose of illustration or clarification; rather, they constitute Newman's defense or justification of his analysis. He has carefully picked out certain bits of everyday experience and invited us to reflect on them. He believes that after we have looked inward and looked outward, we shall (perhaps suddenly) "grasp" the reasonableness of placing various beliefs under the same head. Newman speaks of the following beliefs of profession:

> A. "the assents made upon habit and without reflection; as when a man calls himself a Tory or a Liberal, as having been brought up as such; or

18 O.Ar. A.30.11: untitled paper on faith, dated 13 May 1853. See *Theological Papers*, 11-13.

again, when he adopts as a matter of course the literary or other fashions of the day, admiring the poems, or the novels, or the music, or the personages, or the costume, or the wines, or the manners, which happen to be popular, or are patronized in the higher circles." (53)

B. "the assents of men of wavering restless minds, who take up and then abandon beliefs so readily, so suddenly, as to make it appear that they had no view (as it is called)[19] on the matter they professed, and did not know to what they assented or why." (53)

C. the assent of "[m]any a disciple of a philosophical school, who talks fluently, [but] does but assert, when he seems to assent to the *dicta* of his master, little as he may be aware of it. . . . This practice of asserting simply on authority, with the pretence and without the reality of assent, is what is meant by formalism. . . . It is thus that political and religious watchwords are created; first one man of name and then another adopts them, till their use becomes popular, and then every one professes them, because every one else does. Such words are "liberality," "progress," "light," "civilization;" such are "justification by faith only," "vital religion," "private judgment," "the Bible and nothing but the Bible." Such again are "Rationalism," "Gallicanism," "Jesuitism," "Ultramontanism"—all of which, in the mouths of conscientious thinkers, have a definite meaning, but are used by the multitude as war-cries, nicknames, and shibboleths . . . ." (53-54)

D. certain assents imposed on us by Inference. "For instance, it can be proved by irrefragable calculations, that the stars are not less than billions of miles distant from the earth; . . . yet who can say that he has any real, nay, any notional apprehension of a billion or a trillion? We can, indeed, have some notion of it . . . but I am speaking of the vast number in itself." (55)

The connection between Newman's phenomenological analysis and his apologetical strategy is not hard to perceive. Newman wants to depreciate the religious beliefs of certain people, such as Protestants who have little regard for traditional Christian teachings that have been able to survive the test of time (B), Protestants who proclaim the importance of "private judgment" (C), Roman Catholic Ultramontanist extremists (C), and intellectual liberals who attack religious dogma and argue for a "purely rational" religion (C and D). He does so by showing that these religious beliefs are significantly similar to certain secular beliefs that are both relatively uncontroversial and easily recognizable as "superficial," e.g., foolish, conventional judgments about wine (A).

Why are beliefs of type A so "feeble" and "superficial" even when compared to other notional beliefs? Consider two of the many items on Newman's list of type A beliefs. If you were to ask them about the quality of Canadian wines, most Canadians would probably say, with a sad smile, "The best Canadian wines are not comparable in quality

---

19 On Newman's use of "view," see Nicholas Lash, *Newman on Development: The Search for an Explanation in History* (London: Sheed and Ward, 1975), 35.

to the best European wines." Here is an assertion, and we would normally assume that such an assertion is backed up by the speaker's belief. (It is hard to believe that these Canadians are trying to deceive us about Canadian wine, or that they are incapable of finding the proper words for articulating their belief.) Yet most Canadians know very little, and indeed *think* very little, about the quality of different wines; they are familiar with only a very limited range of wines and have trouble specifying their criteria for distinguishing between good wines and excellent wines. And when one points these facts out to them, most are likely to give this sort of reply: "Now that I think about it, you are quite right; my judgment was a rather gratuitous one based on my acceptance of conventional opinion or the opinion of certain supposed experts." Political preferences are usually taken more seriously than wine preferences, but a good many people who assert that they are Liberals or Conservatives have thought very little about what being a Liberal or Conservative involves. Many professed Liberals cannot tell you to what programs or principles their party (or any other party) is committed. And when one points this fact out to such Liberals, they are apt to be touchy and defensive at first, but after reflecting on the matter may well give this sort of reply: "Now that I think about it, your point is a fair one; my commitment to the Liberal party is not a very profound one. Instead of being based on a sound understanding of important political disagreements, it is based on my acceptance of the judgment of my parents, teachers and friends."

Assents of type A are "feeble" and "superficial," then, because they have some combination of the following characteristics: (1) The assertion they supposedly "back up" contains one or more terms that correspond to a rather indistinct notion (e.g., "best wines," "Liberal"); (2) They are made after little or no reflection; (3) They are easily recognized as unwarranted; (4) A reasonable person will, after reflection, quickly surrender them; and (5) They are based on the speaker's uncritical acceptance of either conventional belief or the belief of certain supposed authorities. (Because of his interest in the "notional" nature of these beliefs, Newman must regard the first characteristic as most basic.) But there is, I think, a sixth characteristic that the practical-minded Newman sees beliefs of type A as having. When we put Newman's analysis of these beliefs together with other things that he says in the *Grammar*, we find that it implicitly suggests that assents of type A have a relatively limited influence on the speaker's behaviour. Granted, many Canadians will continue to buy the "best" European wines, and many uncritical "Liberals" will continue to vote for Liberal party candidates. But if a person has not bothered to think very much about a certain "belief," has made his assent on the basis of minimal apprehension of some fuzzy, imprecise notion, and is willing to surrender it after only a small amount of reflection, then can his behaviour have been profoundly influenced by it? A man who has no conception of what a "good" or "excellent" wine is can continue to buy the "better" European wines, but he will have a hard time, for example, determining whether an unidentified glass of Italian wine is better than an unidentified glass of Canadian wine; and a man who has little idea of what being a Liberal involves can continue to vote for Liberal party candidates, but he will have a hard time in consistently supporting Liberal principles in everyday life.

Newman has not argued that all judgments about wine and political parties are feeble and superficial; he has carefully supplied the necessary provisos: "made upon habit and without reflection," "as having been brought up as such," "adopts as a matter of course," "fashions of the day," "which happen to be popular, or are patronized in the higher circles." Newman knows that many oenophiles and many Liberals can give elaborate and reasonable defenses of their beliefs and can even give clear descriptions of what they mean by such terms as "good wine" and "Liberal." He regards these facts as irrelevant to the subject under discussion, and rightly so. Moreover, in discussing beliefs of type C, he carefully admits that he is only speaking about *many* a disciple of a philosophical school, and that terms like "private judgment" have a definite meaning "in the mouths of conscientious thinkers."

Newman, of course, is very partisan in picking his examples of beliefs of type C; he emphasizes Protestant profession and all but ignores Roman Catholic profession. The narrowness of his examples is somewhat disconcerting to the non-Catholic reader; even one who is aware of Newman's apologetical aims may be disappointed by the gracelessness of Newman's one-sided list. Still, Newman's comparison of types A and C beliefs is reasonable enough to warrant his having grouped them together under a common head. He rightly suggests that many of the Protestants who proclaim the importance of "private judgment" have an imperfect notion of "private judgment," much as most men who praise European wine have an imperfect notion of "good wine," and many defenders of the Liberal party have a fuzzy notion of what being a Liberal involves. He is probably right in suggesting that assents of type C resemble those of type A in having a relatively limited influence on the speaker's behaviour; if one has no clear idea of what "private judgment" is, then his belief in its importance may lead him to call himself a "Protestant" rather than a "Catholic," but it will not in itself lead him to perform acts of Christian charity. And Newman is justifiably sensitive here to the dangers of empty sloganizing and labeling, and is right in observing that certain religious assertions are "backed up" by something that barely merits the name of "assent" (being based, as it is, on a *highly* indistinct notion).

Newman's choice of the term "profession" is, if somewhat infelicitous, not altogether mysterious. Newman's main interest is in religious beliefs, and we tend to associate the act of professing with religious commitment. One "professes his faith" by announcing it, avowing it, declaring it openly. Such profession involves a combination of bold assertion and either genuine, counterfeit, or confused belief. Since the beliefs that Newman is discussing here are primarily assertions ("little more than assertions"), and since it is widely recognized that men often profess to believe things that they do not really believe, the term "profession" is no less appropriate in this context than any other Newman could have chosen.

Not much will be gained by trying to determine whether Newman's analysis of profession is correct or incorrect in some objective sense. Newman may have made some false statements in his discussion of profession, and the very use of the term "profession" may be questioned; but Newman has given us what is, on the whole, an interesting and reasonable *comparison* of certain beliefs (or certain assertions), a comparison that provides us with a certain way of viewing those various beliefs. As we have seen, Newman has apologetical motives for encouraging us to view these beliefs as similar instances of profession. One can compare a red apple with a red fire engine or with a green apple, and the comparison that one makes will depend on the particular point that one wishes to convey in a specific situation; to say that a red apple and a red fire engine have something important in common is not to give the "correct" analysis of "things" but to give a valuable and perhaps appropriate one, and it will not do for a critic to say that such an analysis is invariably useless because of the significant differences between an apple and a fire engine. But is Newman's analysis *appropriate*?

A principal objective of the *Grammar* is to establish the superiority of the pious Catholic's "real" belief to the liberal's weaker notional belief. But Newman's comments on profession may not serve his purpose well. If the typical Protestant user of the term "private judgment" has an indistinct notion of "private judgment," then his belief may well deserve a low place in Newman's hierarchy of beliefs; and let us assume for the sake of argument that the average Protestant's notion of "private judgment" *is* indistinct. But how much more distinct is the Roman Catholic factory-girl's notion of love or grace or even God? Are not most of the Catholic's assents "made upon habit and without reflection," asserted "simply on authority," etc.? If Newman's aims were purely philosophical, he would have no prob-

lem here; but he is trying to establish that the simple Catholic peasant's religious beliefs are more profound than those of the Protestant
multitude. Liberal intellectuals may not be better Christians than
Catholic peasants, but they are more reflective, and they make more of
an effort to think *clearly*. Newman would probably reply to this
objection in the following way: the Catholic peasant's notions may be
as indistinct as the religious liberal's, but unlike the liberal, the
peasant makes a real assent rather than (or as well as) a notional one
("As to Catholic populations, . . . among them assent to religious
objects is real, not notional" [62]). But such a reply would not solve all
of Newman's problems.

Consider these three remaining difficulties. (1) Many important
religious propositions contain terms of a highly abstract nature. It is
hard to believe that the typical Catholic factory-girl or peasant is
capable of associating such propositions with any experience or
image at all. Newman himself asks, "What sense, for instance, can a
child or a peasant, nay, or any ordinary Catholic, put upon the Tridentine canons, even in translation? . . . Or again, consider the very
anathematism annexed by the Nicene Council to its Creed, the language of which is so obscure . . ." (126). And yet, according to Newman, "These doctrinal enunciations are *de fide*: peasants are bound to
believe them as well as controversialists, and to believe them as truly
as they believe that our Lord is God" (126-27). For the peasant, can
such beliefs ever be "little more than assertions?" (2) A simple person
can attach inappropriate images to certain terms in a religious proposition. To devout peasants, "the Supreme Being, our Lord, the Blessed
Virgin, Angels and Saints, heaven and hell, are as present as if they
were objects of sight . . ." (62). Maybe so, but a foolish peasant may
associate the supreme being with an image of his kindly grandfather,
or he may associate heaven with an image of a king's court. When a
peasant associates heaven with an image of a king's court, his idea of
heaven may be very sharp and distinct in one sense, but as an idea *of
heaven*, it is of dubious value. Now, since the peasant's assent in such
a case is accompanied by vivid images, it is in one sense "stronger"
than mere "profession"; but does it really deserve a higher place in a
hierarchy of beliefs?; is a foolish image-laden notion more respectable
than a confused abstraction? (3) The beliefs of "profession" have a
relatively limited influence on behaviour, but they do have *some*
influence on behaviour. They lead a man to continue to buy European
wines, to continue to vote for Liberal party candidates, to continue to
call himself a Protestant. It is possible for a belief of profession to have
a healthy influence on behaviour, just as it is possible for a "real"
belief to have an unhealthy one. Say, for example, that in a particular
riding, the Liberal party candidate is a decent and competent man

while his opponents in the election are hacks. The man who is a Liberal, "having been brought up as such," will do more to promote civilization than the man who makes a real assent to the proposition "All Liberals are agents of the devil."

In his comments on profession, Newman is drawing our attention to the importance of *clarity*; as he rightly observes, we ought to know what we mean when we use various terms, especially when we are engaged in a religious controversy. Newman has rightly condemned certain kinds of sloganizing, and in doing so, he has scored a point against woolly-headed critics of Catholicism. But the implications of his comments are more complex than he realizes. Consider again problems 1, 2, and 3. (1) If the paradigm of a clear belief is a "real" one, then a simple Catholic cannot be very *clear* about some of the most important teachings of the church; (2) If an ordinary Catholic associates an important religious term with vivid but inappropriate images, then in a very important sense he has an *unclear notion*, even though he has made a real assent; (3) Clarity is not enough, for a man may have clear beliefs that are not only false but maleficent. Moreover, Newman himself has suggested the proper remedy for the confusion of profession: "reflection" or "conscientious" thinking. Newman has rightly observed that many liberal intellectuals are not as reflective as they think they are. But instead of imitating the unreflective, uncritical peasant, these men should be *more* reflective, as should the peasant himself. So while Newman has cleverly attacked the liberal intellectuals on their own ground, he has also, without realizing it, played into their hands. His apologetical strategy has backfired.

The larger part of Newman's discussion of profession is devoted to a consideration of "whether belief in a mystery can be more than an assertion" (55); since Newman is concerned here with "mystery" in its theological sense, he must find a way of answering this question in the affirmative. That he is prepared to devote so much attention to this problem is yet another reminder of the supremacy of his apologetical concerns. I shall simply report Newman's conclusions:

§ I consider it [belief in a mystery] can be an assent, and my reasons for saying so are as follows:—A mystery is a proposition conveying incompatible notions, or is a statement of the inconceivable. Now we can assent to propositions (and a mystery is a proposition), provided we can apprehend them; therefore we can assent to a mystery, for, unless we in some sense apprehended it, we should not recognize it to be a mystery, that is, a statement uniting incompatible notions. The same act, then, which enables us to discern that the words of the proposition express a mystery, capacitates us for assenting to it. (55)

§ [W]e feel we are not masters of our subject. We apprehend sufficiently to be able to assent to these theological truths as mysteries; did we not apprehend them at all, we should be merely asserting . . . .

If anything is to be learned from the inappropriateness of Newman's analysis of profession, it is not that the analysis is "incorrect" in some objective sense, or that we need to find a better analysis of profession. As a piece of phenomenological analysis, Newman's story about profession is quite respectable; it is only because of Newman's apologetical and polemical concerns that the story is inappropriate. A person who does not have Newman's apologetical concerns may find the story wholly appropriate and adequate for his everyday life; though perhaps most people simply do not need a concept of profession at all. People who share Newman's special concerns *may* feel the need for a better analysis of profession, but even these people do not *have* to look for one, for they do not have to follow Newman in grouping beliefs in the way he does.

This quick survey of what *is not* to be learned has given us the key to understanding what *is* to be learned. One may have practical as well as purely intellectual motives for seeking a proper analysis of the types of beliefs, or for seeking any proper phenomenological or epistemological analysis. And one way in which we go about determining whether such an analysis is proper is by considering to what extent it serves the purposes for which it was designed. An analysis of certain types of belief may be adequate by purely intellectual or phenomenological standards and yet inadequate by practical or ethical standards. Some philosophers will argue that one ought to be disinterested when one analyzes types of belief, or when one philosophizes in general. But *can* one be wholly disinterested? And even if one can, does it follow that one always *should* be? Newman did not think so, and he had some pretty harsh words for philosophers who "cannot walk straight" (90).

Construction of a plausible and interesting theory of types of belief requires both phenomenological insight and an ability to interpret the everyday language of belief. Practical motives do not necessarily help a philosopher to arrive at a plausible theory, but they do not necessarily prevent him from arriving at one either, and in any case, it is the practical value of the typology that does most to make it interesting. Whatever value Newman's typology has, however, it does not serve the purpose that Newman seems to have intended it to serve.

The four remaining categories of notional belief are ranked in ascending order of strength. *Credence* is "pretty much the same as having 'no doubt'" about propositions. "It is the sort of assent which we give to those opinions and professed facts which are ever presenting themselves to us without any effort of ours, and which we commonly take for granted, thereby obtaining a broad foundation of thought for ourselves, and a medium of intercourse between ourselves and others" (60). The first half of Newman's discussion of credence is rather nebulous, and the second is devoted to contrasting the real belief of Catholic populations with the mere credence of those committed to English Protestant "Bible Religion." Newman here gives us a diatribe disguised as an example. *Opinion* is the name Newman gives to an assent to a proposition, "not as true, but as probably true"; opinion is a notional belief, "for the predicate of the proposition, on which it is exercised, is the abstract word 'probably'" (64-65). *Presumption* is "assent to first principles," to "the propositions with which we start in reasoning on any given subject-matter" (66). Newman's most interesting example of presumption is the belief "that there are things external to ourselves," and we shall be returning to it in the next chapter. Other examples of first principles include "There is a right and a wrong," and "There is a true and a false," which are "abstractions to which we give a notional assent in consequence of our particular experiences of qualities in the concrete, to which we give a real assent" (69). A final example is the principle of causation (70-75). *Speculation* denotes notional beliefs, "which are the most direct, explicit and perfect of their kind, viz. those which are the firm, conscious acceptance of propositions as true" (75). It includes assent to all reasoning and its conclusions, all general propositions, rules of conduct, mathematical propositions, legal judgments, constitutional maxims, determinations of science, and the principles and doctrines of theology (75-76). "As far as these particular subjects can be viewed in the concrete and represent experiences, they can be received by real assent also; but as expressed in general propositions they belong to notional apprehension and assent" (76).

4 Notional and real belief contrasted

"[O]n the whole," Newman writes, "broadly contrasting Belief with Notional Assent and with Inference, we shall not . . . be very wrong in pronouncing that acts of Notional Assent and of Inference do not affect our conduct, and acts of Belief, that is, of Real Assent, do (not necessarily, but do) affect it" (87). When we read such lines and then consider Newman's examples of notional belief, we must follow the Jesuit philosopher M. C. D'Arcy in being critical of Newman's "habitual disparagement" of notional belief.[20] We must marvel at the range and importance of the items on Newman's list of beliefs that supposedly "do not affect our conduct": first principles (e.g., the Moral Law and the principle of causation); conclusions of reasoning; rules of conduct; mathematical propositions; determinations of science, etc. Can Newman be anything but "very wrong" in pronouncing

20 M. C. D'Arcy, *The Nature of Belief* (London: Sheed and Ward, 1937), 148.

that assents to such propositions do not influence our behaviour? Indeed, are there any mental acts that exert a greater influence on our behaviour? When we reflect on Newman's examples of notional belief, we may wonder whether he has unwittingly defended the religion of liberals, for religious beliefs that are epistemologically and pragmatically on the same plane as logical, mathematical, and scientific beliefs are hardly to be despised.

Newman probably would have replied to this criticism by arguing that notional beliefs become coupled with real beliefs, with the latter and not the former having the influence on behaviour. As far back as chapter 1 he insists that "in the same mind and at the same time, the same proposition may express both what is notional and what is real," and it is there that he gives his example of the chemistry experiment, in which a physical fact is simultaneously enunciated as an individual thing and generalized into a law of nature (30-31).[21] Throughout the *Grammar*, Newman repeatedly insists that one and the same proposition, such as (and most notably) "There is one God," is subject to both modes of apprehension or interpretation, even by one person at one time. But this coupling is not so common. Though real beliefs may sometimes become coupled with notional ones, what happens more often is that images attach themselves to notional beliefs. And accompanying imagery, no matter how vivid, does not *convert* a notional belief into a real one or in any way *create* a secondary real belief that does the practical work a notional belief cannot do. When a man chooses to make sacrifices for love of country, his nationalistic notions may well become associated with images of the flag, famous national martyrs, or his loved ones at home. But he is making sacrifices here for love of country, *not* for the flag.

We must not make the mistake that Philip Flanagan does when he remarks that, for Newman, "[t]hese names 'real' and 'notional' refer . . . to the impression which the proposition makes on the mind."[22] Newman does not *define* "real" and "notional" in terms of vividness or influence. He defines "real" and "notional" in terms of the *objects* of apprehension; one involves apprehension of "things" and the other apprehension of "notions." According to Newman's analysis, a man who makes sacrifices for love of country does not do so simply for images but *ultimately* for some "thing"; and if he is really making sacrifices for love of country and not *just* for particular national symbols or particular friends and relatives, then that "thing" must be something rather abstract and "notional."

We ought to be worried here about the ambiguity of the key terms "thing" and "notion." We can sympathize with Newman in his inabil-

21 Cf. I. T. Ker, "Recent Critics of Newman's *A Grammar of Assent,*" *Religious Studies* 13 (1977), 70.
22 Philip Flanagan, *Newman, Faith and the Believer* (London: Sands & Co., 1946), 140.

ity to give a precise definition or analysis of "thing"; the greatest metaphysicians have had trouble with this most abstract of notions. Newman probably associates it with the Aristotelian and Lockean concepts of *substance*. But most ontologists will grant that even a notion is in some sense a "thing," even if they will not follow Plato in regarding Ideas or Forms as more real than physical objects and other objects of perception. To make sacrifices for love of one's country is in some sense to sacrifice for a *thing*, a thing that is logically and ontologically distinct from the perceivable objects that may be associated with it. Newman is being metaphysically naïve when he simply *reduces* "love" and "country" to the status of creations of the mind that have no existence or counterpart outside of the mind; love and country usually manage to outlast the individuals who make sacrifices for them, even if they do not have the kind of ontological status that "realists" attribute to them.

We saw earlier that, if Zeno is right, Newman does not offer a precise definition of notion in any of his philosophical works.[23] At the end of his discussion of profession, Newman comments, "Notions are but aspects of things" (60), and this statement only serves to magnify our bewilderment. It is probably safe to assume that Newman's concept of notion is derived mainly from Locke, who writes:

> That the mind, in respect of its simple ideas, is wholly passive, and receives them all from the existence and operations of things, such as sensation or reflection offers them, without being able to *make* any one idea, experience shows us. But if we attentively consider these ideas I call mixed modes, we are now speaking of, we shall find their original quite different. The mind often exercises an *active* power in making these several combinations. For, it being once furnished with simple ideas, it can put them together in several compositions, and so make variety of complex ideas, without examining whether they exist so together in nature. And hence I think it is that these ideas are called *notions*: as if they had their original, and constant existence, more in the thoughts of men, than in the reality of things; and to form such ideas, it sufficed that the mind put the parts of them together, and that they were consistent in the understanding, without considering whether they had any real being . . . .[24]

How much clarification this passage provides is an open question.

In a memo written in the summer of 1868, Newman asked himself, "Should I use 'conception' for 'notion'?"[25] Had he done so, he would have been inviting us to consider the difference between *conception* and *perception*, and so would have been shifting the focus of his distinction from the domain of metaphysics to the domains of phenomenology, epistemology, and physiology. In 1868 he actually

23 Zeno, "Psychological Discovery," 214.
24 John Locke, *An Essay Concerning Human Understanding*, Bk. 2, ch. 22, sec. 2.
25 O.Ar. Gr.M.: memo on certitude and proof, dated 30 July 1868.

characterized the difference between the two modes of apprehension in roughly such terms:

> The apprehension, which is thus a condition of Assent to a proposition, is of two kinds, apprehension of its meaning and of its object; the former of these is mainly an act of pure intellect, the latter an act of experience, present or past and in memory in aid of experience; and according, and so far as, the apprehension is of the former or the latter kind, so is the assent languid or energetic.
>   . . . If the faculty of imagination may be taken to stand, not for an inventive power, but for the power, which attends on memory, of recalling to the mind and making present the absent, then, while the former kind of apprehension by the pure intellect may be fitly called notional, the latter may be called by way of contrast imaginative.[26]

The distinction in the *Grammar* emphasizes the difference between notions and things, but this earlier distinction contrasts meaning with object, intellect with experience and imagination. Why did Newman eventually decide to contrast the notional with the real rather than with the imaginative? Was it perhaps because of his realization that the contrast between the real and the non-existing is more impressive than that between experience and intellect or object and meaning? Near the end of chapter 4, he writes, "No one, I say, will die for his own calculations; he dies for realities" (89). It would have been far less dramatic for him to have said that martyrs die for their perceptions or for the images in their mind. Unfortunately, Newman did not take seriously the interesting possibility that some men die for their *ideals*.

Newman's discussion of real belief is not even half as long as his discussion of notional belief. He does not attempt any classification of real beliefs, and he confines himself to giving a few new examples and making some explanatory remarks. In what is probably his clearest example, he points out that many people who believed that slavery is wrong were only moved to act forcefully against the institution by tracts and speeches that appealed to their imagination and thereby roused them "from their dreamy acquiescence in an abstract truth . . ." (78). Real belief is not "intrinsically operative" but "accidentally and indirectly affects practice"; it is "the images in which it lives, representing as they do the concrete" that "have the power of the concrete upon the affections and passions, and by means of these indirectly become operative" (86-87). If, as I have suggested, images can become attached to notional beliefs without converting those beliefs into real beliefs, and if notions are "intrinsically operative" in their own right, then Newman's real/notional distinction loses all of its apologetical significance.

26 O.Ar. A.30.11: "On apprehension and assent through the imagination . . . .," dated 26 April, 5 May, and 7 September 1868. See *Theological Papers*, 135.

As Newman rightly observes: "The fact of the distinctness of the images, which are required for real assent, is no warrant for the existence of the objects which those images represent. A proposition, be it ever so keenly apprehended, may be true or may be false" (80). Images can be, in their own way, conceptions, and "the mind is ever exposed to the danger of being carried away by the liveliness of its conceptions, to the sacrifice of good sense and conscientious caution . . ." (81). Newman is, in effect, conceding to the rationalistic liberals that, since the things that images stand for may not exist, reason ("good sense and conscientious caution") must keep the imagination in check. He adds, in the manner of Locke, that we should not be overly impressed with special cases or ignore the "natural and rightful effect of acts of the imagination upon us" according to the "normal constitution" of our minds (81); and few of us would disagree with him that a vivid and distinct image "carries with it . . . some sort of presumption of its truth."[27] Still, he does recognize that there is an important gap between the realm of "things" and the realm of "images," one which at times he finds it convenient to ignore.

In his second explanatory remark, Newman observes that even real assent is not necessarily practical. Here he qualifies his earlier comments about the power of images: "Strictly speaking, it is not imagination that causes action; but hope and fear, likes and dislikes, appetite, passion, affection, the stirrings of selfishness and self-love. What imagination does for us is to find a means of stimulating those motive powers . . ." (82). Newman does not explain why notions and reasons cannot stimulate the motive powers, and he does not consider the more disturbing implications of his view that human action is invariably rooted in irrational emotions and appetites. It is now clear that he follows such empiricists as Hobbes and Hume in seeing reason as playing only a minor role in behaviour. By the end of 1866, he had already reduced his theory of action to a neat formula: "Strictly speaking, imagination does not lead to action; it is rather to be considered as a *sine qua non*. It awakens emotion, and from emotion we are impelled to act . . . ."[28]

In his final remark on real belief, Newman presents us with a thesis that is plainly and significantly false. He tells us that while real beliefs are of a "personal" character, notional beliefs are not. Considering notions first, he writes, "All of us have the power of abstraction, and can be taught either to make or to enter into the same abstractions; and thus to cooperate in the establishment of a common measure between mind and mind." In contrast, he writes, "Real assent, . . . as the experience which it presupposes, is proper to the individual, and, as

27 O.Ar. Gr.M.: part of a rough section on certitude, dated 1-6 November 1868.
28 O.Ar. Gr.M.: paper on distinct assents, dated 12 December 1866.

such, thwarts rather than promotes the intercourse of man with man."
Like the images that are its objects, it is a matter of "personal experience" (82-83). Newman is right in arguing that there is a personal or
subjective dimension to perception and imagination; but there is an
important sense in which notional beliefs are far more personal than
those more directly based on experience. As Newman has himself
observed, the terms of many real propositions are such that "we can
actually point out the objects which they indicate" (39). We can point
to the pear about which we are thinking or to an apple that looks like
the apple about which we are thinking; two people can simultaneously look at the same pear or apple. "Things" are thus public objects
in a way that "notions" are not. If we cannot even be sure that two
people are having similar perceptions of the pear they are examining
(or similar beliefs about that pear's shape or colour), then how can
Newman be so sure that we can "enter into the same abstractions"?
How can Newman be sure that other people share his particular
notion of justice, evil, liberalism, notion, chair, or redness?

I must be careful not to overstate my point here. Newman is right in
believing that real belief has a "personal" dimension. People view
objects somewhat differently. And if two people have never seen Lake
Louise, or last saw it many years ago, they are likely to think of it in
very different ways. Moreover, Newman is right in believing that our
conceptions of justice and evil, and especially chair and redness, have
a great deal in common. But notional beliefs are far from impersonal.
Judgments like "Newman is kind" seem to be rather more "personal"
than judgments like "Newman is wearing a red skullcap." One person
may associate Newman's kindness with a memory of his smile, while
another may associate it with a memory of his gift to a certain factory-
girl; and these two people may have very similar or very different
notions of kindness. While the images that we associate with Lake
Louise may be quite different, it is unlikely that the images we associate with a red skullcap will be very different. And we can go to see
Lake Louise in a way that we cannot go to see the concept of kindness.
So Newman's claim that real belief is significantly more personal than
notional belief is gratuitous.

It is not hard to understand why Newman wants us to regard real
belief as personal. If Newman can establish that the real belief of the
simple Catholic believer is personal, he will have placed that belief
beyond rational criticism; he will have shown the irrelevance of the
cold, impersonal, rational arguments of sceptics, liberals, and
atheists. But Newman's plan has not worked: it is easier for a sceptic to
attack beliefs about "things" than abstract beliefs. His first question to
the simple believer will be "Where can we find these 'things' that you
believe in?"

Newman closes chapter 4 with his 1841 attack on the "liberalism" of Brougham and Peel. He tells us that even then he had insisted on "this marked distinction between Beliefs on the one hand, and Notional Assents and Inferences on the other," and that he is quoting his earlier words because "they present the doctrine on which I have been insisting, from a second point of view, and with a freshness and force which I cannot now command . . ." (88). Newman should have saved this passage for a later chapter, since it contrasts belief and inference rather than notional and real belief; but even though it has been inserted at an inappropriate place, it gives us much insight into Newman's philosophical project. It shows the relevance of the *Grammar* to Newman's lifelong crusade against "liberalism," and it draws our attention to the pragmatic dimension of the project:

§ Many a man will live and die upon a dogma: no man will be a martyr for a conclusion. A conclusion is but an opinion; it is not a thing which *is*, but which we are *"quite sure about;"* . . . . No one, I say, will die for his own calculations: he dies for realities. This is why a literary religion is so little to be depended upon; it looks well in fair weather; but its doctrines are opinions, and, when called to suffer for them, it slips them between its folios, or burns them at its hearth. (89)

§ To most men argument makes the point in hand only more doubtful, and considerably less impressive. After all, man is *not* a reasoning animal; he is a seeing, feeling, contemplating, acting animal. He is influenced by what is direct and precise. (90)

§ Life is not long enough for a religion of inferences; we shall never have done beginning, if we determine to begin with proof. . . . Life is for action. If we insist on proofs for every thing, we shall never come to action: to act you must assume, and that assumption is faith. (91)

§ I only say, that impressions lead to action, and that reasonings lead from it. Knowledge of premises, and inferences upon them,—this is not to *live*. It is very well as a matter of liberal curiosity and of philosophy to analyze our modes of thought: but let this come second, and when there is leisure for it, and then our examinations will in many ways even be subservient to action. But if we commence with scientific knowledge and argumentative proof, or lay any great stress upon it as the basis of personal Christianity, or attempt to make man moral and religious by libraries and museums, let us in consistency take chemists for our cooks, and mineralogists for our masons. (91)

§ So well has this practically been understood in all ages of the world, that no religion yet has been a religion of physics or of philosophy. It has ever been synonymous with revelation. (91)

While these powerful remarks contrast belief with inference, they do serve to underscore a central theme of the chapter they close. For they passionately assert what has been dispassionately argued, that there is no adequate substitute for the real belief needed for action.

We can all agree with Newman that life is for action, though we may also be inclined to agree, with Plato and Aristotle, that the contemplative life has much to be said for it. But we should not accept Newman's claim that "notions" contribute little to practice, action, and life. And while Newman is right in insisting that images have a powerful influence on behaviour, he has shown contempt for the finer features of human thought and personality. His treatment of the modes of apprehension and belief is, as we have seen, seriously flawed, both in itself and as an apologetical maneuver.

Chapter Three

Religious Belief as "Real"

1 Real belief in God

In chapter 5, the last of part I, Newman discusses "apprehension and assent in the matter of religion." Religious considerations are never far from his mind, but in this chapter he gives them special attention. His main aim here is to show how it is possible to give a real assent to religious propositions; and in his opening remarks, he goes to great pains to indicate that he is not setting himself up as a rival to the church's theologians. A dogma of faith, he tells us, is a proposition that may be apprehended and believed in either of the two modes: "To give a real assent to it is an act of religion; to give a notional, is a theological act. It is discerned, rested in, and appropriated as a reality, by the religious imagination; it is held as a truth, by the theological intellect" (93). There is no "party-wall" between these two modes of assent; intellect and imagination are both common to all religious believers. But we may still hold that the theological and religious habits of mind are in some sense distinct. Newman insists that he is not doing natural theology: "I am not proposing to set forth the arguments which issue in the belief of these doctrines, but to investigate what it is to believe in them, what the mind does, what it contemplates, when it makes an act of faith" (93-94). But after making what is, in effect, a useful distinction between phenomenology and metaphysics-cum-epistemology, he immediately goes on to blur the distinction: "It is true that the same elementary facts which create an object for an assent, also furnish matter for an inference: and in showing what we believe, I shall unavoidably be in a measure showing why we believe; but this is the very reason that makes it necessary for me at the outset to insist on the real distinction between these two concurring and coincident courses of thought, and to premise by way of caution, lest I should be misunderstood, that I am not considering the question that there is a God, but rather what God is" (94). He puts

66

more distance between himself and the theologians by observing that considerations of revelation, paramount though they are, do not "enter into the scope of the present inquiry" (94).

Newman starts by considering the proposition "There is one God," which may be regarded as "the foundation of all religion" (94). *All religion?* Even with his failings as a student of comparative religion, Newman could not have been blind to the fact that this statement is false. Here, as so often in his writings, he is letting us know that he does not take the Eastern religions seriously. Moreover, he is not happy with the way that many professed believers think of "one God" (e.g., as a "mere *anima mundi*" or "collective humanity"); he is only interested in "the God of the Theist and of the Christian," a God who is

> numerically One, who is Personal; the Author, Sustainer, and Finisher of all things, the life of Law and Order, the Moral Governor; One who is Supreme and Sole; like Himself, unlike all things besides Himself which all are but His creatures; distinct from, independent of them all; One who is self-existing, absolutely infinite, who has ever been and ever will be, to whom nothing is past or future; who is all perfection, and the fulness and archetype of every possible excellence, the Truth Itself, Wisdom, Love, Justice, Holiness; One who is All-powerful, All-knowing, Omnipresent, Incomprehensible. (95)

I suspect that most Christians do not have exactly the same view of God that Newman does; there is, as Newman is so fond of observing, something personal about religious apprehension. Even those who accept Newman's list of God's attributes may see some of those attributes as being more important than Newman allows; as Sillem observes, "Newman always sees God first and foremost in His moral attributes, and not as Infinite Being...."[1] And although Newman casually remarks that belief in God "admits without difficulty of being what I have called a notional assent" (95), the fact remains that the concept of God is more complex and more obscure than most.

Newman's interest in the concept of God is secondary here; his main concern is the "image" of God:

> Can I attain to any more vivid assent to the Being of a God, than that which is given merely to notions of the intellect? Can I enter with a personal knowledge into the circle of truths which make up that great thought. Can I rise to what I have called an imaginative apprehension of it? Can I believe as if I saw? Since such a high assent requires a present experience or memory of the fact, at first sight it would seem as if the answer must be in the negative; for how can I assent as if I saw, unless I have seen? but no one in this life can see God. Yet I conceive a real assent is possible, and I proceed to show how. (96)

Newman draws a strange analogy:

> When it is said that we cannot see God, that is undeniable; but still in what sense have we a discernment of His creatures, of the individual

---

1 Sillem, *Notebook*, vol. 1, 127.

beings which surround us? The evidence which we have of their presence lies in the phenomena which address our senses, and our warrant
for taking these for evidence is our instinctive certitude that they are
evidence. By the law of nature we associate those sensible phenomena or
impressions with certain units, individuals, substances, whatever they
are to be called, which are outside and out of the reach of sense, and we
picture them to ourselves in those phenomena. The phenomena are as if
pictures; but at the same time they give us no exact measure or character
of the unknown things beyond them;—for who will say there is any
uniformity between the impressions which two of us would respectively
have of some third thing, supposing one of us had only the sense of
touch, and the other only the sense of hearing? Therefore, when we
speak of our having a picture of the things which are perceived through
the senses, we mean a certain representation, true as far as it goes, but not
adequate.

And so of those intellectual and moral objects which are brought home
to us through our senses:—that they exist, we know by instinct . . . . (96)

The point of this analogy is that while we cannot see God, we
cannot—strictly speaking—see any external objects, "the individual
beings which surround us"; hence, real apprehension and knowledge
of God are on this level no more mysterious than real apprehension
and knowledge of any other external object. Newman does not see his
observation as opening the door to Berkeleian idealism or Humean
scepticism; he has rejected idealism and scepticism on the grounds
that we have *evidence* for the existence of external objects, evidence
that "lies in the phenomena." But he says that our warrant for taking
these phenomena as evidence is nothing more than an "instinctive
certitude that they are evidence," and here he echoes something that
he has said in his discussion of presumption in chapter 4: "[T]hat
there are things existing external to ourselves, this I do consider a first
principle, and one of universal reception. It is founded on an instinct;
I so call it, because the brute creation possesses it" (67).

We have not yet considered what Newman regards as the
"phenomena" in which evidence for God's existence lies. But before
we consider this aspect of his analogy, let us look at some weaknesses
in his position as it now stands. First, Newman may be much closer to
Berkeleian idealism and Humean scepticism than he thinks. After
reading sheets of the *Grammar*, Meynell actually warned Newman, "I
fear for your Idealism."[2] Newman rightly observes in chapter 4, "The
fact of the distinctness of the images, which are required for real
assent, is no warrant for the existence of the objects which those
images represent" (80); but he now argues that images or phenomena
constitute the sole evidence we have of the presence of external
objects. Many contemporary epistemologists would argue that New-

2 Letter, Meynell to Newman, 16 August 1869, in *The Letters and Diaries of John
Henry Newman*, vol. 24: *A Grammar of Assent*, ed. Charles Stephen Dessain and
Thomas Gornall (Oxford: Clarendon Press, 1973), 306.

man has not adequately distinguished, phenomenologically or physiologically, between perceiving an object and having phenomena or images before one's mind. We do not associate all our images with external objects, and our ideas of external objects are more than just pictures based on phenomena. As for Newman's talk about "instinctive certitude," it is both nebulous and half-hearted. Newman has not yet discussed certitude, and when he finally does, he makes it clear (at least sometimes) that the feeling of certitude occasionally misleads us. The term "instinct" itself raises serious problems. Newman had written to Meynell, "By instinct I mean a realization of a *particular*; by intuition, of a *general* fact—in both cases without *assignable* or *recognizable* media of realization."[3] If this is so, then for Newman, "explaining" something by appealing to instinct is tantamount to admitting that it is inexplicable.

In arguing that phenomena constitute evidence of the existence of external objects, Newman is sliding somewhat casually from phenomenology to epistemology. Most of us agree with Newman that the senses are usually reliable sources of knowledge about the world; but the senses and the imagination do deceive us, and some of the great philosophers (e.g., Plato, Descartes, and Spinoza) have pointed out that this is a far more interesting fact than naïve empiricists have realized. On the other hand, certain sophisticated empiricists have argued that belief in external objects is neither epistemologically nor pragmatically warranted. If they are right, then the brute creation's belief in external objects is one more of many unscientific naïvetés that the civilized person can leave behind him. Finally, as Cameron notes, "[T]he analogy between trusting our senses and trusting our tendency to religious faith breaks down because there is no general human tendency to religious faith, at least not in any form which would have satisfied Newman, whereas we all trust our senses."[4] As Newman well knows, the existence of God is not universally received; the brute (or civilized) creation does not instinctively accept the dogmas of Christian faith.

Newman completes his analogy by telling us what he regards as the "phenomena" in which evidence for God's existence lies:

> Now certainly the thought of God, as Theists entertain it, is not gained by an instinctive association of His presence with any sensible phenomena; but the office which the senses directly fulfil as regards creation that devolves indirectly on certain of our mental phenomena as regards the Creator. Those phenomena are found in the sense of moral obligation. As from a multitude of instinctive perceptions, acting in particular instances, of something beyond the senses, we generalize the notion of an external world, and then picture that world in and according to those

3 Letter, Newman to Meynell, 17 August 1869, ibid., 309.
4 Cameron, *Battle*, 211-12.

particular phenomena from which we started, so from the perceptive power which identifies the intimations of conscience with the reverberations or echoes (so to say) of an external admonition, we proceed on to the notion of a Supreme Ruler and Judge, and then again we image Him and His attributes in those recurring intimations, out of which, as mental phenomena, our recognition of His existence was originally gained. (97)

If he is to have an analogy here, Newman must be able to identify those mental phenomena that enable us to picture God in roughly the same way as sensible phenomena enable us to picture the external world. He thinks he has uncovered them in the "intimations of conscience" that are found in the "sense of moral obligation." From these mental phenomena, he argues, we proceed not only to a *notion* of "Supreme Ruler and Judge," but to an *image* of "Him and His attributes."

In order to explain "how we gain an image of God and give a real assent to the proposition that he exists," Newman must "start from some first principle . . . viz., that we have by nature a conscience" (97-98). Newman readily admits that this first principle is something "which I assume and shall not attempt to prove" (97):

I assume, then, that Conscience has a legitimate place among our mental acts; as really so, as the action of memory, of reasoning, of imagination, or as the sense of the beautiful; that, as there are objects which, when presented to the mind, cause it to feel grief, regret, joy, or desire, so there are things which excite in us approbation or blame, and which we in consequence call right or wrong; and which, experienced in ourselves, kindle in us that specific sense of pleasure or pain, which goes by the name of a good or bad conscience. (98)

This is "taken for granted" (98) as Newman proceeds to explain how "in this special feeling, which follows on the commission of what we call right or wrong, lie the materials for the real apprehension of a Divine Sovereign or Judge" (98).

Newman stresses that the feeling of conscience is twofold, "a moral sense, and a sense of duty; a judgment of the reason and a magisterial dictate"; it has "both a critical and judicial office" (98). Earlier British moral philosophers usually emphasized the former aspect of conscience, but Newman is mainly concerned with the latter: "Here I have to speak of conscience in the latter point of view, not as supplying us, by means of its various acts, with the elements of morals, such as may be developed by the intellect into an ethical code, but simply as the dictate of an authoritative monitor bearing upon the details of conduct as they come before us, and complete in its several acts, one by one" (98-99). This is the "primary and most authoritative aspect" of conscience; "[h]alf the world would be puzzled to know what was meant by the moral sense; but every one knows what is meant by a good or bad conscience" (99).

But what is the connection between conscience and the image of God? Newman reminds us that "we are accustomed to speak of conscience as a voice, a term which we should never think of applying to the sense of the beautiful; and moreover a voice, or the echo of a voice, imperative and constraining, like no other dictate in the whole of our experience" (99). "If, on doing wrong, we feel the same fearful, broken-hearted sorrow which overwhelms us on hurting a mother; if, on doing right, we enjoy the same sunny serenity of mind, the same soothing, satisfactory delight which follows on our receiving praise from a father, we certainly have within us the image of some person, to whom our love and veneration look, in whose smile we find our happiness, for whom we yearn, towards whom we direct our pleadings, in whose anger we are troubled and waste away" (101). And it is thus that we come to have in our minds an *image* of God and not just an abstract notion:

> "The wicked flees, when no one pursueth;" then why does he flee? whence his terror? Who is it that he sees in solitude, in darkness, in the hidden chambers of his heart? If the cause of these emotions does not belong to this visible world, the Object to which his perception is directed must be Supernatural and Divine; and thus the phenomena of Conscience, as a dictate, avail to impress the imagination with the picture of a Supreme Governor, a Judge, holy, just, powerful, all-seeing, retributive, and is the creative principle of religion, as the Moral Sense is the principle of ethics. (101)

Notice that Newman sees his observations as having more than phenomenological significance; again he is sliding from phenomenology to epistemology and metaphysics. He is saying, in effect, that when we reflect on the phenomena of conscience, we are led to real religious belief by a kind of rational necessity, the need for an explanation. "I have already said I am not proposing here to prove the Being of a God; yet I have found it impossible to avoid saying where I look for the proof of it" (97). For years Newman had felt that the traditional scholastic proofs only bring men to notional religious belief at best; the more "concrete" argument from conscience had always been Newman's preferred proof of theism.[5] His student Caswall had written in his lecture notes: "The Father thinks that the whole world of religion comes from conscience, and this was the opinion of S. [Saint] Anselm. The argument from final causes never satisfied the Father; that from conscience appeared to him stronger."[6] Walgrave concludes, "The philosophy of conscience is, undoubtedly, what underlies Newman's entire thought. All his greater works are ramifications and extensions of what he holds to be the significance of conscience in the life of man."[7] While endorsing this view, Thomas

5 See Adrian J. Boekraad and Henry Tristram, *The Argument From Conscience to the Existence of God According to J. H. Newman* (Louvain: Nauwelaerts, 1961).
6 O.Ar. B.7.4: Edward Caswall's notes on 1851 lectures by Newman on faith and reason.
7 Walgrave, *Theologian*, 342.

Vargish adds that "of all his psychological theories his theory of conscience is perhaps the most alien, certainly the most readily suspect, to uncommitted twentieth-century readers."[8] And as we shall now see, there is plenty of reason to be suspicious.

In assessing Newman's claims about the significance of the intimations of conscience, we should begin by noting that Newman himself regards as notional, as a "presumption," the belief that we have by nature a conscience (66, 97-98). His subsequent analysis and argument is based on a belief that is, in his own words, "taken for granted," a belief to which we do not give real assent. Newman does not expect his assumption to be challenged, for "every one knows what is meant by a good or bad conscience" (99). But perhaps Newman is being too presumptuous. Conscience seems to be more of a "notion" than a "thing," and people who talk about it often have very different views of it. Intimations of conscience are certainly not as natural as the perceptions of the five ordinary senses, and many thinkers have argued that we have to be trained to develop a conscience. We sometimes hear people say that a certain person "has no conscience." And it is certainly not obvious that conscience is an irreducible or inexplicable phenomenon, one that cannot be explained away in terms of more basic elements, such as belief, reason, memory, and desire.

Newman tells us that the intimations of conscience are found in the sense of moral obligation, and a page later he analyzes conscience in terms of a moral sense and a sense of duty. What are we to make of all this talk about a moral "sense"? Commentators have warned us not see Newman as undervaluing the role of reason in moral judgment. Sillem, for example, writes that "the reader must be on his guard against the common error of treating conscience as a mere irrational instinct. Newman, following the universal teaching of the Fathers and Doctors of the Church, sees it as 'a constituent element of the mind' and therefore as an intellectual power 'whose operations admit of being surveyed and scrutinized by Reason'."[9] In describing the feeling of conscience as twofold, Newman does indeed associate the moral "sense" with a "judgment of the reason" (98). In his discussion of the illative sense in chapter 9, he draws our attention to the use of the word "sense" in such expressions as "good sense" and "common sense" (271), and his use of it in the expressions "sense of moral obligation," "moral sense," and "sense of duty" may be no more technical. Still, Newman seems to have chosen the term quite deliberately. Walgrave points out, "'Sense' [for Newman] is applied to a mental function by analogy with the bodily senses. Newman, in fact,

8 Thomas Vargish, Newman: The Contemplation of Mind (Oxford: Clarendon Press, 1970), 58.
9 Sillem, Notebook, vol. 1, 115.

distinguishes between 'bodily senses' and 'mental senses'...."[10] In Walgrave's view, the term "moral sense" may designate "that ethical knowledge obtained by deduction from individual experiences of conscience,"[11] or "*phronesis*, the virtue which perfects moral judgment."[12] But if Newman was influenced here by the scholastic teachers of his church, he would seem to have been influenced even more by the moral philosophy of the British empiricists. As Cameron has observed, such quasi-technical terms as "moral sense" and "moral perceptions" are "drawn from the tradition of British empiricism. They had become so much a part of educated speech that it is a nice question whether they ought to be considered technical terms at all."[13]

Much of eighteenth-century British moral philosophy is a reaction to the gloomy psychology of Hobbes's *Leviathan*. In his *Inquiry Concerning Virtue or Merit* (1699), Shaftesbury criticizes Hobbes for not properly acknowledging the fact of human benevolence, and he theorizes that men possess a natural moral sense that enables them to regulate the passions or "affections." There are, he tells us, three kinds of affections: natural affections that lead to the public good; self-affections that lead only to private good; and unnatural affections that lead to neither public nor private good. It is not unnatural for one to be concerned with his own private good, and there are actually cases in which the individual's public affections are too strong and his private affections too weak; but the plainer and more essential part of vice is that which involves the public affections being too weak, or the private affections being too strong, or the affections being unnatural. The moral sense enables people to bring about the proper balance between their public and private affections. A person, however, may come to lose much natural moral sense through "Custom" or by "licentiousness of Practice, favour'd by Atheism." To have the natural, kindly, or generous affections that lead to the public good is to have the chief means and power of self-enjoyment, and to lack these affections is to be miserable.[14]

Shaftesbury's theory of the moral sense was developed by Hutcheson, who carried it a step further by arguing that, "in equal Numbers, the Virtue is as the Quantity of the Happiness, or natural Good; or that the Virtue is in a compound Ratio of the Quantity of Good, and Number of Enjoyers ... so that, the Action is best, which procures the greatest Happiness for the greatest Numbers; and that, worst, which,

10 Walgrave, *Theologian*, 352.
11 Ibid., 353.
12 Ibid., 354.
13 Cameron, *Battle*, 204.
14 Anthony Ashley Cooper, Third Earl of Shaftesbury, *Inquiry Concerning Virtue, or Merit* (1699, 1714), bk. I, pt. 1, sec. 3.

in like manner, occasions Misery." Hutcheson inferred that one could actually apply a mathematical calculation to moral subjects, determining how much happiness or natural good results from various alternative courses of action.[15] According to Hume, "Reason is, and ought only to be the slave of the passions, and can never pretend to any other office than to serve and obey them."[16] He thus followed Shaftesbury and Hutcheson in seeing a special kind of sentiment or feeling, and not reason, as the ultimate basis of morality; and he also followed them in arguing that human beings have a natural feeling of benevolence. For Hume, sympathy with the pleasures and pains of other people is an undeniable fact of human nature.

In spite of their repudiation of Hobbes's view that humans are thoroughly selfish and unsympathetic beings, the moral-sense philosophers accepted Hobbes's claim that human beings are ultimately governed by their passions and sentiments rather than by reason; they did not take seriously the scholastic theory of human nature that Hobbes himself had attacked. And in spite of the efforts of such philosophers as Wollaston and Price to change its course, British moral psychology after Shaftesbury continued to emphasize feeling at the expense of reason. One development of this tendency was Bentham's hedonistic utilitarianism, which Newman rejected. Newman was more sympathetic to the moral-sense theory of Bishop Joseph Butler, who saw the moral sense or conscience as including both a "sentiment of the understanding" and a "perception of the heart."[17]

It would be wrong to treat Newman's moral psychology as simply one more version of British moral-sense theory. Newman attaches great importance to the moral teachings of his church in a way that Shaftesbury and Hume do not, and he never divorces morality from religion. He also sometimes attempts to promote reason to its proper place in the act of moral judgment. But his use of such code words as "moral sense" and "moral perceptions" reminds us that in his ethic as well as elsewhere in his philosophy he works largely within the framework of traditional British empiricism. Cameron, who feels that "the philosophical affinities of Newman are peculiarly with one philosopher in the British empiricist tradition, namely, David Hume,"[18] observes that for both philosophers "a destructive philosophical analysis is a moment in an argument designed to show that we have no alternative to putting our trust in 'nature'."[19] Although the two "could scarcely be more different" in their views of "what putting our

15 Francis Hutcheson, *Inquiry Concerning the Original of our Ideas of Virtue or Moral Good* (1725, 1738), sec. 3, pts. 8-15.
16 David Hume, *A Treatise of Human Nature* (1740), bk. II, pt. 3, sec. 3.
17 Joseph Butler, *Dissertation II: Of the Nature of Virtue* (1736, 1740).
18 Cameron, *Battle*, 220.
19 Ibid., 223.

trust in 'nature' commits us to,"[20] they both feel that recognition of moral perception as natural is the appropriate starting point for ethical theory. So as Hume regards sympathy as an undeniable fact of human nature, Newman believes it must be taken for granted that we have by nature a conscience. In addition, Newman follows the empiricist moralists in seeing moral perception as analogous to visual perception.

In chapter 5 of the *Grammar*, Newman concentrates on the sense of moral *obligation*, the sense of *duty*; his interest here is more in the "judicial" office of conscience than in the "critical." Well aware that the moral "sense" leads people to radically different moral judgments, he directs our attention to something that does not look very controversial, the "fact" of the "dictate of an authoritative monitor." But since he clings to the analogy between moral and visual perception, he leaves his theory open to the standard objections raised against all moral-sense theories. We all know what types of sensations correspond to each of the five ordinary senses; we know, for example, that our vision enables us to have sensations of redness, darkness, and roundness. But what exactly are intimations of conscience? Is *feeling* that one should pay one's taxes really much more than *being aware* that not paying them will result in certain negative consequences? Does the *sense* of guilt involve some kind of twinge or itch?

People not only are led to different moral judgments by their moral sense but also feel morally obliged under very different circumstances. The five ordinary senses are seen as providing us with knowledge of an external world partly because there is a very impressive degree of agreement on empirical matters. But is there an analogous consensus in the area of moral obligation? Newman feels guilty when he disagrees with the Roman Catholic hierarchy; others feel guilty when they *agree* with the Roman Catholic hierarchy; and still others rarely feel guilty at all. Given his serious disagreement on moral questions with so many of his fellow citizens, Newman must regard forty, fifty, or sixty per cent of his fellow Englishmen as having seriously *defective* moral senses. Interestingly enough, however, few people will admit to having a defective moral sense as readily as the blind, colour blind, or hard of hearing will admit to their physical defects.

When we have a sensation of redness, we do normally associate that sensation with a "thing," as Newman argues; we regard the sensation as corresponding to one of the *qualities* of that substance or object. But if Newman is to make a fair analogy, he should see us as associating our "intimations" of rightness and wrongness with things that have the qualities of rightness and wrongness, *acts*, and not with a

20 Ibid.

supreme ruler and judge. This analogy is not a very exciting one, and it is by no means obvious that acts are actually "things" or objects that have qualities in the way that apples or fire engines do. But if Newman is going to draw an analogy here, this is the kind that he has to draw. Of course, Newman may feel that God is the *cause* of our sense of guilt in the way that the (redness of the) apple is the *cause* of our sensation of redness; but this analogy is also not so exciting, because not only must Newman regard God as the cause of *all* things, but he has not established that only God can be the *immediate* cause of our intimations of conscience.

Newman himself sometimes recognizes that moral sensation has something to do with a judgment of the reason. At one level, empirical judgments do not require a background of knowledge; to see the redness of an apple, the sighted person normally needs only to open his eyes (provided, of course, that there is enough light). Moral perception, on the other hand, demands prior knowledge of the facts of a particular situation, of the interests of other human beings, and so on. Newman has not adequately explored the possibility that moral sentiments are derivative. He simply assumes that the moral sentiments are natural; and having never considered how they originate, he cannot give a satisfactory explanation of why reflective, educated people are generally more benevolent or sympathetic than infants or brutes.

Though Newman was influenced by the ideas of the British moral-sense philosophers, he still regards his talk about conscience as relatively straightforward: "Half the world would be puzzled to know what was meant by the moral sense; but every one knows what is meant by a good or bad conscience." So even if the concept of a moral sense is vague and problematic, and even if the analogy between moral and visual perception is unsatisfactory, the fact remains that most of us do have some idea of what Newman means by "intimations of conscience." But it is still not clear how we get from such "intimations" to an "image" of God. Given the way intimations of conscience vary from person to person and culture to culture, there is no reason to believe that there will be a substantial uniformity in the images people form of God in their minds. If someone like Torquemada or Eichmann is *conscientiously* committed to burning heretics or liquidating Jews, what is his image of God? Does he see God as super-Inquisitor, super-Nazi, super-torturer? And how is Newman to explain the fact that many an atheist feels a moral obligation to do x and refrain from y but does not form an image of God or give any assent whatsoever to God's existence? It will not do for Newman to argue here that the atheist *ought* to form such an image, for he is speaking here mainly on a phenomenological level, not a metaphysical one.

And this leads us to a wider consideration. As many people do not identify the intimations of conscience with the reverberations of an external admonition, they are quite prepared to offer alternative explanations of these intimations. Some men feel guilty because they are worried about their reputation, or because they fear revenge or punishment by their fellow human beings, or because their self-respect has been diminished. In that fountainhead of moral philosophy, the *Republic*, Plato developed powerful arguments to establish that justice pays even if the gods are not watching,[21] and generations of philosophers have added to these arguments; and if Newman cannot understand or appreciate such arguments, so much the worse for his view of morality.

" 'The wicked flees, when no one pursueth;' then why does he flee? whence his terror? Who is it that he sees in solitude, in darkness, in the hidden chambers of his heart?" The cause of the wicked man's emotions here may well belong to this visible world. Moreover, if the wicked man could give a real assent to God's existence, then why is he so consistently wicked? Surely a real belief ought to be effective enough to dissuade him from doing bad things, especially if it has been strong enough to bother him after he has already done other bad things. We can agree with Newman that throughout history, ethics and religion have been intimately related; but Newman's Christian faith may well have led him to see them as more intimately related than they really are. Perhaps only those who are low on the scale of civilization *require* belief in a supreme governor as an impetus to being moral. Exactly how Newman sees us as being able to jump from the awareness of conscience to an image of God is not clear. Copleston points out that "Newman seems to be primarily concerned with personal insight into the 'significance' or 'implications' of the awareness of obligation in a sense of these terms which it is difficult to define"; moreover, a mere *inference* from the sense of obligation to religious belief is not satisfactory for Newman, who insists on the importance of real belief and not just the notional belief of conclusion.[22] I suspect that for most people—and for most genuine religious believers—the image of God is more akin to what Newman calls a "notion" than to a picture. For the average believer, God is indeed a being, but a being *conceived* of as the subject or holder of certain attributes (such as love and justice). I also suspect that those who do associate the intimations of their conscience with some picture of the supreme governor already have an effective idea or notion of God before making this association.

21 Plato *Republic* 365-367, 576-592.
22 Copleston, *History*, vol. 8, pt. 2, 282-83.

2 Conscience as a source of justified belief in God

Newman has told us that his main aim in chapter 5 is to show how real assent to religious propositions is possible, not to prove that God exists: "I am not proposing to set forth the arguments which issue in the belief of these doctrines, but to investigate what it is to believe in them, what the mind does, what it contemplates, when it makes an act of faith." But we should not be surprised to find Newman sliding from phenomenology to a more aggressive style of apologetics, one that seeks to establish what traditional natural theology aims at proving, that God exists and that we can know that he does. Newman has not scored a big point against the liberals if he has merely shown that some religious believers can associate God with vivid but wild and silly images, perceptual *or* moral. If some people associate intimations of conscience with a super-torturer or some other dark force, is this not all the more reason to regard real religious belief as less reliable than notional? And if some people think of God as a super-torturer or even just as an angry old man or a gaseous vertebrate, why is their faith so admirable? So Newman owes us an explanation of why it is *proper* for people to move from intimations of conscience to real religious belief, and especially to Catholic belief. Newman feels that "the same elementary facts which create an object for an assent, also furnish matter for an inference: and in showing what we believe I shall unavoidably be in a measure showing why we believe . . . ." But why should those who do *not* move—and cannot see any reason for moving—from awareness of conscience to an image of God, regard intimations of conscience as constituting a *reason* for anyone's believing in God? If the overwhelming majority of people did make such a move, we might be inclined to think twice here; but they do not.

Newman himself had long believed that a full awareness of conscience gives us *justified* belief in God, or even knowledge of God. In the opening lines of his 1859 "proof of theism," he writes, "Ward thinks I hold that moral obligation is, because there is a God. But I hold just the reverse, viz. there is a God, because there is a moral obligation."[23] For Newman, then, insight into conscience gives us not only an *image* of God but an *awareness* of God; Sillem sees Newman's argument as "a making manifest of a Presence, concealed behind a veil of 'mental phenomena', by a method of phenomenological analysis."[24] If Sillem is right, Newman knows that non-believers will not be very impressed by such an argument, for the argument is designed primarily to impress the person who believes in God but

23 John Henry Newman, "Proof of Theism" (1859), in Boekraad and Tristram, *Argument From Conscience*, 103.
24 Sillem, *Notebook*, vol. 1, 125.

does not know how to think of him.[25] But such an interpretation undervalues the importance that Newman attaches to the implications of conscience, especially if Newman thinks that "the whole world of religion comes from conscience" and that the way of conscience is the only way to *real*, effective belief in God. Cameron remarks that Newman "thought that in a way one could not argue for Christianity: one could only make it clear what Christianity was and in what ways it differed from its rivals for men's attention; and then leave the issue to Divine Grace and human freedom."[26] But I do not see how we can reconcile such an interpretation with the apologetical emphasis that characterizes all of Newman's writings. The way from conscience to religious belief is not just described by Newman but recommended.

For obvious reasons, then, Newman is deeply troubled by the fact that conscience and Catholicism do not fit together like hand and glove. When Walgrave tells us that Newman always "emphasizes" that conscience is not infallible,[27] he overstates the point, for the logic of Newman's argument requires him to play down the unreliability of conscience. But Newman knows that there are "false consciences," and he is well aware that conscience goes along with a wide variety of world-views. In some 1865 notes, he gives this clear statement of the problem:

> The moral sense seems to be in consequence not a natural possession of the mind but the creation of schools and sects. Its varieties, it may be said, may be logically traced to the external circumstances and influences in which they are found. There is a law of society, a law of honor, a barbarian, a civilized law, and consciences are what these laws severally make them. Virtue and vice are regulated by latitude and longitude. Our Asiatic has one conscience, a European another. Each man takes for the voice of God the sentiments which he has been brought up in. Did not the preceding generation form the conscience of the next, those contrarieties in the moral code, which at present run with time and places, would occur confusedly and at random in all societies and systems; whereas they are determined by the state of the local atmosphere, . . . national tradition, the hereditary maxims, . . . prejudices of the nursery and school room, . . . religious creed, political party or philosophical sect.[28]

So if all people everywhere did associate intimations of conscience with the "voice of God," it would seem that God is saying different things to different people. Or must we believe that there are many gods doing the talking?

Since Newman cannot accept such conclusions, he must find an explanation of how conscience can be checked or controlled. He

25 Sillem, "Way to God," 382.
26 Cameron, *Battle*, 206.
27 Walgrave, "Religious Experience," 110.
28 O.Ar. A.30.11: 1865 paper on the moral sense.

concludes his discussion of conscience in chapter 5 by admitting that "in religion the imagination and affections should always be under the control of reason" (109). This is a bigger concession to the rationalistic liberals than he seems to realize; for how can we expect the factory-girl and *charbonnier* to summon up the reasoning necessary for doing such checking, and why should we regard their reasoning as superior to that of non-Catholic intellectuals?

Newman seems to be faced here with the problem of relativism. As a committed Catholic, Newman believes that certain metaphysical and moral propositions are true in the most objective, absolute sense possible; and as an apologist, he wants other people to accept these propositions as such. He is deeply antipathetic to what he perceives as the excessive tolerance of the liberals. He is quite willing to be regarded as a bigot (in one sense, at least) and he is a champion of dogmatism. In one of the most famous lines of the *Apologia*, he writes, "From the age of fifteen, dogma has been the fundamental principle of my religion: I know no other religion; I cannot enter into the idea of any other sort of religion; religion, as a mere sentiment, is to me a dream and a mockery...."[29] Many Newmanists have decried attempts by commentators to portray Newman as a relativist, and there is much truth to claims like Fey's that "Newman's constant talk of man's duty to truth; his description of faith as obedience to the authority of revealed truth; his attack against 'private judgment' of revelation; his defense of dogma and creed; and his defense of certain knowledge about matters of fact in general—can all be understood as a defense of objective truth."[30] Still, for a variety of reasons, some of which have already emerged, Newman attaches far more importance to subjectivity than traditional Catholic apologists have, so much so that he has sometimes been regarded as a precursor of such semi-apostate Catholic "modernists" as Loisy and Tyrrell. There is a genuine tension between Newman's dogmatism and his subjectivism, and we shall consider it at some length when we examine his views on informal inference and illative judgment. But here we want to give special attention to the emphasis he places on the subjectivity of moral judgment.

Newman knew that his subjectivism posed problems long before he wrote the *Grammar*. In an 1839 Oxford sermon on love, faith, and superstition, he acknowledges that there is a danger that some will misuse his analysis of the subjective dimension of faith:

> Now, there is one very serious difficulty in the view which I have taken of
> Faith, which most persons will have anticipated before I refer to it: that
> such a view may be made an excuse for all manner of prejudice and
> bigotry, and leads directly to credulity and superstition; and, on the

29 Newman, *Apologia*, 163.
30 Fey, *Faith and Doubt*, 5.

other hand, in the case of unbelief, that it affords a sort of excuse for impenetrable obduracy. Antecedent probabilities may be equally available for what is true, and what pretends to be true, for a Revelation and its counterfeit, for Paganism, or Mahometanism, or Christianity. They seem to supply no intelligent rule for what is to be believed, and what not; or how a man is to pass from a false belief to a true. If a claim of miracles is to be acknowledged because it happens to be advanced, why not in behalf of the miracles of India, as well as those of Palestine? If the abstract probability of a Revelation be the measure of genuineness in a given case, why not in the case of Mahomet, as well as of the Apostles? How are we to manage (as I may say) the Argument from Presumption in behalf of Christianity, so as not to carry it out into an argument against it?[31]

We can see from this passage that even at the time of the *University Sermons*, Newman realized that the charge of relativism would be directed against his theory of faith. Just as Newman argues that the uneducated Christian has exercised "implicit reason," so can the pagan, Moslem, and atheist also argue that *they* have exercised an "implicit reason." If the reason involved in faith is implicit, how can any particular faith be known to be more rational than any other? In defending the reasonableness of the simple Christian's faith, Newman seems to have given the non-Christian a new and ingenious excuse for "credulity" and "obduracy." For how can we challenge a reason that is implicit, personal, private? "It is plain," Newman concludes, "that some safeguard of Faith is needed, some corrective principle which will secure it from running (as it were) to seed, and becoming superstition or fanaticism."[32]

In the 1839 sermon, however, Newman argues against the fashionable view of the rationalists that "Faith is built upon Reason, and Reason is its safeguard." According to the rationalistic liberals, the proper way to prevent faith from becoming superstition, to erect a bulwark against infidelity, is to get men to cultivate their reason: "Give them, then, education; open their minds; enlighten them; enable them to reflect, compare, investigate, and infer; draw their attention to the Evidences of Christianity." Newman rejects the rationalists' candidate for the proper safeguard of faith and gives an interesting reason for doing so. According to the rationalists, that which forms the foundation of faith is also its corrective. If they are right, then "nothing can be more extravagant than to call Faith an exercise or act of Reason, as I have done, when, in fact, it needs reason."[33] Newman's argument, then, takes the following form: if reason forms the foundation of faith, if faith is an exercise of reason, then reason has already played its part; reason cannot be called upon

31 John Henry Newman, "Love the Safeguard of Faith Against Superstition," *University Sermons*, 3rd ed. (London: S.P.C.K., 1970 [1843, 1871]), 232. This sermon was preached on 21 May 1839.
32 Ibid., 232-33.
33 Ibid., 233.

to curb or correct itself, for if it cannot be trusted at one level, it can hardly be trusted at another; so if the rationalist insists on maintaining that reason is the safeguard of faith, he must abandon his belief that faith is built upon reason, that faith is an exercise of reason; but anyone who understands the nature of reason, and can see that reason can be implicit as well as explicit, can also see that faith *is* an exercise of reason. The linchpin of Newman's argument is his claim that faith involves a special kind of reason, implicit reason, and he believes that he has already established the truth of this claim in his earlier Oxford sermons.[34] (Nevertheless, recognizing the need to strengthen this key part of his argument, Newman went on in the next year to deliver his important sermon entitled "Implicit and Explicit Reason.")

Newman must now produce his own candidate, for he has not yet disposed of his "serious difficulty":

> What, then, is the safeguard, if Reason is not? I shall give an answer, which may seem at once common-place and paradoxical, yet I believe is the true one. The safeguard of Faith is a right state of heart. This it is that gives it birth; it also disciplines it. This is what protects it from bigotry, credulity, and fanaticism. It is holiness, or dutifulness, or the new creation, or the spiritual mind, however we word it. . . . It is Love which forms it out of the rude chaos into an image of Christ . . . .[35]

In support of his candidate, Newman presents various passages from the New Testament:

§ "I am the Door of the sheep . . . . I am the Good Shepherd, and know My sheep, and am known of Mine."[36]

§ "Ye believe not, because ye are not of My sheep, as I said unto you. My sheep hear My voice, and I know them, and they follow me. . . ."[37]

§ It was from lack of love towards Christ that the Jews discerned not in Him the Shepherd of their souls. . . . It is the new life, and not the natural reason, which leads the soul to Christ. Does a child trust his parents because he has proved to himself that they are such, and that they are able and desirous to do him good, or from the instinct of affection? We *believe*, because we *love*.[38]

§ This means, not love precisely, but the virtue of religiousness, under which may be said to fall the *pia affectio*, or *voluntas credendi*.[39]

§ It [i.e., a passage in I Corinthians] teaches the nothingness of natural Reason, and the all-sufficiency of supernatural grace in the conversion of the soul.[40]

After giving a few more references, Newman concludes: "Right Faith is the faith of a right mind. Faith is an intellectual act; right Faith is an

34 Also in this sermon, 222-32.
35 Ibid., 234.
36 Ibid.
37 Ibid., 234-35.
38 Ibid., 235-36.
39 Ibid., 236.
40 Ibid., 236-37.

intellectual act, done in a moral disposition. Faith is an act of Reason, viz. a reasoning upon holy, devout, and enlightened presumptions. . . . As far as, and wherever Love is wanting, so far, and there, Faith runs into excess or is perverted."[41]

Newman now offers some illustrations of how love prevents faith from becoming superstition or fanaticism. Superstition in its grossest form is worship of evil spirits: "Love towards man will make [Faith] shrink from worship."[42] Another kind of superstition is payment of religious honour to forbidden things; so when the Israelites worshipped the golden calf, they evinced a deficiency in their love of God.[43] "The woman with the issue of blood, who thought to be healed by secretly touching our Lord's garment" had a faith which "did not rise to the standard of her own light. She knew enough of the Good Shepherd to have directed her faith to Him as the one source of all good, instead of which she lingered in the circumstances and outskirts of His Divine Perfections."[44] Faith, then, "becomes superstition or credulity, enthusiasm or fanaticism, or bigotry, in proportion as it emancipates itself from this spirit of wisdom and understanding, of counsel and ghostly strength, of knowledge and true godliness, and holy fear." Real faith is itself an intellectual act, but one which "takes its character from the moral state of the agent" and is perfected by obedience rather than by intellectual cultivation. It is a presumption of a "serious, sober, thoughtful, pure, affectionate, and devout mind."[45]

We expect a Christian philosopher to assign to love a conspicuous place in his philosophy, but in this Oxford sermon, Newman has gone above and beyond the call of duty by assigning to it the highest place in his epistemology: he has argued that love is the safeguard of faith and reason. The love he has in mind is not simply the *agape* or *caritas* that we are accustomed to hearing Christian teachers praise: "love" here is a catch-all for a wide range of loosely related qualities: a right state of heart, holiness, dutifulness, the new creation, the spiritual mind, the instinct of affection, "a certain moral disposition," the "spirit of wisdom and understanding, of counsel and ghostly strength, of knowledge and true godliness, and holy fear," obedience, seriousness, sobriety, thoughtfulness, purity, devoutness, religiousness, the gift of supernatural grace. Newman was wise to add, in revising his original sermon, that when he speaks of love in this context, he does not mean "love precisely."[46] What do the qualities associated here with love have in common? Viewed negatively, they are things that cannot be counted as reason or rationality, which

41 Ibid., 239.
42 Ibid., 240.
43 Ibid., 241-42.

44 Ibid., 244-45.
45 Ibid., 249-50.
46 Ibid., 236.

Newman has rejected as a candidate for the proper safeguard of faith; viewed positively, they are praiseworthy dispositions, *virtues*. When we look over the range of items on this list of qualities, we see that Newman regards *virtue* as the proper safeguard of faith. With an eye appropriately fastened on the teachings of the New Testament, Newman identifies all the virtues with loving God and loving one's neighbour. The man who loves God and his neighbour, the virtuous man, will hold all (and only) those religious and moral beliefs that a man ought to hold. He will have *right* faith.

In developing a theory of the relation of faith to reason, Newman has found himself confronted with the problem of relativism and has attempted to dispose of it by bringing in a third element, love or virtue; so he now has a theory of the relations of love, faith, and reason. Faith involves reason; right faith involves both reason and virtue. But has Newman successfully disposed of his "serious difficulty"? Pagans, Moslems, or atheists will almost certainly insist that they, and not Christians, personify the correct combination of implicit reason and virtue. They too can argue that they have a right state of heart, the instinct of affection. Pagans may well regard themselves as obedient, serious, and sober. Many Moslems will be quick to point out that they are as pure, devout, and religious as most Christians. Christians are not the only people who regard themselves as gifted with supernatural grace. And to a neutral third party, it is not always obvious that the typical Christian is more virtuous (obedient, sober, and so on) than the typical Buddhist. Newman sees his view of love as a safeguard of faith as a way of freeing himself from the charge that he has given non-Christians an excuse for all manner of prejudice, superstition, or "impenetrable obduracy." But he seems to have ended up in his sermon by giving them still another excuse. The rationalist's candidate for the proper safeguard of faith, explicit reason, has at least this much to be said for it: being "explicit," it is public, out in the open. Demonstrations, proofs, and formal arguments are relatively objective in that they can be discussed, evaluated, taken into consideration. So even if Newman is right in saying that love is the ultimate safeguard of faith, which is not so obvious, he has not disposed of his original difficulty. Logic, inference, and natural reason may do rather little to bring people to Christianity; but non-Christians are not likely to be any more impressed by Newman's arbitrary characterization of them as vicious, thoughtless, lacking the gift of supernatural grace, and so forth.

By associating virtue with grace in the particular way that he does here, Newman all but rules out the possibility that people can be persuaded to accept Christianity. If the proper functioning of an individual's implicit reason depends wholly on grace, there is little point in the Christian's witnessing, and even the value of religious and moral education becomes questionable. Newman himself usually realizes that religious and moral education can and often do help to make people more religious and more virtuous; so his 1839 view of the relation of virtue to faith and reason is rather narrow. This loss of peripheral vision is a symptom of his anti-intellectualism.

One question that arises here is what the proper safeguard of *virtue* is. The answers "faith" and "reason" do not seem wholly irrelevant. Newman has told us that virtue, "love," is the safeguard of faith; but many committed Christians will insist that it is their faith that protects their virtue. Similarly, while Newman has argued that virtue keeps implicit reason under control, a good many people will insist that reason has played a large part in keeping them virtuous. It is tempting to wonder whether perhaps Newman's disagreement with all these people is just a semantic one; but Newman's terminology in the *University Sermons* is derived almost exclusively from ordinary language. In any case, Newman's association of a "right state of heart" with Christian commitment is gratuitous: many good-hearted people are not Christians, and as Newman himself knew from bitter personal experience, many Christians, Catholic and non-Catholic, are not good-hearted.

And so we are finally brought back to Newman's approach to conscience in chapter 5 of the *Grammar*. Here Newman presents us with one version of a theory that runs through the entire corpus of his writings, the theory that phenomenological insight into morality provides us with the key to a proper appreciation of religion. Newman's concern with what, why, and how we believe is not that of the disinterested psychologist, anthropologist, or philosopher of mind; Newman's aim is to establish that religious belief is epistemically justified, even for those Catholics who cannot possibly understand the complex demonstrations of medieval Christian philosophy. Having attached so much importance to conscience, Newman is understandably troubled by the striking differences between his own conscience and that of a pagan or Moslem, a liberal or atheist, a Laud or Kingsley. Recognizing that conscience, the immediate source of moral "intimations," must be checked or controlled, he makes the concession that "in religion the imagination and affections should always be under the control of reason." (We must remember that in chapter 5 Newman is primarily concerned with *moral* affections, though he has not ignored the *visual* images that people associate with God.) Newman warns us that "we must know concerning God, before we can feel love, fear, hope, or trust towards Him" (109). Intimations of conscience, then, are no substitute for knowledge of God, and in the last analysis, they do not even constitute a necessary condition of it.

Compare now the positions Newman takes in chapter 5 of the *Grammar* and in the 1839 sermon. In both, much importance is attached to a human being's moral disposition. Yet, in one sense, the two positions seem to be diametrically opposed. In the 1839 sermon, Newman argues that virtue *rather than reason* is the safeguard of faith; but in the *Grammar*, he calls upon reason to do the job of keeping the moral affections in check. By emphasizing the subjective dimension of faith, reason *and* morality, Newman's philosophy is in constant peril of degenerating into relativism. Whenever Newman feels the need to free it from this danger, he points to something that can hold a particular subjective element in check: since faith involves *implicit* reason, it must be kept in check by virtue, morality, a right state of heart; but if the core of morality is subjective conscience, then reason itself must be called upon to keep morality in check. Is this a vicious circle?

Perhaps not. There is nothing intrinsically inconsistent in the view that religious commitment involves a system of checks and balances between rational and sentimental elements. Newman is equally antipathetic to pure religious rationalism and pure religious sentimentalism, and he often makes it quite clear that he is faithful to traditional Catholic teaching in refusing to analyze right faith in terms of a single element. Moreover, he never denies that reason and conscience both have an objective as well as a subjective dimension. Newman's main problem here may be that his immediate polemical aims often lead him to offer various simplistic analyses of faith. Newman never simply argues against relativism *per se*; he always argues against particular theories of faith and possible misinterpretations of his own theory. Newman must emphasize the subjective aspects of faith because other apologists and theologians have traditionally undervalued them. In the 1839 sermon, he emphasizes virtue, a right state of heart, because rationalists have undervalued it. In chapter 5 of the *Grammar*, he talks about rational control over the affections only after he has assigned to these affections a very important role in religious faith. To some extent, Newman's analysis of faith is an attempt at the reconciliation of its elements. In one place he writes that theology cannot always have its own way and must make a "truce" with the "rival forces" of "religious sentiment" and "ecclesiastical interests."[47]

Was Newman wrong in 1839 to reject reason as a safeguard of faith? Newman regards faith as an *exercise* of reason, so he can hardly be regarded as a fideist. Still, he has certainly undervalued reason in the 1839 sermon. He seems to have fallen into the trap of setting up an artificial hierarchy of the elements of faith. We can all see that in many instances reason combined with virtue yields right faith; but we cannot allow this fact to blind us to equally important facts: reason

47 Newman, *Via Media*, 3rd ed., vol. 1, xlix.

helps to promote virtue; right faith contributes to the cultivation of virtue; and right faith promotes or at least aids reason. Newman's artificial hierarchy is at the heart of his rejection of the rationalists' candidate: "What, according to them, forms the foundation of Faith, is also its corrective." Since faith is already, by its very nature, an exercise of reason, how can we turn to reason as a corrective to itself? Newman theorizes that once reason has played its part, we have no more use for it. So why plague the simple, devout peasant with logical proofs and demonstrations when he has already made the best possible use of his reason? We must respond to Newman in this way: reason does not simply "play a part" and then cease to have value; and indeed reason can be self-correcting. A man can have rationally concluded that such-and-such is the case and then, faced with compelling evidence, rationally conclude that his original opinion, though reasonable before, is no longer acceptable. If we agree with Newman's thesis that Christian faith is not blind but involves implicit reason, must we then also accept Newman's assumption that explicit reason cannot overrule the kind of personal reason that involves verisimilitude and antecedent probabilities? And even if we accept this questionable assumption, must we then follow Newman in assuming that implicit reason cannot be self-correcting but can only be corrected by a virtue wholly or partly dependent on the gift of supernatural grace?

Repelled by the hypocrisy of certain liberal élitists, Newman announces to us in both the 1839 sermon and the *Grammar* that the religious commitment of intellectuals and rationalists falls short of that of devout peasants and factory-girls. But here the rationalist has several pointed questions to raise: (1) How can Newman be sure that the simple believer's virtue is primarily a cause rather than a concomitant by-product (albeit an important one) of his right faith? Christ *teaches* his followers to love God and their neighbour. Is it love of God and their neighbour that makes them take Christ's teaching seriously? (2) How can Newman explain the fact that every church, including his own, takes its teaching mission very seriously, and how can he explain the great importance that churches have traditionally attached to the writings of philosophers, doctors, and logicians who present formal, explicit arguments? (3) How can Newman be sure that in all cases implicit reason and virtue are both *necessary* conditions of right faith? Is it not possible that supernatural grace and virtue, supernatural grace alone, or even virtue alone can, without the aid of reason, directly yield right faith? Is Newman's talk of implicit reason not already a very big concession to the rationalist? On the other hand, is it not possible that in some cases unaided reason can lead a person to right faith? (4) Is Newman's analysis of faith as an "exercise of reason" really compatible with our ordinary understanding of faith? (5) How can Newman explain that the highest leaders of his church have rarely been recruited directly or immediately from the peasantry? (6) How can Newman ignore the fact that devout peasants are more likely to be superstitious and fanatic than liberal intellectuals are?

Several things can be said in Newman's defense here. One is that he is certainly not alone in having difficulty reconciling the need for grace with the need for study, guidance, and reflection; every Christian philosopher and theologian has to deal with this problem. Another is that there is a very fundamental way in which virtue is a condition of the rationality that enables people to arrive at sound conclusions. An intemperate person, one whose soul is corrupted by an obsession with pleasure, honour, or material wealth, generally cannot reason well enough to arrive at sound conclusions, implicitly or explicitly. Being virtuous is not simply living well; it is having the dispositions that enable a man to live well. But the greatest strength of Newman's two analyses is that they draw our attention to the inadequacies of narrow, one-dimensional conceptions of faith. Though both of the analyses are themselves inadequate, they provide us with useful phenomenological data. We appreciate Newman's insight here when we view his phenomenological approach to the act of faith as a forerunner of a more sophisticated one like Paul Tillich's. When Tillich complains about various common distortions of the meaning of faith, he is following in Newman's footsteps: "Faith as ultimate concern is an act of the total personality. It happens in the center of the personal life and includes all its elements. Faith is the most centered act of the human mind. It is not a movement of a special section or a special function of man's total being. They all are united in the act of faith."[48] Tillich goes on to show how faith involves intellect, will, *and* emotion, and that any phenomenological analysis of the act of faith that ignores one or more of these elements is inadequate. While Newman's criticisms of pure religious rationalism and pure religious sentimentalism involve a less sophisticated analysis, they resemble Tillich's criticisms in style as well as in spirit.

Still, the analysis of faith in chapter 5 of the *Grammar* is, like the rather different analysis in the 1839 sermon, quite unsatisfactory as theory. We saw earlier that it is phenomenologically unsound; and we have now seen that it is also epistemologically unsound. Just as it is not clear how conscience leads us to an image of God, it is not clear how it leads us to a knowledge of God or a justified belief in God. When Newman tacks on to his discussion of conscience and God the proviso that reason is needed to keep the imagination and affections

48 Paul Tillich, *Dynamics of Faith* (New York: Harper & Row, 1958), 4. Cf. pp. 30–40.

under control, he gives us too little too late. He has already left unsympathetic readers with "an excuse for all manner of prejudice and bigotry . . . and . . . for impenetrable obduracy."

Perhaps it is a mark of Newman's uneasiness that after formally introducing his next subject of discussion, belief in the Holy Trinity (109), he attempts to strengthen the argument of the preceding section. Admitting that he "cannot hope to carry all inquiring minds" with him and that there are those "whose experience will not respond to the appeal," he goes on to point out that universal reception of his position is not a necessary condition of its being regarded as sound. He then makes an interesting appeal to *conventional* opinion: "[I]t must be considered sufficient in any inquiry, if the principles or facts assumed have a large following. This condition is abundantly fulfilled as regards the authority and religious meaning of conscience;—that conscience is the voice of God has almost grown into a proverb" (109-10). We can all agree with Newman that a position can properly be regarded as reasonable even if it is not universally accepted; in fact, sometimes people have had good reason to hold beliefs that have been universally rejected. Part of the greatness of great teachers is their ability to make us overcome our inclination to agree uncritically with conventional opinion. But why then does Newman attach so much importance here to conventional opinion? The answer lies in Newman's appreciation of the peculiarity of his own method. Newman realizes that in chapter 5 he has not been giving formal arguments and explicit reasons but has been analyzing the subjective dimension of the act of faith. His phenomenological analysis is not of much value if most readers are left cold by it. The test of the adequacy of a phenomenological analysis is subjective in a way that the test of the adequacy of a formal argument is not. But Newman's analysis of the religious meaning of conscience does not meet the subjective test as satisfactorily as he has assumed. Even if most people regard conscience as the voice of God, which is itself questionable, most people do not give a real assent to the existence of the God of Roman Catholicism in the way that certain Spanish peasants and English factory-girls do. Newman is well aware of this fact: why else does he see a need for apologists like himself to set things straight? While most people in Newman's own society had some idea of what conscience is and why it is important, few saw it as having the implications that Newman did.

3 Phenomenology of the Christian faith

Complex though it is, belief in God is one of the simpler beliefs that a Roman Catholic is obliged to hold. The remainder of chapter 5 deals

with the possibility of real assent to the more abstruse dogmas of the
Catholic faith; Newman first considers belief in the Holy Trinity and
then moves on to a wider discussion of belief in dogmatic theology.
Newman has already signaled his concern about such beliefs in chapter 2 (33-35) and chapter 4 (55-60); but he must now reconsider them
with regard to the possibility of their being grasped by real apprehension.

> Now it is the belief of Catholics about the Supreme Being, that this
> essential characteristic of His Nature is reiterated in three distinct ways
> or modes; so that the Almighty God, instead of being One Person only,
> which is the teaching of Natural Religion, has Three Personalities, and is
> at once, according as we view Him in the one or the other of them, the
> Father, the Son, and the Spirit—a Divine Three, who bear towards Each
> Other the several relations which those names indicate, and are in that
> respect distinct from Each Other, and in that alone. (111)

> Indeed, the Catholic dogma may be said to be summed up in this very
> formula, on which St. Augustine lays so much stress, 'Tres et Unus,' not
> merely 'Unum;' hence that formula is the key-note, as it may be called, of
> the Athanasian Creed. (112)

> That this doctrine, thus drawn out, is of a notional character, is plain; the
> question before me is whether in any sense it can become the object of
> real apprehension, that is, whether any portion of it may be considered as
> addressed to the imagination, and is able to exert that living mastery over
> the mind, which is instanced as I have shown above, as regards the
> proposition, 'There is a God.' (112)

> Let it be observed, it is possible for the mind to hold a number of
> propositions either in their combination as one whole, or one by one; one
> by one, with an intelligent perception indeed of all, and of the general
> direction of each towards the rest, yet of each separately from the rest, for
> its own sake only, and not in connexion and one with the rest. (114-15)

> [A] man of ordinary intelligence will be at once struck with the apparent
> contrariety between the propositions one with another which constitute
> the Heavenly Dogma, and, by reason of his spontaneous activity of mind
> and by an habitual association, he will be compelled to view the Dogma
> in the light of that contrariety,—so much so, that to hold one and all of
> these separate propositions will be to such a man all one with holding
> the mystery, as a mystery; and in consequence he will so hold it;—but
> still, I say, so far he will hold it only with a notional apprehension. (115)

> That systematized whole is the object of notional assent, and its proposi-
> tions, one by one, are the objects of real. (119)

> Religion has to do with the real, and the real is the particular; theology
> has to do with what is notional, and the notional is the general and
> systematic. Hence theology has to do with the Dogma of the Holy Trinity
> as a whole made up of many propositions; but Religion has to do with
> each of these propositions which compose it, and lives and thrives in the
> contemplation of them. (112)

Let us consider some curious features of Newman's latest analysis.
First, Newman says nothing here in defense of his claim that we are

capable of giving a notional assent to the dogma of the Trinity as a whole. There are a good many people in the world who believe that the dogma of the Trinity is sufficiently mysterious, obscure, and incoherent to be thoroughly unbelievable; and in the view of such strict monotheists as Jews, Moslems, and Unitarians, the doctrine is absurd and even odious. Newman thought that he had successfully explained belief in mysteries in chapter 4; but his explanation there was not convincing. Even if it had been, there is still much to be disturbed about in his latest analysis. For one thing, Newman may be unfaithful to traditional Catholic teaching in reducing the "whole" dogma of the Trinity to the "inferior" phenomenological and pragmatic status of a notion. Newman realizes that to believe in the dogma of the Trinity is not simply to accept the nine constituent propositions into which he has analyzed it. A Catholic is obliged to recognize the mystery involved in the juxtaposition of the propositions. But given Newman's disparaging remarks about notional belief, particularly about how notional belief does not influence behaviour, we may have to see Newman as regarding the whole dogma of the Trinity as rather less important than the many religious propositions that are capable of being grasped by real apprehension. Moreover, Newman seems to be trying to put some sort of conceptual and temporal distance between the various propositions that make up the dogma; but exactly how separate are such propositions as "The Father is God," "The Son is God," and "The Father is not the Son" (119-21)? Is the Catholic not obliged to believe them simultaneously? And if so, will his images not clash? To believe simultaneously the separate propositions of the dogma of the Trinity may be like trying to believe simultaneously that a certain object is both completely blue and completely red (not-blue).

Another disturbing feature of Newman's analysis of belief in the Trinity is that it indirectly suggests that no compound proposition can be grasped by real apprehension. Newman does not simply argue that a mystery cannot be apprehended "really"; he suggests that no complex or system of propositions can be grasped by real apprehension. To believe in the dogma of the Trinity "as a whole" is to believe nine particular propositions and to perceive the general direction of each towards the rest. Newman regards as notional any perception of the relation between propositions, regardless of what the particular propositions are and whether their relation is mysterious or not. Any complex or system of nine propositions, or even of two propositions, would seem to lack the particularity necessary for an object of real apprehension. If this is indeed Newman's position, then he is committed to the view that one cannot give a real assent to the ordinary compound proposition "Mike is singing, and Judy is dancing," for to accept this proposition is to grasp a certain relation between the simple propositions "Mike is singing" and "Judy is dancing." This is an odd view, and we must conclude that Newman has overstated—or at least not explained clearly enough—the difference between believing a particular proposition and believing a combination of propositions.

Newman's main point, of course, is that the nine particular propositions that make up the dogma of the Trinity are such that there is no problem in apprehending each individual one "really." Even this thesis is questionable. Newman takes as his principal example the dogmatic proposition "The Son is God." "What an illustration of the real assent which can be given to this proposition, and its power over our affections and emotions, is the first half of the first chapter of St. John's gospel! or again the vision of the Lord in the first chapter of the Apocalypse! or the first chapter of St. John's first Epistle" (121). But the proposition "The Son is God" is quite different, on many levels, from the propositions "This apple is red" or "Philip was the father of Alexander." To believe any *son*, whether Jesus or Alexander, to *be God*, is *itself mysterious*, regardless of the relation of this belief to other beliefs. It is hard enough to understand what images we are supposed to associate with someone's being the son of Alexander; but how much harder it is to associate images with someone's being the son of God! Furthermore, it is not clear that the dogmatic proposition "The Son is God" can be properly apprehended without at least some minimal apprehension of the other eight propositions that make up the dogma of the Trinity. To apprehend the term "Son" here, it is necessary to have some view of the relation of the Son to the Father and the Holy Spirit. So if we isolate this particular proposition from the other propositions making up the dogma, it is incomprehensible in yet another way.

Newman's problems mount as he tries to explain how the peasant and factory-girl give a real assent to the most abstruse teachings of his church. "It is a familiar charge against the Catholic Church in the mouths of her opponents, that she imposes on her children as matters of faith, not only such dogmas as have an intimate bearing on moral conduct and character, but a great number of doctrines which none but professed theologians can understand, and which in consequence do but oppress the mind, and are the perpetual fuel of controversy" (123). "What sense, for instance, can a child or a peasant, nay, or any ordinary Catholic, put upon the Tridentine Canons, even in translation? such as, 'Siquis dixerit homines sine Christi justitiâ, per quam nobis meruit, justificari, aut per eam ipsam formaliter justos esse, anathema sit;' or 'Siquis dixerit justificatum peccare, dum intuitu aeternae mercedis bene operatur, anathema sit.' Or again, consider the very anathematism annexed by the Nicene Council to its Creed, the language of which is so obscure, that even theologians differ about its meaning" (126). Yet, according to Newman, "These doctrinal enunciations are *de fide*; peasants are bound to believe them as well as controversialists, and to believe them as truly as they believe that our Lord is God. How then are the Catholic *credenda* easy and within reach of all men" (127)?

Newman's solution, a taste of which we have already been given in chapter 2 (33-35), is remarkably simple: "The difficulty is removed by the dogma of the Church's infallibility, and of the consequent duty of 'implicit faith' in her word" (129). This dogma "stands in the place of all abstruse propositions in a Catholic's mind, for to believe in her word is virtually to believe in them all. Even what he cannot understand, at least he can believe to be true; and he believes it to be true because he believes in the Church" (129). He now gives us the "rationale of this provision for unlearned devotion":

> It stands to reason that all of us, learned and unlearned, are bound to believe the whole revealed doctrine in all its parts and in all that it implies according as portion after portion is brought home to our consciousness as belonging to it; and it also stands to reason, that a doctrine, so deep and so various, as the revealed *depositum* of faith, cannot be brought home to us and made our own all at once. . . . Thus, as regards the Catholic Creed, if we really believe that our Lord is God, we believe all that is meant by such a belief; or, else, we are not in earnest, when we profess to believe the proposition. In the act of believing it at all, we forthwith commit ourselves by anticipation to believe truths which at present we do not believe, because they have never come before us;—we limit henceforth the range of our private judgment in prospect by the conditions, whatever they are, of that dogma. . . . This virtual, interpretative, or prospective belief is called a believing *implicitè* [sic]; and it follows from this, that, granting that the Canons of Councils and the other ecclesiastical documents and confessions, to which I have referred, are really involved in the *depositum* or revealed word, every Catholic, in accepting the *depositum*, does *implicitè* accept those dogmatic decisions. . . . That the Church is the infallible oracle of truth is the fundamental dogma of the Catholic religion; and "I believe what the Church proposes to be believed" is an act of real assent, including all particular assents, notional and real . . . . (130-31)

In examining chapter 2 of the *Grammar*, we took note of Newman's mistaken view that to believe a proposition true simply on someone's authority is to have the apprehension necessary for believing the proposition itself. In the closing pages of chapter 5, Newman revives his argument that one can believe what one cannot understand, and now he makes explicit reference to the simple Catholic's ability to believe the more abstruse teachings of his church: in giving a real assent to the dogma of the church's infallibility, the peasant or philosopher is also believing *implicité* all of the church's teachings, regardless of whether they are too abstruse for him to understand. Now, take some very recondite Catholic doctrine, *d*, that a peasant overhears his priest teaching to a theology student. There is indeed a sense in which the peasant believes that *d* is true; and the plasticity of our language is such that we may even say that the peasant believes *d*. But the kind of belief that is involved here is not the kind that Newman has in mind when he speaks earlier of belief requiring apprehension; for here there is neither understanding nor apprehension. So what is the importance of such belief, and why does Newman's church bother to demand it? Throughout the *Grammar*, Newman is concerned with the ranking of beliefs; he repeatedly insists that the devout peasant's real belief is more genuine and more effective than the liberal intellectual's notional belief. But what is genuine or effective about the peasant's belief that *d* is true? Of what value or significance is it when measured on the same scale as the religious rationalist's beliefs?

But Newman has gone much further here than he did in chapter 2. First, there is an interesting ambiguity in his claim that "all of us, learned and unlearned, are bound to believe the whole revealed doctrine in all its parts." Newman sees this obligation as satisfied by the peasant's belief in the dogma of the church's infallibility. Perhaps, however, his point has more profound implications. Perhaps a peasant cannot be as good a Christian as one who is capable of understanding a much larger part of the whole revealed doctrine. And perhaps the well-meaning peasant is obliged to undergo the rigorous intellectual training of a theology student so that instead of merely believing *implicité*, he can believe truly and with understanding.

More disturbing is Newman's remark that "if we really believe that our Lord is God, we believe all that is meant by such a belief; or, else, we are not in earnest, when we profess to believe the proposition." This claim is problematic on two levels. The phrase "all that is meant by such a belief" is ambiguous, and it can be taken to mean something that Newman surely does not want it to convey. Newman cannot mean by it awareness of all possible implications of the proposition, and given his views on the value and efficacy of real apprehension, we can hardly see him as thinking here of the kind of abstract intellectual insight or understanding that he loves to contrast with imaginative apprehension. So it is not at all clear what he does mean by the phrase. Moreover, Newman is being offensively presumptuous in attributing hypocrisy or lightness of mind to those believers who do not associate the proposition under consideration with other propositions that Catholic theologians associate with it.

"In the act of believing it at all, we forthwith commit ourselves by anticipation to believe truths which at present we do not believe, because they have never come before us. . . ." Here Newman is suggesting that believing *implicité* is not really believing at all but only being *prepared* to believe, which is a very different propositional attitude. And when Newman tells us that the devout peasant gives a *real* assent to the dogma of the infallibility of the church, he does not go very far towards explaining how "images" and "things" come to be associated with so abstract a proposition.

What is most fascinating in Newman's latest analysis, however, is his sudden announcement of the "fundamental" nature of the Catholic's belief in the infallibility of his church. He writes:

> I say, "granting these various propositions are virtually contained in the revealed word," for this is the only question left; and that it is to be answered in the affirmative, is clear at once to the Catholic, from the fact that the Church declares that they really belong to it. To her is committed the care and the interpretation of the revelation. The word of the Church is the word of revelation. That the Church is the infallible oracle of truth is the fundamental dogma of the Catholic religion; and "I believe what the Church proposes to be believed" is an act of real assent, including all particular assents, notional and real.... (131)

This passage brings to mind an observation by Inge: "[W]hen, after an acute analysis of the processes by which beliefs come to be held, he [Newman] takes us with breathless haste, by a series of leaps and bounds, into the heart of Roman Catholic orthodoxy, we follow with undiminished admiration of his dialectic, but with no inclination towards conversion."[49] But since Newman is the Roman Catholic apologist par excellence, why should Inge and I be so fascinated?

We have to remember that, for Newman, a central aim of the *Grammar* is to show how faith is rational, an exercise of reason. Such a position is incompatible with the view that faith is ultimately a matter of blind submission to authority. In chapter 10 of the *Grammar* and in many of his other works, especially in the *Essay on Development*, Newman does give us some idea of why he thinks we should take the judgment of the Catholic hierarchy as seriously as he does. Such an explanation is not offered in chapter 5, for Newman seems to feel it is irrelevant. Indeed, the main aim of the last part of chapter 5 is phenomenological or descriptive: Newman is trying to describe how the Roman Catholic's mind works. We may still wonder, however, whether Newman's description is accurate; and in light of Newman's wider objectives, we cannot be blamed for asking ourselves whether the commitment Newman *is* describing is rational.

I have to speak now on a personal level: *cor ad cor loquitur*. The Roman Catholics with whom I am acquainted on a relatively intimate basis do not seem to me to regard the church or the pope as infallible in the way that *I* understand the concept of infallibility. I do not

49 Inge, *Faith*, 235.

know whether these people should be regarded as good and loyal Catholics, even though some of them are priests and nuns. They do appear to take their Catholic faith quite seriously, and some of them even seem to be willing to die for it. Still, they occasionally have grave doubts about some of the things that popes and bishops have taught. And I suspect that most of them would disagree with Newman's claim that the *fundamental* dogma of *their* Catholic faith—if that faith is genuinely Catholic—is that the church is the infallible oracle of truth. More fundamental to them are their beliefs in a just and loving God, in the soundness of the moral teachings of the New Testament, in the unique value of the Catholic church as an instrument of enlightenment and civilization, and in the immortality of the soul. If they do not consider the church infallible in Newman's sense of the word, they still have a deep respect and affection for it that non-Catholics are unable to share. And they are not all that troubled by the fact that the spiritual leaders of their church have taught many things that they are simply unable to believe. Moreover, it is worth noting here that the Roman Catholic church is not the monolithic institution that its more naïve critics have often taken it to be: priests (and popes, too) have disagreed on some very fundamental doctrinal matters, even in spite of Newman's insistence that "there cannot be two rules of faith in the same communion" (129). Newman himself knew from bitter personal experience how easy it is for an obedient, loyal Catholic to disagree with the leaders of the Catholic hierarchy.

But let us assume that there are peasants and philosophers in the world who do have the unusual psychogenic capacity of being both willing and able to believe that their church is the infallible oracle of truth, and not just in some very abstract sense. Consider again that particular peasant who wants to believe that particular doctrine d, which has been pronounced as true by a particular priest, who represents the "church" in the peasant's eyes. How can the non-Catholic, or the kind of Catholic with whom *I* associate, view that peasant's faith as an act of reason? Newman knows that he has not yet answered this question. However, the first part of the *Grammar* deals primarily with assent in relation to apprehension, not with assent in relation to inference or reason; and so we have a right to expect that in the second part of the *Grammar*, the part that deals with assent and inference, Newman will indeed face this kind of question. For the time being, then, we must be patient.

Although the *Grammar* is a book about assent, Newman's main interest here, as in his other works, is not belief per se but religious faith. As Horgan observes, "Whether it be a sermon or a lecture or a poem, faith for Newman is always the dominant interest...."[50] So

50 Horgan, "Faith and Reason," 132.

Newman is interested in belief mainly because faith involves belief. What is the precise nature of the involvement? Newman realizes that faith is not simply a *kind* of belief. At the beginning of chapter 5, he writes, "I mean by belief, not precisely faith, because faith, in its theological sense, includes a belief, not only in the thing believed, but also in the ground of believing; that is, not only belief in certain doctrines, but belief in them expressly because God has revealed them" (94). Still, it is clear even from this statement that Newman sees assent to propositions as being at the heart of faith; and this view is consistent with his claim that faith is an exercise of reason and not just a matter of sentiment.

John Hick criticizes Newman for treating faith as essentially a matter of believing religious propositions. In several important works, Hick draws our attention to the inadequacy of this kind of analysis; and while he has some generous words for Newman's theory of the illative sense, he thinks that Newman has unwisely assumed that belief in divine existence and divine revelation is of the same logical type as belief in such propositions as "New York is to the north of Washington."[51] Pailin is also critical of Newman for "restricting his treatment of faith to assent to propositions."[52] While Hick and Pailin are right to argue that Newman does not fully acknowledge certain aspects of faith, several points can be made in Newman's defense. The first is that propositional belief is certainly at the heart of faith; Newman's analysis is congruent with ordinary usage in treating assent as the primary condition of faith. A second is that Newman's discussion of faith in the *Grammar* is shaped by his specific apologetical objectives in the work, and especially that of showing the rationality of faith. He warns us that there is an aspect of faith that "does not enter into the scope of the present inquiry" (94), and while he is not thinking here of those particular aspects of faith that Hick and Pailin have in mind, he is at least aware of the fact that the *Grammar* does not offer a complete analysis of faith. Moreover, the *Grammar* is just one of many works in which Newman discusses the nature of faith, and in some ways it is the most unusual. Finally, in spite of his emphasis on faith as propositional belief, he repeatedly insists, as we have seen, on the inadequacy of purely rationalistic, intellectualistic analyses of faith.

Hick correctly perceives Newman as comparing belief in God, the Trinity, and dogmatic theology to belief in such propositions as "New York is to the north of Washington." And Hick is right in insisting that the two kinds of belief are not established by wholly comparable procedures.[53] We must remember, however, that if Newman exagger-

51 Hick, *Faith and Knowledge*, 86-91.
52 Pailin, *Way to Faith*, 193.
53 Hick, *Faith and Knowledge*, 90.

ates the importance of certain features of religious faith, it is partly because of the nature of his philosophical project. Newman never forgets that there is something "obscure" about religious commitment that makes it very different from ordinary belief;[54] and as a believing Catholic, he cannot help regarding with awe a commitment that he sees as "supernatural, and a divine gift."[55] So when Newman compares belief in God to belief in external objects, or demystifies the Catholic's belief in mysteries, or blurs the distinction between believing *implicité* and believing that which we can apprehend, it is not because he does not regard religious faith as something special, but because he wants to show that old-fashioned religious commitment is not quite as obscure as certain liberals would have us believe. Nevertheless, the fact remains that the analysis of religious belief that Newman gives us in chapter 5 of the *Grammar* is bad phenomenology and bad epistemology. It is also marred by errors in ethics, theology, psychology, and anthropology. It magnifies and compounds the central weakness of the whole first part of the *Grammar*, the subordination of notional apprehension to real apprehension.

Fey tells us that "Newman did not define the nature of faith according to some *a priori* theory. He took faith as he found it—described in Scripture, lived by saints, expressed in creeds, and practiced in the Church from Apostolic times to his own day."[56] This is misleading; for although Newman practises phenomenology and the analysis of ordinary language, he tends to find what he wants to. He has remarkable trouble finding faith among Protestants and Jews, liberals and progressives, Buddhists and Moslems. He interprets the words of prophets and saints in ways that even his ecclesiastical superiors cannot understand, much less outsiders. He so idealizes the religious commitment of his peasants and factory-girls that he leaves the real peasants and factory-girls of the world in the background. Perhaps the problem here is that Newman, plagued by what Bremond has characterized as "autocentrism," always ends up "finding" things in his own mind.[57] In any case, his theory of faith is a good deal closer than most to being an *a priori* one.

54 O.Ar. B.9.11: paper on faith, n.d.
55 Ibid.
56 Fey, *Faith and Doubt*, 28.
57 Henri Bremond, *The Mystery of Newman*, trans. H. C. Corrance (London: Williams and Norgate, 1907), viii, *passim*.

Chapter Four

Degrees of Belief

1 The unconditionality of belief

The second part of the *Grammar* is by far the larger, being more than twice as long as the first. It is the more interesting and more insightful part, and its main themes are rarely related to the phenomenology of apprehension in the first part. When they are, it is only indirectly, so that one is almost tempted to see the *Grammar* as made up of two separate books. But the *Grammar* is one book and embodies a single, clearly defined philosophical project.

This larger part of the *Grammar* deals with the relation of belief to inference. In the earliest pages of the *Grammar*, Newman contrasts unconditional belief with conditional inference, treating them as two distinct mental acts or propositional attitudes. He states there that "assent" is the holding of a categorical proposition, while "inference" is the holding of a conditional one. He does not offer an elaborate defense of this claim and postpones further discussion of it so that he can concentrate on the more basic matter of the role of apprehension in belief. Now, while still insisting that the unconditionality of belief is "obvious," he acknowledges a certain "difficulty":

> As apprehension is a concomitant, so inference is ordinarily the antecedent of assent;—on this surely I need not enlarge;—but neither apprehension nor inference interferes with the unconditional character of the assent, viewed in itself. The circumstances of an act, however necessary to it, do not enter into the act; assent is in its nature absolute and unconditional, though it cannot be given except under certain conditions.
> This is obvious; but what presents some difficulty is this, how it is that a conditional acceptance of a proposition,—such as is an act of inference,—is able to lead as it does, to an unconditional acceptance of it,—such as is assent; how it is that a proposition which is not, and cannot be, demonstrated, which at the highest can only be proved to be truth-like, not true, such as "I shall die," nevertheless claims and re-

ceives our unqualified adhesion. To the consideration of this paradox, as it may be called, I shall now proceed; that is, to the consideration, first, of the act of assent to a proposition, which act is unconditional; next, of the act of inference, which goes before the assent and is conditional; and, thirdly, of the solution of the apparent inconsistency which is involved in holding that an unconditional acceptance of a proposition can be the result of its conditional verification. (135)

Newman now declares "simple assent" as his new subject, but this concept is not defined until the next section, where he contrasts it with "complex assent." There he tells us, "That mode of Assent which is exercised thus unconsciously, I may call simple assent, and of it I have treated in the foregoing Section; but now I am going to speak of such assents as must be made consciously and deliberately, and which I shall call complex or reflex assents" (157). However, the real purpose of the first section of chapter 6 is to defend the "obvious" doctrine that belief is unconditional, and Newman does this by attacking Locke's view that belief admits of "degrees."

This doctrine was not always so obvious to Newman himself, who in notes and papers does not hesitate to speak of "conditional assent." In an undated fragment, he writes, "The assent, which the mind gives to its thoughts as being true, is either absolute and simple, or conditional and complex."[1] In a manuscript of 1853, he writes, "*Assent* is the acceptance of a proposition as true. Assent is either *absolute* or *conditional*."[2] And in a later manuscript, he writes, "The assent, which I give to my thoughts as true, is either absolute and simple, or conditional and complex. . . . Conditional or complex assent is that which I give to a thought as true, viewed with and in another thought."[3]

Although he has now come to regard the doctrine as obvious, he admits that certain "writers of great ability . . . have put it aside in favour of a doctrine of their own," and he even allows that their own view "carries with it a show of common sense":

> The authors to whom I refer wish to maintain that there are degrees of assent, and that, as the reasons for a proposition are strong or weak, so is the assent. It follows from this that absolute assent has no legitimate exercise, except as ratifying acts of intuition or demonstration. What is thus brought home to us is indeed to be accepted unconditionally; but, as to reasonings in concrete matter, they are never more than probabilities, and the probability in each conclusion which we draw is the measure of our assent to that conclusion. . . . Such is what may be called the *a priori* method of regarding assent in its relation to inference. It condemns an unconditional assent in concrete matters on what may be called the

1 O.Ar. A.18.11: fragment, n.d.
2 O.Ar. A.30.11: untitled paper on faith, dated 13 May 1853. See *Theological Papers*, 11.
3 O.Ar. A.18.11: material for an introduction, n.d.

nature of the case. Assent cannot rise higher than its source, inference in such matters is at best conditional, therefore assent is conditional also. (136)

Rejecting this theory, Newman insists that it "cannot be carried out in practice" and that "it debars us from unconditional assent in cases in which the common voice of mankind, the advocates of this theory included, would protest against the prohibition":

> There are many truths in concrete matter, which no one can demonstrate, yet every one unconditionally accepts; and though of course there are innumerable propositions to which it would be absurd to give an absolute assent, still the absurdity lies in the circumstances of each particular case, as it is taken by itself, not in their common violation of the pretentious axiom that probable reasoning can never lead to certitude. (136)

When Newman tells us here that there are many propositions to which it would be absurd to give an absolute assent, he seems to be implying that it would be absurd to give them *any* assent, for he has just argued that all assent is "absolute" in the sense of being unconditional. When he refers to "certitude," he does not suggest that this mental act differs from belief, though a quick examination of the *Grammar*'s table of contents tells us that Newman does not consider "certitude" a mere *synonym* of "assent." We may even be inclined to reflect here that if the terms "belief" and "certitude" have a different force in ordinary language, it is precisely because we regard certitude as being "unconditional" in a way that belief is not.

In attacking the view that there are degrees of belief, Newman takes Locke as the principal spokesman for the position. He acknowledges his high respect "for the character and the ability of Locke, for his manly simplicity of mind and his outspoken candour," and he says that he feels no pleasure in criticizing a philosopher with whom he agrees on so much (137-38). Still, in Newman's view, Locke is the English Protestant philosopher par excellence; and Newman is perceptive here, for we can see from Locke's writings on politics and religion that this most influential of English philosophers is indeed a precursor, even a founder, of the liberalism Newman so much deplores. Moreover, it is not hard to understand Newman's apologetical motive for attacking the doctrine of degrees of belief, for his criticism of Locke is clearly an attempt to show that the simple, unreflective Catholic believer has a right to assent fully and firmly to those Catholic teachings for which he has limited evidence. If belief is unconditional and does not admit of degrees, then it makes little sense to criticize the simple, devout believer for believing to a "degree that is unwarranted by the strength of the evidence." As H. H. Price has observed, if Newman "can show that Locke has confused assent with inference, he thinks the doctrine of degrees of assent will lose any plausibility it has; and with the collapse of that doctrine, Locke's *Ethics of Belief* will collapse too."[4]

The point of departure for Newman's attack on the doctrine of degrees of belief is his consideration of some remarks by Locke in the *Essay Concerning Human Understanding* (137-38). After telling us that Locke is not consistently wrong about the matter at hand, he singles out for criticism the following passage:

> How a man may know, whether he be so [i.e., a lover of truth], in earnest, is worth inquiry; and I think, there is this one unerring mark of it, viz. *the not entertaining any proposition with greater assurance than the proofs it is built on will warrant*. Whoever goes beyond this measure of assent, it is plain, receives not truth in the love of it. . . . For the evidence that any proposition is true (*except such as are self-evident*) lying only in the proofs a man has of it, whatsoever degrees of assent he affords it *beyond the degrees of that* evidence, it is plain *all that surplusage of assurance* is owing to some other affection, and not to the love of truth; it being as *impossible* that the love of truth should carry *my assent above the evidence* there is to me that it is true, as that the love of truth should make me assent to any proposition for the sake of that evidence which it has not that it is true. . . .[5]

Setting aside Newman's apologetical motive for disapproving of this view, let us consider Newman's philosophical reasons for rejecting it.

Before introducing his four main lines of argument, Newman makes the preliminary point that Locke contradicts himself; by doing so, Newman gives support to his claim that even advocates of the doctrine of degrees of assent would protest against its consistent application. Newman cites these passages from Locke's *Essay*:

> § Most of the propositions we think, reason, discourse, nay, act upon, are such as we cannot have undoubted knowledge of their truth; yet some of them *border so near* upon certainty, that we *make no doubt at all* about them, but *assent* to them *as firmly*, and act according to that assent as resolutely, *as if they were infallibly demonstrated*, and that our knowledge of them was perfect and certain.[6]

> § [W]hen any particular thing, consonant to the constant observation of ourselves and others in the like case, comes attested by the concurrent reports of all that mention it, we receive it as easily, and build as firmly upon it, as if it were certain knowledge, and we reason and act thereupon, *with as little doubt as if it were perfect demonstration*. . . . These *probabilities* rise so near to certainty, that they *govern our thoughts as absolutely*, and influence all our actions as fully, as *the most evident demonstration*; and in what concerns us, we make little or no difference between them and certain knowledge. *Our belief thus grounded, rises to assurance.*[7]

---

4 H. H. Price, *Belief* (London: George Allen and Unwin, 1969), 138.

5 Locke, *Essay*, ch. 19, sec. 1. This chapter was added in the fourth edition. The transcription of the passages from Locke is not completely accurate; most of the emphasis has been added by Newman.

6 Ibid., bk. 4, ch. 15, sec. 2.

7 Ibid., bk. 4, ch. 16, sec. 6.

Newman feels that Locke is being inconsistent here:

> How then is it not inconsistent with right reason, with the love of truth for its own sake, to allow, in his words quoted above, certain strong "probabilities" to "govern our thoughts as absolutely as the most evident demonstration"? how is there no "surplusage of assurance beyond the degrees of evidence" when in the case of those strong probabilities, we permit "our belief, thus grounded, to rise to assurance," as he pronounces we are rational in doing? Of course he had in view one set of instances, when he implied that demonstration was the condition of absolute assent, and another set when he said that it was no such condition; but he surely cannot be acquitted of slovenly thinking in thus treating a cardinal subject. A philosopher should so anticipate the application, and guard the enunciation of his principles, as to secure them against the risk of their being made to change places with each other, to defend what he is eager to denounce, and to condemn what he finds it necessary to sanction. (139)

Is not Newman being too severe with Locke? Does a principle collapse as soon as one allows that there are special exceptions to it, exceptions involving borderline cases? If we refused to live by principles that admit of exceptions, we would hardly have enough principles to live by. But Newman's point is more profound: Locke may well have been arbitrary in drawing the borderline where he found it convenient to do so. If there has to be a borderline, why not draw it somewhere else? Or why not replace the original rule with a more realistic one? As Newman observes:

> He [Locke] takes a view of the human mind, in relation to inference and assent, which to me seems theoretical and unreal. Reasonings and convictions which I deem natural and legitimate, he apparently would call irrational, enthusiastic, perverse, and immoral; and that, as I think, because he consults his own ideal of how the mind ought to act, instead of interrogating human nature, as an existing thing, as it is found in the world. Instead of going by the testimony of psychological facts, and thereby determining our constitutive faculties and our proper condition, and being content with the mind as God has made it, he would form men as he thinks they ought to be formed, into something better and higher, and calls them irrational and indefensible, if (so to speak) they take to the water, instead of remaining under the narrow wings of his own arbitrary theory. (139-40)

When Locke admits that we assent to borderline propositions as firmly and absolutely as if they were demonstrated, he is moving from epistemology to phenomenology: he is telling us how the mind works, even in spite of how it ought to work. Newman approves of this move but feels that Locke still does not have enough appreciation of the importance of the phenomenological or psychological data. Though Locke is willing to allow that people must firmly assent to various propositions that are not "certainties" but only "probabilities," he is not nearly as generous as Newman is in admitting propositions into this class.

Locke's inconsistency is less serious than Newman's. In divorcing belief and evidence in the radical way that he does, Newman ends up attaching too much importance to what people already believe and not enough to what they ought to believe. Newman is not simply calling here for an adjustment to the borderline; he is arguing against degrees of assent and the ethics of belief. The irony in this is that Newman, as an apologist, is well aware of the fact that non-Catholics need to be *brought* to believe various propositions that he thinks they *ought* to believe. Newman is no more content with the "mind as God has made it"—the mind of the liberal, Moslem, or atheist—than Locke or anyone else. Like Locke, he "would form men as he thinks they ought to be formed." There are plenty of reasonings and convictions that he himself regards as "irrational, enthusiastic, perverse, and immoral." And dogmatist that he is, Newman is rarely reluctant to consult "his own ideal of how the mind ought to act." But his view of our "proper condition" is not more realistic than Locke's. And even if Locke has overstated his point, we can still approve of his general association of evidence with what we ought to believe strongly. Newman knows that human beings do not have to believe his favourite propositions in the way that they must believe Locke's borderline propositions. Newman's pet propositions are not compelling—phenomenologically, psychologically, or pragmatically—in the same way or to the same degree as are the propositions that Locke has in mind. Moreover, Locke has the option of believing that it is wrong for us to assent as firmly as we do to borderline propositions, even if our doing so must be tolerated, forgiven, or regarded as almost necessary.

Newman now proceeds to give his first main line of argument. Here he lays down as a principle "that either assent is intrinsically distinct from inference, or the sooner we get rid of the word in philosophy the better":

> If it be only the echo of an inference, do not treat it as a substantive act; but on the other hand, supposing it be not such an idle repetition, as I am sure it is not,—supposing the word "assent" does hold a rightful place in language and in thought,—if it does not admit of being confused with concluding and inferring,—if the two words are used for two operations of the intellect which cannot change their character,—if in matter of fact they are not always found together,—if they do not vary with each other,—if one is sometimes found without the other,—if one is strong when the other is weak,—if sometimes they seem even in conflict with each other,—then since we know perfectly well what an inference is, it comes upon us to consider what, as distinct from inference, an assent is, and we are, by the very fact of its being distinct, advanced one step towards that account of it which I think is the true one. (140-41)

Newman goes on to make six points in elaboration and defense of this argument; but before considering them individually, let us take a look at the main theme underlying them. In Newman's view, if assent is conditional and admits of degrees, then it is not significantly different from the propositional attitude of inference. If it "can only be viewed as the necessary and immediate repetition of another act, if assent is a sort of reproduction and double of an act of inference" (140), then the term "assent" does not hold "a rightful place in language and in thought." To have such a place, it must refer to a propositional attitude that is "intrinsically distinct from inference," and it can only do so if it refers to a propositional attitude that is not conditional in the way that inference is.

This is a very curious piece of ordinary-language analysis. It probably did not seem quite as strange to the first readers of the *Grammar*, but nowadays we do not use the terms "assent" and "inference" in anything like the way that Newman describes. Where Newman speaks of "assent," we are more inclined to speak of "belief," and though we do think of belief as a propositional attitude, we often think of it more as a disposition than a mental act.[8] As for inference, we think of it as a process of arriving at belief, not as a rival propositional attitude. When we hear someone say, "The detective infers that Lulu is the culprit," we associate this statement with the idea of the detective having arrived at a belief by means of a certain rational, intellectual process, the idea of his having drawn a conclusion; our attention is not directed to the fact that the conclusion he has arrived at is conditional or in any way inferior to a firm belief. If belief and inference are "distinct," and indeed they are—Locke himself does not use the words "assent" and "inference" interchangeably—it is not because they are rival propositional attitudes, but because one is a propositional attitude and the other is a process by which we arrive at a propositional attitude. (We do sometimes use the term "inference" to refer to a proposition, the conclusion itself, but here again it is not being used to refer to a rival propositional attitude.)

But say that inference *were* a propositional attitude like belief; even then it would not necessarily be the case that the difference between inference and belief is that one is conditional and the other is not. There is an ambiguity in Newman's claim that assent is "intrinsically distinct" from inference. Why cannot "assent" and "inference" refer to two aspects of the same propositional attitude, one term emphasizing the fact of a proposition's being held, the other drawing our attention to both its being held and its having been derived by a certain process? Why must belief and inference be "distinct" in the strong sense Newman has in mind in order for the terms "assent" and "inference" to both have a "rightful place" in language and in thought? Why must they be rival, contradictory propositional at-

8 Cf. Price, *Belief*, esp. series I, lecture 1.

titudes in order to be properly regarded as "distinct"? The term "morning star" deserves a place in our language even though it has the same *reference* as the term "evening star." So why demand that "assent" refer to the opposite of inference? Newman's insight into the nature of language is rather limited here, and it is distorted by a metaphysical presupposition about the nature of "distinctness," one that seems especially odd when made by a philosopher who regards belief and inference as "notions" rather than "things." Furthermore, while Newman objects here to our retaining a word that refers to an "idle repetition," he does not apply so rigorous a standard when he later contrasts belief with certitude. However, this is a point to which we shall have to return.

Newman is indeed left with a "difficulty" and a "paradox." How can belief be both unconditional and the result of the conditional "verification" of inference? There is no problem here for those who believe in degrees of belief, in the conditionality of belief; but there is a problem for Newman. He now makes various points in elaboration and defense of his little piece of linguistic analysis. (1) "First, we know from experience that assents may endure without the presence of the inferential acts upon which they were originally elicited. . . . [W]hen we first admitted them, we had some kind of reason, slight or strong, recognized or not, for doing so. However, whatever those reasons were, even if we ever realized them, we have long forgotten them. . . . Here then is a case in which assent stands out as distinct from inference" (141-42). This case hardly supports Newman's contention that belief is unconditional. Even if we cannot remember our reasons for having come to hold a belief we still hold, we are convinced that we did have reasons. We often try to remember what those reasons were, and if we cannot remember them, we may even abandon the belief or believe it less strongly that we did prior to our latest reflection. (2) "Again; sometimes assent fails, while the reasons for it and the inferential act which is the recognition of those reasons, are still present, and in force. Our reasons may seem to us as strong as ever, yet they do not secure our assent. . . . [W]hat once was assent is gone; yet the perception of the old arguments remains, showing that inference is one thing, and assent another" (142). It is not clear that in cases of this sort the reasons are still "in force" and "seem to us as strong as ever." It would normally seem here that our reasons for holding the belief have come to be outweighed by other considerations, not that we are refusing to believe even in spite of the dictates of reason. Newman has anticipated this response: "[T]his is not always so; sometimes our mind changes so quickly, so unaccountably, so disproportionately to any tangible arguments to which the change can be referred, and with such abiding recognition of the force of the old arguments, as to suggest the suspicion that moral causes, arising out of our condition, age, company, occupations, fortunes, are at the bottom." Now, what we believe—and the strength with which we believe it—is indeed influenced by non-rational factors of the kind Newman has mentioned (and misleadingly classified together under the label of "moral causes"). And sometimes people are actually "irrational" and believe propositions that reason tells them are plainly false. But Newman is dealing here with a relatively small class of beliefs and has not established that most of our beliefs are "unconditional" in the rather narrow sense that he now has in mind. Interestingly enough, in tracing even these beliefs back to non-rational "moral causes," he is drawing our attention to the fact that they too have their own special "conditions," albeit "implicit" ones. But even if Newman can be seen as having established that relatively "irrational" beliefs are relatively "unconditional" in a certain narrow sense, he has not established that belief *as such* is unconditional in the larger and more interesting sense. And why take an "irrational" belief as our model or paradigm? Moreover, in the kind of case Newman has described, inference in *his* sense is absent, for the proposition that is the conclusion of the "old arguments" is no longer *held* by the agent. (If Newman is willing to allow that the agent simultaneously holds and does not hold the same proposition, then his analysis is rather more problematic than he realizes.)

(3) "And as assent sometimes dies out without tangible reasons, sufficient to account for its failure, so sometimes, in spite of strong and convincing arguments, it is never given" (142). We can analyze this case in roughly the same way as we analyzed the previous one. How convincing are the arguments here if they do not lead the agent to believe? And if the same arguments lead different men to believe firmly, strongly, moderately, or even slightly (i.e., with deep reservations), is this not proof that there are degrees of belief? In showing how belief and inference are different or not constantly conjoined, Newman is not establishing anything that the Lockean does not already know. But it does not follow from the fact that believing is distinguishable from inferring, or from the fact that belief does not always vary in direct proportion with the relative strength of our evidence or reasons, that belief as such is unconditional. Locke is well aware of the fact that people do not always have sufficient respect for the dictates of reason; that is precisely why he speaks of the need for an epistemological ethic of belief. (4) "Again; very numerous are the cases, in which good arguments, and really good as far as they go, and confessed by us to be good, nevertheless are not strong enough to incline our minds ever so little to the conclusion at which they point. But why is it that we do not assent a little, in proportion to those

arguments? On the contrary, we throw the full *onus probandi* on the side of the conclusion, and we refuse to assent to it at all, until we can assent to it altogether. The proof is capable of growth; but the assent either exists or does not exist" (143). To some extent, this argument is open to the same criticisms as the two previous ones. It does not follow from the fact that some people are more rational than others that belief as such is unconditional. A good many people *will* see the arguments here as warranting belief—firm, strong, moderate, or slight. Our recognition of the soundness of the arguments is often capable, even normally capable, of overcoming the non-rational obstacles to our believing. If a person cannot believe, or refuses to believe, even in the face of reasons and arguments that the person regards as intellectually compelling, then the "unconditionality" of the person's doubt would seem to be nothing more than a singularly stubborn irrationality. But Newman has introduced an interesting new theme here: he has drawn our attention to the fact that, in spite of Locke's talk about various degrees of belief, human beings either believe or do not believe a proposition. Ultimately, then, there are only two epistemological options open to the agent. This point merits respectful consideration.

When we ask someone, "Do you believe that free trade benefits the poorer classes?," we may well expect a yes or no answer. If the person hedges, is evasive, and refuses to give a "straight" answer, we may well lose our patience and ask bluntly and with annoyance, "Look, do you believe it or don't you?" While recognizing the value of such answers as "In a way," "In a sense," and "To some extent," we often feel that the people who give such answers are either rather confused or hiding their *ultimate* commitment. And if one believes that, in the last analysis, a person either believes or does not, then in a certain sense one regards belief and doubt as "unconditional" and not admitting of degrees. But look more closely. When people answer "In a way" or "To some extent," they are usually drawing our attention to the complexity of the proposition under consideration. The classic example of a "complex" question is "Have you stopped beating your wife?" If a person answers yes *or* no to this question he condemns himself in a way that may be wholly inappropriate. The question "Do you believe that free trade benefits the poorer classes?" is not "complex" in quite the same way, but like the classic question, it is capable of being broken down into smaller, more detailed questions that the agent will be capable of unhesitatingly answering with a yes or no. It may well be that the agent finds the proposition "Free trade benefits the poorer classes" so vague, so undefined, that that individual is not in the position to believe or doubt it, or cannot take it seriously as an object of belief or doubt.

Newman knows full well that there is a difference, phenomenologically and pragmatically, between the commitment of the person who answers, "Yes, I believe that quite strongly," and that of the person who answers, "Yes, I think so, but I have some serious reservations." The difference in the strength of their commitment is reflected in their speech, in their actions, and in their response to discussions of the proposition in question. Neither believes unconditionally in Newman's sense; neither is incapable of appreciating new data that are relevant to the subject at hand. And to have reservations is not to be hypocritical or inconsistent. But consider a curious feature of Newman's analysis. In Newman's view, we cannot see a weak belief as one that is accompanied by a certain amount of doubt, for a person cannot simultaneously believe and doubt a proposition. For Newman, if a weak assent were simply a belief accompanied by a certain amount of doubt, then a person who weakly assented to a proposition would be in the position of simultaneously believing and not believing the proposition. The problem here is that, for Newman, to *doubt* a proposition, to have a reservation about it, is to *withhold assent*. You will recall that at the beginning of the *Grammar*, Newman writes: "To doubt . . . is not to see one's way to hold, that Free-trade is or that it is not a benefit; . . . to assent to the proposition, is to hold that Free-trade is a benefit" (26). For Newman, belief and doubt are conflicting mental acts.

H. H. Price criticizes Newman for failing to notice "that propositions about which we have some doubt are nevertheless relied upon" in that they "give us some guidance both in thought and in action. . . ."[9] To counter such an objection, Newman must refuse to count "relying upon" or "being guided by" as genuine belief. Price does not consider belief and doubt to be conflicting mental acts, and he writes, "When our evidence for a proposition, though not conclusive, is favourable, or favourable on balance when any unfavourable evidence there may be is taken into account, we can assent to that proposition with a limited degree of confidence. . . ."[10] For Price, then, to have a doubt or reservation that limits one's confidence is to have a certain attitude towards the available evidence and to adjust one's degree of belief accordingly; and according to such a view, to doubt is not necessarily to withhold assent. When we reflect on the disagreement here between Newman and Price, we are reminded of a certain ambiguity in the word "doubt" as it is used in ordinary language. Newman is right in believing that when someone says, "I doubt that free trade benefits the poorer classes," that person is normally indicating that he does not believe the proposition. But when

9 Ibid., 153.
10 Ibid., 155-56.

people say, "I believe that free trade does *in a sense* (more or less; on the whole; to a great extent) benefit the poorer classes, but I do have my doubts, at least sometimes," they are indicating that there is "unfavourable" evidence that prevents them from believing the proposition as strongly as they believe certain other propositions. If we keep pressing them and ask, "Look, do you believe it or don't you?," they can sincerely answer, "Yes; I do," even though their belief is not unconditional in Newman's sense. The key point, then, is this: though the word "belief" does designate a particular propositional attitude, one that is distinguishable from others, the attitude it signifies is subject to various modalities.

(5) "I have already alluded to the influence of moral motives in hindering assent to conclusions which are logically unimpeachable. According to the couplet,—

> 'A man convinced against his will
> Is of the same opinion still;'—

assent then is not the same as inference" (143). This brief and somewhat cryptic observation constitutes the whole of Newman's fifth point. Newman's talk about the role of the "will" in belief has been of great interest to certain scholars, and in one recently published study of Newman's thought the author has placed this talk at the centre of Newman's philosophical project.[11] Such an interpretation gives us a distorted view of the project, for it exaggerates the importance of one of many themes. Newman here associates the role of the will in belief with the "influence of moral motives" to which he had alluded on the previous page. He directs our attention there to the influence on belief of non-rational "moral causes," which arise "out of our condition, age, company, occupations, fortunes" (142). Newman has not told us very much about these "moral" motives or causes, but even though he will have more to say about them later in the *Grammar*, it is not too early for us to note how little they have to do with either morality or the will. Newman's immediate aim here, of course, is to reinforce his argument that what we believe depends on non-rational factors as well as on inference and reasoning. I have already admitted that Newman is quite right in seeing these factors as major influences on belief. Ironically, however, this very point has implications that would have made Newman most uncomfortable. For one thing, we can now see that in associating condition, age, and other such factors with the will, Newman is being naïvely voluntaristic. We have a good deal less control over the non-rational influences on belief than we do over the rational ones. Freedom is rooted in reason, not in causal factors of which we are largely unaware. Scholars like Gerrard are very perceptive when they observe that much of Newman's teaching

11 Ferreira, *Doubt*.

in the *Grammar* anticipates the philosophy of the unconscious;[12] but anyone who has read the major psychoanalytical theorists is apt to associate talk about unconscious, non-rational motives with radical determinism, not with the will, or at least not with the innocent sort of will that the moralizing Newman has in mind. Moreover, there is a serious inconsistency in Newman's treatment of the non-rational influences on belief. Here in chapter 6, Newman draws our attention to such influences in order to separate inference from belief, to show that believing is something independent of inferring and reasoning. But soon Newman will argue that the "moral motives" play a large role *in* "informal inference" and "inference in concrete matter," and he will refer to them in explaining how such inference differs from the dry "formal" inference of the philosophers, logicians, and intellectuals. So Newman will end up with two conflicting models: in one, "moral motives" are at the heart of informal inference; in the other, "moral motives" *combine* with inference in the act of illative judgment.

But what does Newman's talk about the role of the will actually accomplish here in chapter 6? In spite of the importance that he attaches to his couplet, Newman knows full well that the will alone does not ordinarily lead us to belief. All along he has insisted that inference normally precedes belief, and indeed a main aim of the *Grammar* is to show the rationality of faith. He can hardly be arguing then that inference is really "after the fact," and that reasoning merely supports what the will has already determined we should believe. Newman also knows that we all believe things that we would rather not believe; he cannot be ignorant of the fact that the "will to believe"—understood in an innocent, non-deterministic way—only carries us so far and even then only in a very limited number of cases. Besides, even if the will is as powerful as Newman feels, and even if non-rational motives do not do their work *within* the process of informal inference, Newman has not supported his claim that belief is unconditional. For just as evidence varies in degrees, so does the influence of most of Newman's "moral motives." We speak of people as strong-willed and weak-willed; as a sort of spiritual horsepower, willpower admits of countless gradations. So does morality, which, after all, involves evaluation, valuing. And unless one is a very strict determinist, one will allow that there are degrees to which one can be influenced by something like condition, occupation, or fortune. It is not at all clear then why Newman thinks we should expect the non-rational "moral" conditions of belief to be more successful than evidence is in yielding a uniform, unconditional acceptance of propositions.

12 Gerrard, "Sure Future," 311.

(6) "Strange as it may seem, this contrast between inference and assent is exemplified even in the province of mathematics. Argument is not always able to command our Assent, even though it be demonstrative" (143). In arguing that we can only give absolute assent to demonstrations, Locke lends considerable prestige to the highly formal argumentation that baffles peasants and factory-girls and is consequently an object of Newman's scorn. The logic of Newman's general argument requires him to hold that mathematical inference is no more a matter of believing than any other kind of inference, even though the propositions on which its conclusions depend are almost universally accepted. And indeed a person might arbitrarily make it his rule never to assent to mathematical conclusions without the corroboration of others, "at least before the lapse of a sufficient interval" (144). Still, Newman recognizes that mathematical inference often *commands* our belief: "Certainly, one cannot conceive a man having before him the series of conditions and truths on which it depends that the three angles of a triangle are together equal to two right angles, and yet not assenting to that proposition" (143). Locke would add that a belief that is thus "commanded" is clearly stronger than any other belief, so much so that it alone represents an absolute or resolute belief. Newman does not directly attack this position and must fall back here on his other arguments.

In concluding his first main line of argument against the doctrine of degrees of belief, Newman repeats his point about the distinctness and "substantiveness" of the mental act of belief, but he also attempts to give inference its due. He warns that he must not be taken to deny that there is a "legitimate or actual connexion" between inference and belief, "as if arguments adverse to a conclusion did not naturally hinder assent; or as if the inclination to give assent were not greater or less according as the particular act of inference expressed a stronger or weaker probability; or as if assent did not always imply grounds in reason, implicit, if not explicit, or could be rightly given without sufficient grounds" (144-45). Carrying this caveat a step further, he writes:

> So much is it commonly felt that assent must be preceded by inferential acts, that obstinate men give their own will as their very reason for assenting, if they can think of nothing better; "stat pro ratione voluntas." Indeed, I doubt whether assent is ever given without some preliminary, which stands for a reason. . . . (145)

Still, "it does not follow from this, that it may not be withheld in cases when there are good reasons for giving it to a proposition, or may not be withdrawn after it has been given, the reasons remaining, or may not remain when the reasons are forgotten, or must always vary in strength, as the reasons vary . . ." (145). Does the Lockean deny any of this? As an epistemologist, Locke knows just as well as Newman does that belief is not always rational; he even believes that there are "very few lovers of truth, for truth-sake" who consistently refrain from entertaining propositions with greater assurance than the proofs they are built on will warrant (138). Where Locke disagrees with Newman is in believing that people are *capable* of giving different degrees of belief; and in a sense, he believes that people can be more rational than Newman thinks they can.

Newman commences his second main line of argument by asking whether we can cite instances of a belief's coexisting with doubt. People may think that they can give such examples, but do they not invariably end up giving examples of inference rather than belief?

> Usually, we do not assent at all. Every day, as it comes, brings with it opportunities for us to enlarge our circle of assents. We read the newspapers; we look through debates in Parliament, pleadings in the law courts, leading articles, letters of correspondents, reviews of books, criticisms in the fine arts, and we either form no opinion at all upon the subjects discussed, as lying out of our line, or at most we have only an opinion about them. (146)

"Only" an opinion? In chapter 4, Newman characterizes opinion as a kind of assent, albeit only assent to a proposition that such-and-such is probable. So is opinion assent or not? Newman anticipates this question and says that when we have an opinion we do not have reservations about the *probability* of x, only about x itself, and x itself is not a proposition to which we *assent* (147). Newman then turns his attention to the following passage by Gambier, who "expresses himself after Locke's manner":

> Moral evidence may produce a variety of degrees of assents, from suspicion to moral certainty. For here, the degree of assent depends upon the degree in which the evidence on one side preponderates, or exceeds that on the other. And as this preponderancy may vary almost infinitely, so likewise may the degrees of assent. For a few of these degrees, though but for a few, names have been invented. Thus, when the evidence on one side preponderates a very little, there is a ground for suspicion, or conjecture. Presumption, persuasion, belief, conclusion, conviction, moral certainty,—doubt, wavering, distrust, disbelief,—are words which imply an increase or decrease of this preponderancy. Some of these words also admit of epithets which denote a further increase or diminution of the assent.[13]

Newman, of course, will have none of this. Gambier's "assents," he tells us, are "really only inferences," and for Gambier, "assent is a name without a meaning, the needless repetition of an inference." The items on Gambier's list—suspicion, conjecture, presumption, and the like—"are not 'assents' at all; they are simply more or less

13 Newman gives as his source: "Gambier on Moral Evidence, p. 6."

strong inferences of a proposition" (147). Newman adds that he cannot think of any case where we "deliberately profess assent to a proposition without meaning to convey to others the impression that we accept it unreservedly" (147). Even our use of a term like "half-assent" is nothing more than an attempt to indicate that we "feel drawn towards assent" (148).

When modern readers substitute the term "belief" for Newman's term "assent," they can hardly see Newman's linguistic analysis here as satisfactory. Newman must do considerably more than explain away the occasional special use of "belief"; he must deal with the larger part of its usage. Although Newman is constantly urging us to focus our attention on concrete cases rather than abstract principles, his linguistic analysis in this section gives us little concrete with which to work. Consider then a case like the following, which does not seem to be special or unusual. When someone asks us, "Is it raining outside?" or "Is Birmingham a larger city than Manchester?", we may well answer, "I believe so" or "I believe that it is," and in giving such an answer, we do not at all mean to convey that we accept some proposition unreservedly; indeed, there is nothing at all contradictory in the common answer, "I believe so, but I am not sure." We even contrast belief with knowledge, much as the ancient Greek philosophers contrasted *doxa* with *episteme* and *gnosis*, so that when articulating our view in a discussion of some serious matter, we may well say something like, "That, of course, is just my belief; I do not really know." We would rarely if ever say, "I believe that it is raining," if we actually *knew* or *felt certain* that it is. Granted, to know or feel certain is also to believe; but when we know or feel certain, we simply say, "It is raining," without using the introductory phrase, "I believe that . . . ." We usually use this phrase to *hedge*, although there is a special use of it in which it does serve to indicate our deep or even absolute commitment to a certain religious or philosophical creed. Newman would seem to have been so much concerned with this special use of the phrase that he took it for the ordinary one.

Nor would we ordinarily say, "I infer that it is raining," or "I have inferred that it is raining," to indicate that we have reservations; and if someone tells us that this is what we really mean when we say, "I believe that it is raining," we would probably feel that this person has confused belief and inference, not us. We would not understand what was meant when it was said that in using the term "belief" here, we had used it "without a meaning," and we would probably protest that it is this person who has wrongly reduced belief to inference. To say that suspicion, conjecture, presumption, and the like are not really modes of belief is to show a certain contempt for ordinary language. But Newman cannot argue here that the ordinary language of belief is confused and needs to be replaced by a technical language of belief, for this whole argument against Locke and Gambier is based on an *appeal* to ordinary language. Newman has argued that it is perfectly consistent with ordinary usage to say that "I suspect that it is raining, but I do not really believe that it is." This argument is unsound.

Newman, of course, discusses "assent," not "belief," and the linguistic usage of his age also differs somewhat from our own. If Newman's use of "assent" is *radically* different from our contemporary use of "belief," then the *Grammar* is a dead book and embodies a project that is of purely historical interest to the contemporary philosopher or theologian. But the difference, I think, is not so radical; Newman not only uses a phrase like "inclined to believe" interchangeably with one like "inclined to assent" (146) but also gives us innumerable reasons for believing that the words "assent" and "belief" in *his* age played essentially the same role in language that the word "belief" now plays in the language of our own.

Consider now Newman's analysis of *opinion*. It is not clear why Newman thinks he is justified in analyzing the opinion "I believe that it is raining" as "I believe that the proposition 'It is raining' is probable." That he feels obliged to offer such an analysis is itself noteworthy: for having announced that Gambier's "assents" are really inferences, he is now hedging by allowing that they are indeed beliefs, albeit only in a certain sense. Thus he writes:

> There is only one sense in which we are allowed to call such acts or states of mind assents. They are opinions; and, as being such, they are, as I have already observed, when speaking of Opinion, assents to the plausibility, probability, doubtfulness, or untrustworthiness, of a proposition; that is, not variations of assent to an inference, but assents to a variation in inferences. When I assent to a doubtfulness, or to a probability, my assent, as such, is as complete as if I assented to a truth; it is not a certain degree of assent. (147)

This analysis has some remarkable features. One is that it blurs the very distinction between inference and belief that Newman has laboured so hard to draw. For, according to this analysis, inferring a proposition is substantially the same as believing a related proposition, the proposition that the main proposition is probable. So even if inferring a proposition is not a way of believing that proposition, it is a way of believing *some* proposition. Inference itself has been shown to be reducible to belief; and suspicion, conjecture, presumption, and the like have turned out to be beliefs after all. Moreover, as suspicion and other modes of inference all involve some assessment of probability, the supposedly unconditional acts of belief that correspond to them turn out to admit at least indirectly of degrees. This is an important point, and we shall return to it when we consider Newman's fourth line of argument, particularly his analysis of *prima facie* belief. Another feature of Newman's analysis is that it treats opinions as beliefs about propositions rather than beliefs about things. Newman, of course, warns us earlier that his use of the term "opinion" is a personal one (64). Still, there is a larger issue here: Newman is engaged in some questionable linguistic analysis, and some questionable phenomenology, too, when he treats a statement like "I suspect that it is raining" as a statement wholly about evidence and not at all about the weather. When someone says nowadays, "I believe that it is raining, but I am not sure," he is not *merely* hedging but is also providing us with what he takes to be useful information about the weather. Furthermore, when a person makes such a statement, he may very well have in his mind the images that Newman associates with real belief. When a person says, "I suspect that it is raining," the images in his mind are apt to be no less vivid than those that accompany his belief when he asserts more forcefully, "It is raining." So even by Newman's own phenomenological criteria, it is not clear why Gambier's "assents" should be demoted to the rank of notional beliefs about the probability of propositions.

Newman begins his second main line of argument by challenging us to give an example of a belief that coexists with doubt. Realizing that most of us think we can produce many such examples, he immediately warns that what passes for belief is often just inference; and he follows up this point by arguing that what appears to be conditional "belief that *p*" is really unconditional "belief that *p* is probable." According to Newman's analysis, to suspect or presume *p* is not to believe *p* but rather to infer *p* and to believe *p* probable. Why then do so many people who merely infer *p* and believe *p* probable keep saying, "I believe *p*"? We are not, after all, dealing here with an occasional lapse but with ordinary language at its most ordinary. How can Newman dismiss our ordinary understanding of "belief" as a simple confusion? Contemporary epistemologists and analytical philosophers may have some sympathy for Newman here; our ordinary language of belief does indeed have some disturbing characteristics. But Newman does not openly call for conceptual revision or linguistic reform; on the contrary, he attacks the Lockes and Gambiers for not doing justice to the ordinary language of belief. Here he is on weak ground, for his own concepts of belief, inference, and opinion are not nearly as close as the Lockean's are to those of peasants, factory-girls, parish priests, and liberals. Yet, if our ordinary language of belief is sometimes imprecise and misleading, it does not follow that the conceptual revisions that Newman indirectly recommends leave us with a language or theory of belief that is phenomenologically or pragmatically superior to what we now have.

Whatever sympathy we may have for Newman's attempt to protect the "surplusage of assurance" that marks the simple believer's religious faith, we cannot endorse Newman's claim that Locke has demanded the *impossible* in calling upon us to believe certain propositions less strongly than others. Moreover, our language possesses a term that has served long and efficiently to designate the firm belief that Locke and Gambier contrast with other degrees of belief; that term is "certitude," and no one is less anxious to do away with it than Newman is. Finally, even if Newman *had* successfully established that all belief is necessarily absolute, unconditional, and unreserved, he would not have thereby shown that the simple Catholic believer has a right to assent fully and firmly to those Catholic teachings for which he has limited evidence. For it can be argued that it is wrong to believe p at all if it is both possible and rational to hold instead simply that p is probable. Newman himself would have had to admit that there is a sense in which believing p probable is "weaker" than directly believing p itself, a sense of "weaker" that has little or nothing to do with images. So by associating inference with opinion in the way he has, Newman has indirectly implied that there are at least two epistemologically significant "degrees" of belief. In Newman's view, a true Catholic believes dogmatic propositions p, q, and r; such a person does not simply infer p, q, and r, and he does not simply believe p, q, and r probable. Newman cannot think very highly of the person who defends his claim that he is a true Catholic by pointing to the fact that he firmly, absolutely, unconditionally believes that p, q, and r are probable.

In his third main line of argument, Newman gives a list of "some of those assents, which men give on evidence short of intuition and demonstration, yet which are as unconditional as if they had that highest evidence" (148). He begins by pointing to beliefs derived from self-consciousness and quickly goes on to mention our beliefs that other people exist, that there is an external world, that the universe is "carried on by laws," and that the future is affected by the past. We also hold "with an unqualified assent" that the earth is a globe, that all its regions see the sun by turns, that it has really existing cities which go by the names of London and Paris, that we had parents, that we shall depart this life, that we cannot live without food, and so on (149). "On all these truths we have an immediate and an unhesitating hold, nor do we think ourselves guilty of not loving truth for truth's sake, because we cannot reach them through a series of intuitive propositions" (150). Moreover, even the Lockes and Gambiers, after having "made their protest, . . . subside without scruple into that same absolute assurance of only partially-proved truths, which is natural to the illogical imagination of the multitude" (152).

What exactly is the argument here? As Newman well knows, Locke himself observes that there are certain propositions that *"border so near upon certainty, that we make no doubt at all about them"* (137). But in Newman's view, Locke is still too demanding. Commenting on the motive of the Lockeans, Newman writes:

> They warn us, that an issue which can never come to pass in matter of fact, is nevertheless in theory a possible supposition. They do not, for instance, intend for a moment to imply that there is even a shadow of a doubt that Great Britain is an island, but they think we ought to know, if we do not know, that there is no proof of the fact, in mode and figure, equal to the proof of a proposition of Euclid; and that in consequence they and we are all bound to suspend our judgment about such a fact, though it be in an infinitesimal degree, lest we should seem not to love truth for truth's sake. (151-52)

For Newman, however, "[a]ssent on reasonings not demonstrative is too widely recognized an act to be irrational, unless man's nature is irrational, too familiar to the prudent and clear-minded to be an infirmity or extravagance":

> None of us can think or act without the acceptance of truths, not intuitive, not demonstrated, yet sovereign. If our nature has any constitution, any laws, one of them is this absolute reception of propositions as true, which lie outside the narrow range of conclusions to which logic, formal or virtual, is tethered; nor has any philosophical theory the power to force on us a rule which will not work for a day. (150)

Whatever value there is in Newman's latest reflections, they can hardly be seen as constituting an argument against the doctrine of degrees of belief. For even assuming for the moment that Newman is right in believing that we all give an unconditional assent to the various items on his list, the fact remains that we do not give such an assent to many or most propositions. It is the countless number of items that Newman has carefully *left off* his list that represents the Lockean's major concern here.

Since Newman has now accused the school of Locke of hypocrisy as well as philosophical naïveté, we owe it to Locke to consider how flagrantly Newman has distorted his position. Newman sees the Lockeans as having robbed us of our right to believe things we need to believe and have always believed; he tells us that they have insisted that "we are all bound to suspend our judgment" on the existence of an external world and the necessity of food for life. But Locke has done nothing of the kind; his credentials as a common-sense realist and enemy of scepticism are impeccable and far more impressive than Newman's. It is Newman, not Locke, who insists that belief is an all-or-nothing matter, and that the slightest doubt prevents us from believing. It is Newman, not Locke, who argues that people do not believe all sorts of things that they need to believe and have always believed, the countless number of things that Newman denies the status of belief and relegates to the inferior class of "inferences." In Locke's view, we need to believe and do believe innumerable propositions that Newman carefully leaves off his latest list of unconditional beliefs. Who, then, makes the harsh and impossible demands?

Newman seems to have no understanding of the epistemological value of Locke's normative doctrine of degrees of belief. Locke never denies that human beings are capable of believing that the world is round, that it will rain tomorrow, that London is larger than Paris, that Paris is larger than London, and that the moon is made of green cheese; but Locke rightly insists that only some of these beliefs should be held and that some should be held more strongly than others. In contrast, Newman holds, in theory if not in practice, that our beliefs that the world is round and that it will rain tomorrow must be equally unconditional and equally strong. But how can a person lead a normal life if he cannot have more reservations about tomorrow's weather than about the roundness of the world? And when a day passes and the weather turns out to be lovely, will such a person be as shocked and disoriented as if he had learned that the world is flat?

Consider some of the countless beliefs that Newman has kept off his list, our beliefs that it is raining outside, that it rained last Tuesday, that it will rain tomorrow, that our landlord is an honest man, that our uncle is still vacationing in Florida, that more Europeans go to concerts than to football matches, that the government's economic policy is basically sound, and that more people live in metropolitan Toronto than in metropolitan Montreal. Newman knows that most of the people who hold such propositions do not do so unconditionally; they have certain reservations. Newman believes that at most such people have formed "opinions," and have come to believe that these various propositions are quite probable, highly probable, or very highly probable. For Newman, then, they do not really have beliefs at all but make inferences, although corresponding to each inference is a belief in a related proposition, in the proposition that the main proposition is probable. Though Newman allows that people can actually believe these propositions, he thinks that most people simply infer them or believe them probable. Most of us feel as Locke does, however, that people regularly believe such things, even though their belief is rarely absolute and unconditional. Now, when a person believes as strongly in his landlord's honesty as in the roundness of the world, he has almost surely assented "beyond the degrees of his evidence"; such a person not only is not a lover of truth for truth's sake but may well experience various practical difficulties as a result of the "surplusage of assurance" that marks his belief. His excessive confidence in his landlord may lead him to be imprudent in his economic planning. A basic confidence in one's landlord may well be justified, but only if one's landlord is a saintly figure should one believe in his honesty as strongly as one believes in the roundness of the world.

Consider now some items that Newman does include on his list. First, "We accept and hold with an unqualified assent, that the earth, considered as a phenomenon, is a globe" (149). A Lockean will say that we believe this proposition very, very strongly since we regard it as 99.999 per cent probable. In Newman's eyes, the harsh, pedantic Lockean denies us our right to believe this proposition; for even though the Lockean has called our inference "belief," he has implicitly told us that we should only *infer* it very, very strongly and not really believe it. Of course, Locke does not say any such thing. Not only does Locke consider our "inference" here to be genuine belief, but he concedes—perhaps unnecessarily—that when a proposition borders very near to certainty, we make no doubt about it. A proposition that is 99.999 per cent probable would seem to be as near to certainty as it can get. And it is not clear why "merely" believing it to be 99.999 per cent probable—even if so regarding it does fall short of full or genuine belief—is an obstacle to our successfully getting on in the world.

It is worth remembering that many people in the history of the world have believed, even in Newman's strict sense, that the world is flat. Such a belief, whether held absolutely or even just very strongly, can hardly be viewed with the equanimity and tolerance with which Newman views the beliefs on his list. It is precisely because people have held false or questionable beliefs that the epistemological work of philosophers like Locke is so valuable. The practical implications of the absolute or very strong belief in false or questionable propositions have often been far-reaching. So have the practical implications of any excessive belief in propositions that have strong but limited evidence supporting them. The people who laughed at Columbus had some rather impressive evidence for believing the world to be flat: after all, it looks flat. But as some of them eventually admitted, they should have been more open-minded. Some of our most cherished beliefs—even absolute ones—have turned out to be false or questionable. And in believing them as long and as strongly as we have, we have sometimes promoted misery and retarded the advancement of civilization.

Consider another item on Newman's list: belief in the existence of an external world. All but a few philosophers have believed this strongly or even absolutely. Certain philosophical critics of empiricist epistemology (e.g., Moore, Lazerowitz, Bouwsma) have ridiculed those philosophers who have had doubts about the existence of an external world, and sometimes they have even suggested that such philosophers are mentally disturbed.[14] This is not the place for a defense of Cartesian or Humean questions. We should note, however, that it will not do for Newman to join the chorus of scoffers, for, as we have seen, his own approach to the subject of our knowledge of the external world has something of an idealistic ring to it (96). As for the man in the street, if he finds Cartesian and Humean questions to be thoroughly pointless and absurd, perhaps that is simply because he is a good deal less reflective than a philosopher is.

In his fourth and last main line of argument, Newman attempts to explain away "some conversational expressions, at first sight favourable to that doctrine of degrees in assent, which I have been combating" (152). Always mindful of ordinary language, he recognizes the need to translate our various references to belief as "modified," "qualified," "presumptive," and "*prima facie*"; as "conditional"; as "deliberate," "rational," "sudden," "impulsive," and "hesitating"; and as "firm" and "weak." His treatment of *prima facie* belief reflects his earlier analyses of profession and opinion:

> Assent, upon the authority of others is often, as I have noticed, when speaking of notional assents, little more than a profession or acquiescence or inference, not a real acceptance of a proposition. I report, for instance, that there was a serious fire in the town in the past night; and then perhaps I add, that at least the morning papers say so;—that is, I have perhaps no positive doubt of the fact; still, by referring to the newspapers I imply that I do not take on myself the responsibility of the statement. In thus qualifying my apparent assent, I show that it was not a genuine assent at all. In like manner a *primâ facie* [sic] assent is an assent to an antecedent probability of a fact, not to the fact itself.... (152)

We have already considered the inadequacy of Newman's analyses of profession and opinion, and his latest example can only augment our dissatisfaction. It is not clear why a profession that was once considered by Newman as a genuine belief, albeit a notional one, can no longer be regarded as a real acceptance of a proposition; it is not clear how Newman is distinguishing a "positive" doubt from any other kind; it is hard to understand exactly what the connection is that Newman sees here between believing a proposition and taking on oneself the responsibility for it; and it is hard to agree with Newman that our limited doubts about the accuracy of newspaper reports preclude our "genuinely" believing anything we read in newspapers. What is perhaps most interesting, however, is the fact that *prima facie* beliefs at least indirectly admit of degrees.

Say that S holds that there is a 75 per cent chance that it will rain tomorrow, while T holds that there is a 90 per cent chance that it will rain tomorrow. We would ordinarily say that S and T believe the same

---

14 See, for example, "A Defense of Common Sense" and "Proof of an External World," in G. E. Moore, *Philosophical Papers* (London: George Allen and Unwin, 1959).

proposition and that T believes it more strongly. While allowing that S and T both do believe something, Newman insists that they unconditionally believe that "the proposition 'It will rain tomorrow' is probable." The logic of Newman's argument, however, requires him to admit that S and T actually believe two different propositions: S believes "the proposition 'It will rain tomorrow' is 75 per cent probable," while T believes "the proposition 'It will rain tomorrow' is 90 per cent probable." By allowing—even encouraging—this kind of analysis, Newman is able to dispose of certain criticisms of his view that belief is unconditional; but he pays a great price for allowing it. His latest analysis belies his simplistic theory in chapter 4 that it is the presence or absence of images in apprehension that leads people to speak of strong and weak beliefs. For even if Newman were right in believing that there are no degrees of belief, clearly people are *led to speak* of strong and weak beliefs by their recognition of considerations of probability. Newman has thus undermined his defense of the pious peasant's right to believe firmly or unconditionally. For even if it were wrong to attack the peasant for assenting to a "degree that is unwarranted by the evidence," it would not necessarily be wrong to criticize him for assenting to proposition p ("Proposition x is 90 per cent probable") or to proposition x itself when he should be assenting instead to proposition q ("Proposition x is 75 per cent probable"). We could still attack the peasant for assenting to a *proposition* (p or x) that is unwarranted by the evidence, one that has a great deal in common with q but is "stronger." We could even revise the contentious passage in Locke's *Essay* in such a way as to accommodate Locke's point to Newman's conceptual scheme. The point that Locke has made in terms of "greater assurance," "measure of assent," "degrees of assent," and "surplusage of assurance" can be made instead in terms of propositions, probabilities, and *prima facie* beliefs. Newman, then, does not gain as much as he thinks he does by attacking the doctrine of degrees of belief. Those who share Locke's view about the importance of evidence need not talk about how strongly we have a right to believe but can talk instead about *which* propositions we have a right to believe. Moreover, while Locke is willing to allow that the peasant may have a right to believe x, although less strongly that he now believes it, Newman is forcing Locke to argue that the peasant has no right to believe x at all, only a weaker proposition like q.

To defend the devout peasant's right to believe x firmly or unconditionally, Newman must ultimately show either that evidence and the ethics of belief are not nearly as intimately related as the Lockeans claim or that the peasant has important evidence of a kind that Lockeans tend to ignore. The first case is not an easy one to make, although Newman has actually started to sketch it out in his various comments about action and the will. Still, no matter how right Newman is in insisting that the ethics of belief involves much more than formal evidence and other impersonal matters, the apologetical strategy of chapter 6 is barren. Even if the theory of chapter 6 were sound, which it is not, it would not further Newman's apologetical aims. Later in the *Grammar* Newman adopts the more sensible strategy of trying to establish that the simple believer has good reasons for believing what he does.

In assessing Newman's criticism of Locke, Pailin suggests that it involves a "bogus dispute arising out of the ambiguity of the term 'assent'":

> When Locke talks about giving "probable assent" to a proposition, he is using a shorthand expression to convey the idea that we accept that it is true that the proposition is probable. Newman has not understood what Locke means by this shorthand expression since he considers that it contradicts his view of assent as the absolute acceptance of a proposition as unconditionally true. In fact the difference between Locke and Newman in the matter of degrees of assent is not material but formal. It concerns the way they use the term "assent." Locke writes of possible and probable assents to a proposition where Newman, describing the same situation, must write about assent to the possibility or probability of the proposition.[15]

While Pailin sees that Newman's criticism is off the mark, here he is too generous towards Newman. The problem is not that Newman "has not understood what Locke means" by a certain "shorthand expression"; it is that Newman's apologetical aims have led him to tamper with our ordinary concept of belief. Locke's talk about degrees of belief does contradict Newman's claim that belief is unconditional; the difference between Locke and Newman in this matter is genuine. In this sense, the dispute is not bogus or a matter of semantics. If the term "assent" was truly ambiguous in Newman's time, then Newman's criticism of Locke has at least some value in that it reminds us of this ambiguity. But if this is the point Newman should have been making, he grossly overstated it in rejecting outright Locke's use of "assent." And, in any case, our contemporary use of "belief" has more in common with Locke's use of "assent" than with Newman's, so that even if the term "assent" was genuinely ambiguous in Newman's time (which is doubtful), this fact is of purely historical interest.

It is difficult to evaluate Newman's translations of such phrases as "conditional assent" and "hesitating assent." However, we still speak quite regularly of "firm" and "weak" belief, as when we say, "I firmly believe that you are doing the right thing" in order to contrast our belief with other weaker beliefs we hold. As Newman rightly ob-

15 Pailin, *Way to Faith*, 133-34.

serves, we often use these terms in characterizing the difference between the religious faith of committed believers and that of casual ones (154). In the first part of the *Grammar*, Newman treats the strength of belief as primarily a matter of apprehension; there he argues that notional belief is weaker than real belief because it is not accompanied by vivid imagery. He also suggests that there is a pragmatic criterion by which to distinguish true religious commitment from its liberal counterpart. But now he offers a broader analysis of our talk about strong and weak beliefs, suggesting that such talk is related to the "circumstances and concomitants" of the belief, "for instance, in the emotions, in the ratiocinative faculty, or in the imagination" (154). Though Newman now acknowledges a wider range of factors as relevant to the popular assessment of the strength of beliefs, he still insists that these factors have nothing to do with the intrinsic character of belief; he still holds that strength and weakness are not characteristics of belief *per se*. Newman might have defended this view by offering a theory of the nature of predication, but this would have required him to do metaphysical and logical theorizing of a kind that he has carefully eschewed throughout most of the *Grammar*. In any case, the analysis of examples from ordinary language does not give him the support he needs.

It is not hard to understand, then, why modern epistemologists like Price are puzzled by Newman's criticism of Locke. Newman's discussion of the unconditionality of belief seems a bit less puzzling when we consider the primacy of Newman's apologetical motives; but, as we have seen, even his apologetical strategy is flawed here. One weakness in that strategy is that it proceeds on the false assumption that once the doctrine of degrees of belief is disposed of, the simple, devout believer can be seen as justified in firmly believing religious propositions even in spite of his limited evidence. Ironically, Newman has demanded that the Lockeans argue that the peasant has no right to believe them at all. Another weakness of Newman's strategy is that it leads him to blur the difference between belief and certitude. Newman actually begins chapter 7 by remarking that "popularly no distinction is made" between assent and certitude (173). Not only is this claim false but, as we shall now see, Newman himself goes on to attach great importance to the distinction between assent and certitude.

2 Certitude

Though chapter 7 bears the title of "Certitude," Newman's discussion of certitude actually begins with his discussion of "complex assent" in the second half of chapter 6. Given the importance of the phrase "I am certain that" in everyday language, we would ordinarily not be surprised to find a long discussion of certitude in a work on the grammar of belief. But since Newman has already argued that all belief is unconditional and does not admit of degrees, what is left for him to say about certitude? We tend to associate being certain with believing very strongly or unconditionally; so if no belief is stronger than any other, how can being certain be different from any other kind of belief?

Newman begins his answer by distinguishing "simple" and "complex" belief. He tells us that up to now he has been considering the former, which is "exercised unconsciously" (157). In contrast with such assent is that which is given "consciously and deliberately." Newman gives the following example of this "complex" or "reflex" belief:

> I have ever believed that Great Britain is an island, for certain sufficient reasons; and on the same reasons I may persist in the belief. But it may happen that I forget my reasons for what I believe to be so absolutely true; or I may never have asked myself about them, or formally marshalled them in order, and have been accustomed to assent without a recognition of my assent or of its grounds, and then perhaps something occurs which leads to my reviewing and completing those grounds, analyzing and arranging them, yet without on that account implying of necessity any suspense, ever so slight, of assent, to the proposition that... Great Britain is an island. (158)

In repeating, after reflection, that assent which I previously made—in assenting to my previous assenting—I have made a complex or reflex assent (158). My new assent differs from the old in that it has the "strength of explicitness and deliberation" that a "mere prejudice" does not. "It is an assent, not only to a given proposition, but to the claim of that proposition on our assent as true; it is an assent to an assent, or what is commonly called a conviction" (162). Moreover, "these reflex acts may be repeated in a series":

> As I pronounce that "Great Britain is an island," and then pronounce "That 'Great Britain is an island' has a claim on my assent," or is to "be assented-to," or to be "accepted as true," or to be "believed," or simply "is true" (these predicates being equivalent), so I may proceed, "The proposition 'that *Great-Britain-is-an-island* is to be believed' is to be believed, &c., &c., and so on to *ad infinitum*. (162)

Once we have realized all this, we are in a position to understand the nature of certitude: "[L]et the proposition to which the assent is given be as absolutely true as the reflex act pronounces it to be, that is, objectively true as well as subjectively:—then the assent may be called a *perception*, the conviction a *certitude*, the proposition or truth a *certainty*, or thing known, or a matter of *knowledge*, and to assent to it is to *know*" (162).

Certitude then is "the perception of a truth with the perception that it is a truth, or the consciousness of knowing, as expressed in the phrase, 'I know that I know,' or 'I know that I know that I know,'—or simply 'I know;' for one reflex assertion of the mind about self sums up the series of self-consciousnesses without the need of any actual evolution of them" (163). The complex act of certitude, combining as it does a simple and reflex assent (177), involves a "confirmation" of what we have already held (176). Here it differs from simple belief *per se*, belief that we "barely recognize . . . or reflect upon, as being assent" (173).

But "what are the tests for discriminating certitude from mere persuasion or delusion?" (162). Here we must consider the "conditions" of certitude. In a summary at the end of chapter 7 he refers to three such conditions: it "follows on investigation and proof," "is accompanied by a specific sense of intellectual satisfaction and repose," and "is irreversible." "If the assent is made without rational grounds, it is a rash judgment, a fancy, or a prejudice; if without the sense of finality, it is scarcely more than an inference; if without permanence, it is a mere conviction" (207-208). Newman begins his discussion of these conditions in chapter 6 and continues it in chapter 7.

Why does Newman, who believes that "popularly no distinction is made" between belief and certitude, attach so much importance to the distinct existence of certitude? Or, to rephrase the question in terms more directly relevant to the exposition of a text by Newman, what are Newman's apologetical motives here? Newman sees himself as defending the orthodox view that certitude is the highest quality of religious faith (174):

> Assents may and do change; certitudes endure. This is why religion demands more than an assent to its truth; it requires a certitude, or at least an assent which is convertible into certitude on demand. Without certitude in religious faith there may be much decency of profession and of observance, but there can be no habit of prayer, no directness of devotion, no intercourse with the unseen, no generosity of self-sacrifice. Certitude then is essential to the Christian; and if he is to persevere to the end, his certitude must include in it a principle of persistence. (180)

Newman, however, is not consistent on this point. For only a few pages earlier, he admits that "multitudes of good Catholics" never attain certitude in religious matters:

> [G]reat numbers of men must be considered to pass through life with neither doubt nor, on the other hand, certitude (as I have used the words) on the most important propositions which can occupy their minds, but with only a simple assent. . . . Such an assent is all that religious Protestants commonly have to show, who believe nevertheless with their whole hearts the contents of Holy Scripture. Such too is the state of mind

of multitudes of good Catholics, perhaps the majority, who live and die
in a simple, full, firm belief in all that the Church teaches, because she
teaches it,—in the belief of the irreversible truth of whatever she defines
and declares,—but who, as being far removed from Protestant and other
dissentients, and having but little intellectual training, have never had
the temptation to doubt, and never the opportunity to be certain. (173)

Any inconsistency is serious enough; but here Newman makes the
additional blunder of suggesting that multitudes of good Catholics,
including his beloved peasants and factory-girls, are incapable of a
habit of prayer, directness of devotion, intercourse with the unseen,
and generosity of self-sacrifice.

Allow me to carry this criticism a step further. All along Newman
has praised and defended the faith of simple, devout Catholics and
has contrasted it with the rationalistic, intellectualistic approach to
religion of the Protestant liberals. But now he is putting rational
reflection in a whole new light. He is now telling us that belief that is
not based on "rational grounds" is a "rash judgment, a fancy, or a prejudice" (207-208). Belief is not enough, regardless of what "moral"
motives had led one to it (cf. 142-43). The man who earlier wrote
The Idea of a University goes on to remind us that "in the case of
educated minds, investigations into the argumentative proof of the
things to which they have given their assent, is an obligation, or rather
a necessity" (160). That the educated are so driven to rational reflection is nothing for them to regret: only such reflection can bridge the
gap between simple assent and certitude; and without certitude, one
may be left with nothing more than "mere prejudice." Realizing that
he has painted himself into a corner, Newman hedges by treating a
simple assent as "material" or "interpretative" certitude (174). But
given the main thrust of his position, we can hardly look at this move
as anything more than a feeble, artificial device.

Having taken note of the inadequacy of Newman's apologetical
maneuver, we can now turn to the fundamental weakness in the
theory itself. It is a serious one indeed: Newman's entire discussion of
certitude is vitiated by a glaring confusion. Newman blurs the distinction between phenomenology and epistemology, alternately treating
certitude as a purely subjective act and an awareness of objective
truth. He tells us that certitude is "the perception of a truth with the
perception that it is a truth"; yet, on the very same page, he admits that
there are "instances of false certitude" (163). Newman begins his
analysis of certitude with the phenomenological analysis of a subjective, mental act, a double assent involving investigation, proof, and a
specific sense of intellectual repose; but then he slides over to an
epistemological use of the term "certitude," and while being well
aware that people often feel certain about false propositions, he goes
on to associate certitude with *knowing*, with perception of *truth*.

Pailin gives a neat statement of this point. He observes that Newman's use of the term "certitude" is "riddled with confusion because
of his failure to make a constant and clear distinction between logical
and psychological issues. To start with, we find that certitude is
claimed both to be restricted to the objectively true and to be capable
of error."[16] "When Newman suggests that certitude necessarily reflects what is objectively correct he shows that he has not fully
grasped the proper logical status of assent. While he recognizes that
certitude is a form of assent, he wants to treat it as if it were concerned
with objective truth-values instead of with the truth-values which the
individual ascribes. Accordingly he tries to place the essence of
certitude in the nature of its object rather than in personal commitment."[17] In his use of the term "certitude," Newman "does not distinguish between the objectively logical and subjectively personal references . . . but moves from the one to the other without any indication
that he is committing a logical type-jump."[18]

How could Newman have allowed his analysis of certitude to get so
muddled? There is a temptation to conclude that the confusion in
Newman's analysis simply mirrors a confusion in ordinary language.[19] However, the word "certitude," unlike "certain," rarely
arises in ordinary language. Newman's use of the term "certitude" is
semi-technical; he admits as much when, in referring to "doubt" and
"certitude," he adds the proviso, "as I have used the words" (173).
And in distinguishing "certitude" and "certainty" in the way he has,
Newman has made it clear that the former is being used to refer to the
subjective act rather than the propositional object. Insofar as "certitude" refers to a kind of assent, to a propositional attitude, it does not
necessarily correlate with an objective "certainty," a true proposition.
Though Meynell had warned Newman, "So far as I know the philosophical hand-books made the objective truth enter into the very
definition of certitude, so as to exclude the notion of a false certitude,"[20] Newman continues to talk about "false certitudes"; and
even though he treats false certitude as counterfeit, as something that
is not genuinely certitude, he freely acknowledges that the three "conditions" that mark the genuine article can also be present when one
believes a false proposition. Since false certitude is *intrinsically* the
same as the genuine article, a person is not necessarily misusing
language when he says, "I am certain that . . ." to characterize his
belief in a particular false proposition.

16 Ibid., 179.
17 Ibid., 181. Cf. Ferreira, *Doubt*, 105.
18 Ibid., 184-85.
19 Ibid., 177.
20 Letter, Meynell to Newman, 4 November 1869, in *Letters and Diaries*, vol. 24, 306.

Ultimately, Newman's problem here is that he has not paid close enough attention to ordinary language. He has paid enough to recognize that there are false certitudes, that the conditions of "being certain" (certitude-qua-act) can be present even when the proposition being held is not a certainty or even a truth. But he slides into treating "certitude" as an epistemological concept, and he does so at least partly because of his tendency to see what he wants to see. An earlier piece of apologetical strategy had led him to argue that *all* belief is unconditional and that there are no *degrees* of belief; so he cannot now simply analyze "being certain" as simply believing very strongly or unconditionally. In this section of the *Grammar*, as in several others, Newman is not faithful to his announced intention to focus on the concrete rather than the abstract. His discussion of certitude is very abstract and gives remarkably few examples of how the words "certain," "certainty," and "certitude" are used in concrete situations. Instead of providing us with a list of representative statements in which these terms are employed, he largely ignores the term "certain" and instead talks abstractly about a "certitude" that is, by his own admission, a semi-technical term.

Let us turn now to his analysis of the *conditions* of certitude. How adequate is Newman's phenomenological analysis? People sometimes say that they are certain even when they have not done the kind of investigation necessary for confirming a prior simple assent. In such cases, people have not simply been too hasty in their confirmation; they have not done any confirmation at all. Newman does not consider such cases but concentrates instead on cases where the investigation is inadequate (165-67). But if a person says, "I am certain that . . ." without having done *any* investigating or reflecting or reconsidering, is he misusing the word "certain"? Newman thinks so; he regards investigation as a necessary condition of certitude, even of false certitude. But in the absence of any detailed ordinary language analysis, it is not obvious that such a use of "certain" should be ruled out of court. Newman himself remarks, "Whatever a man holds to be true, he will say he holds for certain; and for the present I must allow him in his assumption, hoping in one way or another, as I proceed, to lessen the difficulties which lie in the way of calling him to account for so doing" (162-63).

Newman rightly suggests that people, when pressed, will sometimes admit that they were not really certain at a time when they sincerely professed to be (165-67). On the other hand, it is not uncommon for people to say, when their earlier belief has been shown to be false, "But I was *certain* . . .!"

Consider now Newman's second condition of certitude. He tells us that certitude "is accompanied, as a state of mind, by a specific feeling, proper to it, and discriminating it from other states, intellectual and moral, I do not say, as its practical test or as its *differentia*, but as its token, and in a certain sense its form":

> When a man says he is certain, he means he is conscious to himself of having this specific feeling. It is a feeling of satisfaction and self-gratulation, of intellectual security, arising out of a sense of success, attainment, possession, finality, as regards the matter which has been in question. (168)

And "no one can reasonably ignore a state of mind which not only is shown to be substantive by possessing a sentiment *sui generis* and characteristic, but is analogical to Inquiry, Doubt, and Knowledge, in the fact of its thus having a sentiment of its own" (172). Newman surely attaches too much importance to this "feeling," if only because, by his own admission, people will often say they are certain in cases where he himself believes they are *not* really certain. Moreover, when asked whether they are certain about something, people sometimes hesitate, reflect on their evidence, and give an answer like "I think so" or "Pretty well." The line between certitude and other degrees or kinds of belief is not as sharp as Newman's talk about a "special feeling" would suggest.

We come, then, to Newman's last major claim about certitude, that it is "indefectible." Though his discussion of the "indefectibility" of certitude is a long one, he never makes it completely clear what he means by "indefectibility." He associates it with the persistence, irreversibility, and permanence of certitude (180, 197, 205-208); yet much of his discussion actually deals with the reliability, justifiability, or possibility of certitude. That discussion begins by posing some sceptical questions:

> What looks like certitude always is exposed to the chance of turning out to be a mistake. If our intimate, deliberate conviction may be counterfeit in the case of one proposition, why not in the case of another? If in the case of one man, why not in the case of a hundred? Is certitude then ever possible without the attendant gift of infallibility? . . . And, as to the feeling of finality and security, ought it ever to be indulged? Is it not a mere weakness or extravagance; a deceit, to be eschewed by every clear and prudent mind? With the countless instances, on all sides of us, of human fallibility, with the constant exhibitions of antagonist certitudes, who can so sin against modesty and sobriety of mind, as not to be content with probability, as the true guide of life, renouncing ambitious thoughts, which are sure either to delude him, or to disappoint? (182-83)

We have all been "balked by false certitudes a hundred times," and so how is future certitude justified or possible "when it thus manifestly ministers to error and to scepticism?" (186).

In beginning his answer to these questions, Newman does not deny that the false certitudes of the past "are to the prejudice of subsequent ones"; he admits that they constitute an "antecedent difficulty" in our allowing ourselves to be certain of things in the future. "[B]ut antecedent objections to an act are not sufficient of themselves to prohibit its exercise; they may demand of us an increased circumspection before committing ourselves to it, but may be met with reasons more than sufficient to overcome them" (186). Certitude is a "natural and normal state of mind" (172) that deserves its "definite and fixed place among our mental acts" (191):

> It is the law of my mind to seal up the conclusions to which ratiocination has brought me, by that formal assent which I have called certitude. I could indeed have withheld my assent, but I should have acted against my nature, had I done so when there was what I considered a proof; and I did only what was fitting, what was incumbent on me, upon those existing conditions, in giving it. (186-87)

Newman's talk here about the "natural" character of certitude is more than a little disturbing. How "natural" can certitude be if we have the power to withhold it? And if it is only "natural" in the sense of being common, traditional, transcultural, etc., is it any more worthy of maintenance than the many bad things that are "natural" in this sense, such as violence, hatred, and intolerance?

How can we know that our certitude is not a false one? Newman admits, "Certitude does not admit of an interior, immediate test, sufficient to discriminate it from false certitude": "Such a test is rendered impossible from the circumstances that, when we make the mental act expressed by 'I know,' we sum up the whole series of reflex judgments which might, each in turn, successively exercise a critical function towards those of the series which precede it" (205). Certitude-qua-act has the same intrinsic marks whether or not it is genuine certitude-qua-knowledge. Newman has two main responses to this problem; the first is represented by his clock analogy.

In the clock analogy, Newman again draws our attention to the sense or feeling of certitude: "[C]ertitude follows upon examination and proof, as the bell sounds the hour, when the hands reach it,—so that no act or state of the intellect is certitude, however it may resemble it, which does not observe this appointed law. This proviso greatly diminishes the catalogue of genuine certitudes" (191-92). The sense of certitude is "the bell of the intellect" and "that it strikes when it should not is a proof that the clock is out of order, no proof that the bell will be untrustworthy and useless, when it comes to us adjusted and regulated from the hands of the clock-maker" (190). In his talk about a clock, Newman draws our attention to the importance of a certain *faculty*; and he commits himself to the position that the genuineness or reliability of a certitude depends on the proper functioning of that faculty. In attacking scepticism, Newman has just argued that the reliability of that faculty is only one of several factors that we consider prior to allowing ourselves to be certain of a particular proposition. The "antecedent difficulty" of false certitudes of the past being "to the prejudice of subsequent ones" can be *overcome*, he tells us, by sound *reasons* that are in some sense *independent* of the faculty of judgment. But can reasons, even very good ones, really justify or ground certitude when the faculty of judgment is itself defective, unreliable, untrustworthy? Newman seems to want to have his cake and eat it: he says that certitude is possible and warrantable because we possess a faculty of judgment, a "clock"; but he also says that certitude is possible and warrantable because our confidence in that faculty is not a necessary condition of it.

Newman admits that the sense of certitude, the bell of the intellect, often strikes when it should not. Still, according to Newman, that does not mean that the clock-faculty is untrustworthy and useless when it comes back to us "adjusted and regulated from the hands of the clock-maker." This analogy is perplexing. For one thing, Newman earlier claims, "that I am wrong in my convictions about to-day's proposition, does not hinder my having a true conviction, a genuine certitude, about to-morrow's proposition" (185). But in the case of a clock, when we know that it has misled us once, we will not trust it again *until it has been repaired*. So if the clock analogy is to hold, then if I am wrong in my convictions about today's proposition, I should not trust my faculty of judgment until it has been "adjusted and regulated." But to whom does one go to have his clock-faculty repaired? We can agree with Newman that the faculty of judgment does "require and admit of discipline." But how is it repaired? If inference in concrete matter is really as personal and informal as Newman thinks it is, then studying formal logic will not help us much to adjust our faculty of judgment. Besides, if the simple, unlearned factory-girl and peasant have to go to someone to have their faculty of judgment adjusted, then Newman's general apologetical project has been undermined, for his aim was to show how the simple, unlearned Christian can, without much difficulty, come to be justifiably certain of the truth of religious propositions.

Newman goes on to say later in the *Grammar* that "our possession of certitude is a proof that it is not a weakness or an absurdity to be certain. How it comes about that we can be certain is not my business to determine; for me it is sufficient that certitude is felt" (270). Whether or not Newman really felt this way, he at least attempts in chapter 7 to give a reasonable reply to the challenge of epistemological scepticism. First he tells us that much that passes for the sense of certitude is not the real article; but a feeling is a feeling, nothing more, and if the only thing that counts against a particular certitude is that it has turned out to be false, then that does not say much for the value of our sense or feeling of certitude. Newman then says that the past unreliability of our faculty of judgment is only one of several factors to be taken into account and can be outweighed or "overcome" by others in our arriving at a particular certitude. But here we are left with the question of how we *know* that reasons x, y, and z are strong enough to justifiably overcome the "antecedent difficulty" of the past unreliability of our faculty of judgment. That very faculty is actually being called upon to evaluate conditions on which it is itself to be overruled. So Newman is ultimately forced to concede that we cannot throw away the "clock"; we have to have it "adjusted." And by admitting that the clock has to be adjusted, Newman is admitting that the problem of epistemological scepticism still stands. Still, recognizing that our faculty of judgment has misled us itself involves a judgment, a judgment on the faculty. So perhaps the faculty of judgment is self-critical, self-correcting, self-"adjusting." But have we really disposed of the problem of epistemological scepticism when we have acknowledged the existence of a faculty that is so reliable that it even recognizes its own unreliability? Clearly the clock analogy is not very helpful.[21]

Newman's other main response to the problem is to appeal to the "indefectibility" of certitude: "[I]f it is the general rule that certitude is indefectible, will not that indefectibility itself become at least in the event a criterion of the genuineness of the certitude?"; "I observe that indefectibility may at least serve as a negative test of certitude, or *sine quâ non* condition, so that whoever loses his conviction on a given point is thereby proved not to have been certain of it" (206). Here Newman is associating "indefectibility" with the certitude's persistence, irreversibility, and permanence. But what has been established here? It looks as if Newman is saying that we are justified in feeling certain until our belief has been shown to be false or questionable, at which point we are obliged to admit that we were never really certain at all. This latest "defense" of our right to feel certain is something of an *argumentum ad ignorantiam*, and a radical one too, since being certain is the strongest of all positive propositional attitudes. Moreover, as we have seen, many people will insist that though they were wrong to feel certain at an earlier time, they nevertheless *were* certain at that time; in so insisting, they are reminding us that "being certain" is as much certitude-qua-act as it is certitude-qua-knowledge, a fact that Newman himself frequently acknowledges.

Newman attempts to show that certitude is natural and normal, that it deserves the place it now enjoys among our mental acts. But in

21 I do not mean to suggest here that there is a simple solution to Newman's problem. Cf. Roderick M. Chisholm, *The Problem of the Criterion* (Milwaukee: Marquette University Press, 1973).

arguing that much of what we regard as certitude does not warrant the name, Newman shows himself to be a good deal more sceptical than the unlearned masses whose judgment he so often wants to defend. In insisting that we tend to be rather promiscuous in using the phrase "I am certain that . . .," he is a true disciple of Locke and Hume and those Protestant empiricist epistemologists whose influence he so much regrets. In his "defense" of our right to feel certain, he has rejected far too many certitudes as pseudo-certitudes. His abstract treatment of certitude does not pay enough attention to the data of phenomenology or ordinary language analysis and ends up as an awkward defense of something that is far different from what he set out to defend. At the heart of his failure lies his rejection of the doctrine of degrees of belief; having rejected this doctrine, he is unable, among other things, to offer the appropriate analysis of "I am certain that . . ." as an indication of our very strong or unconditional belief. He does not err, however, in assigning to investigation, reasoning, or inference a degree of importance that he had previously denied it.

Chapter Five

Formal and Informal Inference

1 The limits of formal inference

In introducing the second part of the *Grammar*, Newman tells us that his aim in the following chapters is to unravel the "apparent inconsistency which is involved in holding that an unconditional acceptance can be the result of its conditional verification" (135). He separates this project into three stages and begins by considering the unconditionality of belief in chapters 6 and 7. In chapter 8 he moves on to the second stage and considers "the act of inference, which goes before the assent and is conditional" (135). What Newman says about inference, however, is largely independent of the theorizing about apprehension, belief, and certitude that precedes it, so that one can accept the main ideas of chapter 8 without accepting the questionable theses of the first seven chapters. Indeed one can see chapter 8 as introducing a whole new dimension to Newman's apologetical strategy, for Newman will now try to show that the simple Catholic peasants and factory-girls of the world are in their own way just as rational as philosophers, intellectuals, and rationalistic liberals. He will argue that there is a kind of inference, "informal" inference, that is not only different than but also superior to the "formal" inference that the myopic rationalists associate with rationality. If he can prove the existence and respectability of this informal inference, he will have taken his biggest step yet towards establishing the rationality of the simple believer's faith. This new argument also comes in stages: first Newman will try to show that formal inference has important limitations that its rationalistic defenders do not recognize; then he will produce examples to show that the inference in concrete matter by which we are able to get along in the world is not "formal" at all.

Though Newman begins chapter 8 by reiterating his frequently made claim that inference is the conditional acceptance of a proposition (209), he soon makes it clear that his main interest in the chapter is inference as a process rather than as a propositional attitude, the movement from premises to a conclusion, the "process of the mind to what is unknown from, besides, and because of what is known."[1] He associates it here with "ratiocination" and "[v]erbal reasoning, of whatever kind, as opposed to mental," and tells us that it "differs from logic only inasmuch as logic is its scientific form" (212).[2] Artz feels that "Newman does not undervalue logically formulated proof; on the contrary: he uses syllogisms himself. What he rejects is only the over valuation of verbal inference and argumentation."[3] Newman does make some attempt to pay formal, verbal reasoning its due, both at the beginning (209-12) and the end (227-29) of his section on formal inference. He points out how it can enlarge our knowledge and admits the need for discovering "an instrument of reasoning . . . which may be less vague and arbitrary than the talent and experience of the few or the common-sense of the many" (210):

> The conclusions of one man are not the conclusions of another; those of the same man do not always agree together; those of ever so many who agree together may differ from the facts themselves, which those conclusions are intended to ascertain. In consequence it becomes a necessity, if it be possible, to analyze the process of reasoning, and to invent a method which may act as a common measure between mind and mind, as a means of joint investigation, and as a recognized intellectual standard,—a standard such as to secure us against hopeless mistakes, and to emancipate us from the capricious *ipse dixit* of authority. (211)

Newman's talk here about the need to "invent" a "common measure" suggests that logic is rather less objective than rationalists think; but Newman is clearly trying, if perhaps half-heartedly, to pay formal reasoning its due. He recognizes that "without external symbols to mark out and to steady its course, the intellect runs wild" (211); and formal reasoning is one of the most important ways in which we use these symbols to keep the intellect under control.

Note here that the symbols Newman is talking about in this passage are *words*; for Newman, reasoning is "formal" when it is *verbal*. Though contemporary logicians regard words as symbols or "forms," they tend to associate the modern discipline of formal logic primarily with such symbols as p, q, $\exists x$, Fx, $\sim$, and $\supset$. Newman had little if any familiarity with the modern formal logic that was beginning to develop in his own age; though a contemporary of such revolutionary logical theorists as George Boole and Augustus DeMorgan, he had not

1 O.Ar. A.18.11: notes for an 1859 lecture on logic. See *Theological Papers*, 53.
2 Newman was well aware of the different meanings attributed to the term "logic" and realized that he himself was using the term in one of many possible ways. See ibid., also O.Ar. A.18.11: fragment, "Definition of logic," n.d.; *Theological Papers*, 52-53.
3 Artz, "Newman as Philosopher," 275.

the slightest awareness of the potential implications of their discoveries. The work of such men has transformed the science of logic, but the view of the science that Newman is working with in the *Grammar* is basically the one that he had learned from Whately as a young Oxonian. True, he does criticize some features of Whately's logic[4] and did have considerable interest in the work of certain later logicians, particularly Mill.[5] Still, his view of the science is, like that of his teachers, essentially Aristotelian and takes the syllogism to be at the heart of all logical inquiry. He quickly identifies logical inference with "Aristotelic argumentation" and "syllogistic reasoning" (214) and concludes his section on formal inference by reminding us, "I have assumed throughout this Section that all verbal argumentation is ultimately syllogistic" (229). This association of logical inference with Aristotelian syllogistic reasoning is a key factor in his criticism of formal inference. Newman would have been dismayed to learn that the kind of reasoning he attacks in the *Grammar* is now regarded primarily as an historical relic, except in certain conservative Roman Catholic institutions of higher learning.

Unlike Artz, O'Donoghue feels that the "whole thrust" of the *Grammar* "tends to discredit the way of formal reasoning,"[6] and the view of formal inference in chapter 8 is basically quite negative. Newman begins his criticism by arguing that while logical inference is partly successful in providing a test and common measure of reasoning, it also "fails on account of the fallacy of the original assumption, that whatever can be thought can be adequately expressed in words." In Newman's view, words cannot be found for representing all of the "countless varieties and subtleties of human thought" (212). He goes on to argue that inference "is hampered with other propositions besides that which is especially its own" and "does not hold a proposition for its own sake, but as dependent upon others"; thus "it is practically far more concerned with the comparison of propositions, than with the propositions themselves" (212-13). Next he argues, "The concrete matter of propositions is a constant source of trouble to syllogistic reasoning," for while, "[w]ords, which denote things, have innumerable implications" (214), it is necessary for inference "to have starved each term down till it has become the ghost of itself, 'omnibus umbra locis,' so that it may stand for just one unreal aspect of the concrete thing to which it properly belongs, for a relation, a generalization, or other abstraction, for a notion neatly turned out of the laboratory of the mind, and sufficiently tame and subdued, because existing only in a definition" (214-15). To the logician, "dog

4 O.Ar. A.18.11: notes for an 1850 lecture on logic. See *Theological Papers*, 52-53.
5 O.Ar. A.30.11: "N.B. on Mill's Logic," dated 4 May 1857. See *Theological Papers*, 39-47.
6 O'Donoghue, "Privileged Access," 248.

or horse is not a thing which he sees, but a mere name suggesting ideas; and by dog or horse universal he means, not the aggregate of all individual dogs or horses brought together, but a common aspect." The logician's aim is "not to ascertain facts in the concrete, but to find and dress up middle terms" and to "enable his pupils to show well in a *vivâ voce* disputation, or in a popular harangue, or in a written dissertation." "Such," Newman concludes, "are the characteristics of reasoning, viewed as a science or scientific art, or inferential process" (215).

If all of these claims are true, then formal inference is of far less value than rationalistic intellectuals would have us believe. "[T]his universal living scene of things is after all as little a logical world as it is a poetical; and, as it cannot without violence be exalted into poetical perfection, neither can it be attenuated into a logical formula. Abstract can only conduct to abstract; but we have need to attain by our reasonings to what is concrete" (215).

But Newman's attack is not yet over; he also wants us to know that inference "can only conclude probabilities: first, because its premisses are assumed, not proved; and secondly, because its conclusions are abstract, and not concrete" (216). "Syllogism . . . does only the minutest and easiest part of the work, in the investigation of truth, for when there is any difficulty, that difficulty commonly lies in determining first principles, not in the arrangement of proofs." Our reasoning ultimately rests on "subtle assumptions" that are traceable to the "sentiments of the age, country, religion, social habits and ideas, of the particular inquirers or disputants," so that "[l]ogic then does not really prove; it enables us to join issue with others; it suggests ideas; it opens views; it maps out for us the lines of thought; it verifies negatively; it determines when differences of opinion are hopeless; and when and how far conclusions are probable; but for genuine proof in concrete matter we require an *organon* more delicate, versatile, and elastic than verbal argumentation" (217). Moreover, inferences and their conclusions are abstract and so "cannot handle and determine the concrete" (222). All formal inferential processes, even induction and analogy, require "general notions" (226) and deal in universals rather than concrete particulars; they allow units to be "sacrificed" to universals (223). We must conclude, then, "that Inference, considered in the sense of verbal argumentation, determines neither our principles, nor our ultimate judgments,—that it is neither the test of truth, nor the adequate basis of assent" (229). "Who would be satisfied with a navigator or engineer, who had no practice or experience whereby to carry on his scientific conclusions out of their native abstract into the concrete and the real?" (223). Even philosophers, scientists, and other advocates of formal reasoning ultimately "judge and determine by common-sense" in concrete matter, though they continue to "speak by rule and by book" (227).

Two or three basic themes underlie Newman's analysis, but the safest path for us to follow here is to examine Newman's points one by one in the order in which he presents them. In the process, we shall find that Newman has committed himself, sometimes unwittingly, to some very strange positions. His first point is that formal reasoning fails because it wrongly assumes that all thought is verbal. Newman seems to me to be confusing two different theses, that all *thought* is verbal and that all *reasoning* is verbal. I suspect that most contemporary psychologists would agree with Newman that not all thought is verbal; but it is hard to see how this point counts against formal inference. First, if thought is not verbal, it still involves symbolism, and the criticisms Newman makes of verbal symbolism may well apply to other forms of symbolism. Secondly, modern formal logic can be divorced from verbal language in a way that Newman could not envision, as in the wholly non-verbal expression $([p \supset q] \cdot p) \supset q$. Thirdly, and most importantly, to regard reasoning as verbal is not to assume that all *thought* is verbal. To have a case against verbal reasoning here, Newman must establish that there is non-verbal *reasoning*; and since he regards formal inference as verbal inference, he must regard informal inference as somehow non-verbal.

While we have not yet considered Newman's discussion of informal inference, it is not too early for us to have grave doubts about his suggestion that the most important reasoning is non-verbal. Newman himself realizes that we reason in order to arrive at beliefs, and he argues right from the first page of the *Grammar* that a conclusion or a belief is the *acceptance of a proposition*. Newman nowhere suggests that a proposition, consisting as it does of "a subject and predicate united by the copula" (25) can be non-verbal. How then can reasoning or inference, which moves us from propositions to another proposition, be anything but verbal? And how can the beliefs to which reasoning aims to lead us be anything but verbal? In contrasting the abstractness of words with the concreteness of "things," Newman is back at his old game of subordinating the notional to the real; but real assent is, by Newman's own admission, as much assent to a *proposition* as notional assent is, and if its terms stand for "things" rather than "notions," they are terms, words, nonetheless. If Newman is going to believe in non-verbal reasoning, he will have to allow that there are premises, conclusions, and beliefs that are not propositions. This will be a hard thesis for Newman to defend, and by advancing it, he will be undermining the simple conceptual framework with which the *Grammar* began. Moreover, he may well be tying his apologetic to a kind of reasoning that is even more abstract and less efficacious than the verbal reasoning he is discrediting.

Though I agree with Newman that much thought is non-verbal, I resent his refusal to elaborate on this claim. The relation of thought to language is a complex philosophical and psychological issue. If thought and language are not identical, as some philosophers and psychologists have actually argued, the fact remains that human thinking is permeated with language.[7] And it is certainly not obvious that verbal thought is significantly less important than some of the other "countless varieties and subtleties of human thought" of which Newman so casually informs us.

It is hard to know what to make of Newman's claims that inference is hampered with other propositions, is not concerned with a proposition for its own sake, and is more concerned with the "comparison" of propositions than with the propositions themselves. It is true that we can get great pleasure from reasoning for reasoning's sake, such as when we work on a crossword puzzle or reflect on the eternal problems of metaphysics. But usually we reason in order to arrive at beliefs, especially at beliefs that can serve as guides to action; Newman himself repeatedly reminds us that acts of inference normally precede the acts of assent that we need to make in order to get on in the world. His reference to the "comparison" of propositions is misleading, for though inferring involves relating various propositions, our primary aim in reasoning is to arrive at new beliefs, to move from the known to the unknown.

We come then to Newman's argument that inference cannot "handle" the concrete because it is forced to work with abstract, general notions. He first advances this position on page 214 and repeats it, with minor changes in emphasis, on page 222. Here his disparagement of formal inference is clearly a mode of his general disparagement of notions and notional apprehension: he tells us that inference starves terms down, reduces things to names, and sacrifices units to universals. We can attack this argument in two ways. First, we can attack the nominalist doctrine that it presupposes.[8] (As in chapter 2, I shall side-step this complicated issue.) Or we can challenge Newman's claim that inference is forced to work with abstract, general notions. Consider the following simple inference of the form *modus ponens*: "If Mr. and Mrs. Brown are hugging and kissing, then they are no longer feuding; they are hugging and kissing; so they are no longer feuding." However questionable the premises of this inference may be, it can hardly be argued that they and the conclusion are so abstract as to have little to do with the "universal living scene of things." The propositions in this inference do not simply refer to

7 A useful though somewhat dated discussion of this subject may be found in George Humphrey, *Thinking* (London: Methuen, 1951), ch. 8.
8 Cf. Horgan, "Faith and Reason," 143.

vague generalities; for not only are the Browns right there in front of us manifesting their affection, but the very ideas of hugging, kissing, and feuding carry with them a considerable degree of emotional force. It is harder to starve down the term "kissing" than the term "horse." Newman, of course, does not associate inference with inference-forms like *modus ponens*; he associates it with the syllogisms of Aristotle and Whately. In traditional syllogistic logic, the propositions of ordinary language must be translated into "categorical" propositions like "All horses are animals," "No dogs are horses," and "Some animals are not dogs." The handling of "particular" propositions like "The Browns are kissing" is more cumbersome and more artificial in traditional logic than in modern formal logic. In associating inference with notional propositions and universal terms, Newman is working on the assumption that formal, verbal reasoning is basically syllogistic. So he has not only failed to consider the possibility of other approaches to the *science* of logic but has also failed to appreciate the importance of a *phenomenological* investigation into what it is that the *mind* does when it reasons formally. In short, his view of the limits of formal inference is as dated as the idea of formal inference it assumes.

We have just been reminded that through much of his analysis, Newman blurs the distinction between being logical and being a logician. In his fourth point, for example, he considers not the aim of formal inference *per se* but the aim of the logician, which we are told is to "enable his pupils to show well" in a disputation, harangue, or dissertation. Here he is almost suggesting that formal inference is really the special preserve of professional logicians and not something with which ordinary reasoners bother much. He also seems to be suggesting that formal inference is always something that goes on in speech and print and never in *thought*. He is not consistent in leaving this impression, and in any event, his characterization of the logician's craft is unjustifiably cynical and narrow. While it is true that many professional logicians have as little interest in the practical applications of their work as do advanced students of "pure" mathematics, the practical value of basic studies in logic is as great as that of basic studies in mathematics. It would be foolish to take mathematics out of the primary and secondary school curricula, and the exclusion of logic from those curricula is something for which our society has paid a high price.

Newman's poetic remark that the living scene of things is not a logical world and cannot be attenuated into a logical formula is a charming piece of rhetoric, the kind for which Newman is so justly famous. But if that world is not logical, is it then illogical? And if so, what does this say for God's competence as a designer? Newman never pretended to take the argument from design seriously.[9] Still, one would think that a believing Christian ought to have as much confidence in the orderliness of the "scene of things" as the scientist or rationalist does. Newman, of course, may simply be suggesting that the "scene" is largely incomprehensible, that its orderliness cannot be grasped by puny mortal minds. But Newman can hardly be willing to deny that scientific reasoning has enabled scientists to make considerable progress towards unraveling the "mysteries" of nature. If the "scene" is still quite incomprehensible, it is rather more comprehensible to us now than it was to the ancients, and that is mainly because generations of intellectuals have been willing to place more confidence in logic than Newman had.

When Newman says that inference can only conclude probabilities because its premises are assumed, we are immediately struck by the epistemological scepticism embodied in his statement. Newman is not saying here that the laws of logic are mere assumptions; he is directing our attention to the premises themselves. But why is a premise merely an assumption? Why can it not be something we *know*? In our earlier example we were not merely *assuming* that the Browns are hugging and kissing; we *saw* the Browns hugging and kissing, and if Newman feels we had no right to trust our senses in this case, then he is being too sceptical for his own (apologist's) good. As Newman himself sometimes says, inference is normally a process that carries us from the *known* to the unknown. This holds true even for traditional syllogistic reasoning. When the Aristotelian logician begins by saying, "If all horses are animals . . . ," he is not warning us that he is merely *assuming* that all horses are animals. So Newman's initial position is misleading.

However, he qualifies it with his talk about "retrospection" and "first principles." His full argument is worth quoting:

> In order to complete the proof, we are thrown upon some previous syllogism or syllogisms, in which the assumptions may be proved; and then, still farther back, to prove the new assumptions of that second order of syllogisms. Where is this process to stop? especially since it must run upon separated, divergent, and multiplied lines of argument, the farther the investigation is carried back. At length a score of propositions present themselves, all to be proved by propositions more evident than themselves, in order to enable them respectively to become premisses to that series of inferences which terminates in the conclusion which we originally drew. But even now the difficulty is not at an end; it would be something to arrive at length at premises which are undeniable, however long we might be in arriving at them; but in this case the long retrospection lodges us at length at what are called first principles, the recondite sources of all knowledge, as to which logic provides no com-

9 O.Ar. A.23.8: note to Ogle on design, dated 4 January 1882. See *Theological Papers*, 157.

mon measure of minds,—which are accepted by some, rejected by others,—in which, and not in the syllogistic exhibitions, lies the whole problem of attaining to truth,—and which are called self-evident by their respective advocates because they are evident in no other way. One of the two uses contemplated in reasoning by rule, or in verbal argumentation, was, as I have said, to establish a standard of truth and to supersede the *ipse dixit* of authority: how does it fulfil this end, if it only leads us back to first principles, about which there is interminable controversy? (216)

Newman's point, then, is not simply that premises are arbitrary and unjustified; this is a silly idea, and Newman's is far more subtle. Though premises are rarely arbitrary, they are normally propositions that we accept on the basis of reasons, evidence. In turn, the reasons that we see as supporting them are *themselves* propositions that we accept for certain reasons, and so on. This process of retrospective justification cannot go on *ad infinitum*, and eventually we shall have to admit that our various chains of reasons rest on propositions that are "first principles," propositions that we cannot defend and must take to be self-evident. So what does logic "prove"? In the last analysis, all logical argument does is lead us back along chains of reasons. If two people arguing happen to share a key belief at a particular stage of retrospection, they may be able to resolve their original disagreement and decide who was originally "right." But retrospection may only lead them to recognize that their original dispute rests on conflicting first principles. Formal inference, then, only serves to uncover more fundamental beliefs on which we may or may not agree; it "suggests ideas," "opens views," "determines when differences of opinion are hopeless," and so on. Involving as it does all sorts of "subtle assumptions" traceable to sentiments of age, religion, and social habit, it does not have the objective validity that rationalists pretend.

Newman is playing with fire here and threatening to destroy all intellectual activity with his scepticism, relativism, and irrationalism. We should begin by noting that Newman suggests—though he does not explicitly state—that most intellectual disputes rest on disagreements about first principles. They do not: a major reason why many of us take verbal argument as seriously as we do is that very often it does help us to resolve disputes. When two people argue, retrospective justification often uncovers a shared belief that supports one of the two original views. Here it is also worth noting that Newman's characterization of "first principles" is rather vague. In discussing presumption in chapter 4, he defines "first principles" as "the propositions with which we start in reasoning on any given subject-matter" (66), and cites as examples our beliefs in external objects, right and wrong, truth and falsity, and causation. But if his earlier talk is vague enough, his new comments about "subtle assumptions" of age and social habit are even more vague. Consider the case of two people arguing about the existence of elves. It will hardly do for the true believer to argue, "I consider the existence of elves to be a first principle. I regard it as self-evident, so there is no point in your arguing with me." Is there anything genuine about this "disagreement in first principles"? Is the true believer being reasonable in refusing to consider evidence that may count against his "first principle"? In the view of most epistemologists and metaphysicians, a first principle is more than just a belief that certain people regard as self-evident and start with in reasoning on a given subject matter: it is a belief that people *must* regard as self-evident and *have a right* to start with in reasoning. Whether or not he is aware of it, Newman has to some extent subjectified first principles. But even if all the people in a society regard the existence of elves as self-evident, it does not follow that it is pointless for an outsider to try to show them that their belief is not a genuine first principle at all.

Newman sees his comments on first principles as constituting a challenge to formal inference. But his comments reach much further: he is actually challenging belief and certitude. For in arguing that premises are "assumptions" that ultimately rest on first principles, he is talking about propositions, many of which we believe or are even certain about. When Newman treats a premise like "The Browns are hugging and kissing" or "Today is Saturday" or "God exists" as something that ultimately rests on arbitrary, unjustified first principles, he is belittling not just inference but belief itself. He is saying that a premise is not simply something believed but something inferred, and as such, a "mere" probability. Not only is he doing what he disapproved of Locke doing, but he is doing it in a far more sceptical spirit. He is saying that all the beliefs that we bring to reasoning are "merely" probable except for first principles, which seem to be arbitrary.

Moreover, Newman's emphasis on first principles has a sharply relativistic ring to it, so much so that he sounds like a precursor of such modern historicists as Dilthey, Croce, and Collingwood.[10] His aim is apologetical, to show that it is arrogant for rationalists to attack religious beliefs that ultimately rest on commitments to first principles. But a Catholic apologist pays a big price for this move: he puts the ultimate commitments of friend and enemy on the same epistemological level. He makes it appear as foolish to criticize a Nazi or a Manichean as a Roman Catholic. He throws the baby out with the bath water, reduces apologetics to rhetoric, and makes the resolution of ideological conflict a matter of *force majeure*. It is moves like this one that have so much alarmed Newman's orthodox Catholic critics.

10 R. G. Collingwood's *Essay on Metaphysics* (Oxford: Clarendon Press, 1940) is perhaps the clearest statement of historicism.

Backtracking now, as Newman does (222-27), let us return briefly to the question of the practical value of formal inference. "Who," Newman asks, "would be satisfied with a navigator or engineer, who had no practice or experience whereby to carry on his scientific conclusions out of their native abstract into the concrete and the real?" Newman is presenting us with a false dichotomy. Inference and experience are far more closely related than Newman's hypothetical question implies. In reasoning we make use of experience; experience provides most of the content of our premises. The problem of the inexperienced navigator is that he does not have the same degree of understanding that the experienced navigator has; he attains greater understanding through experience *and* inference. Set inference aside altogether for the moment: an inexperienced navigator often does not even understand a fact stated in his textbook as well as an experienced one does. In any case, when we need a navigator—or a surgeon—we will be far more satisfied with an inexperienced one who has read the textbooks than with one who has not. As for Newman's claim that even philosophers, experimentalists, and lawyers rely more on common sense than they admit, whatever insight it embodies would seem to depend on what is meant here by "common sense." If my criticisms of Newman's analysis have been fair, then much of what Newman counts as "common sense" is one or another kind of formal or verbal reasoning. Newman, of course, associates common sense with "informal inference," and it is to his view of the latter that we must now turn.

2 Informal inference

Newman's theory of informal inference is so central to his project that I began this study by quoting from the opening paragraph of the section in the *Grammar* in which it is introduced. Here is the complete paragraph:

> It is plain that formal logical sequence is not in fact the method by which we are enabled to become certain of what is concrete; and it is equally plain, from what has been already suggested, what the real and necessary method is. It is the cumulation of probabilities, independent of each other, arising out of the nature and circumstances of the particular case which is under review; probabilities too fine to avail separately, too subtle and circuitous to be convertible into syllogisms, too numerous and various for such conversion, even were they convertible. As a man's portrait differs from a sketch of him, in having, not merely a continuous outline, but all its details filled in, and shades and colours laid on and harmonized together, such is the multiform and intricate process of ratiocination, necessary for our reaching him as a concrete fact, compared with the rude operation of syllogistic treatment. (230)

It may be an overstatement to say that Newman has a "theory" of informal inference. After all, how much can be said about a form of inference or ratiocination that is non-verbal, cannot be analyzed in terms of rules, and varies with the nature and circumstances of the particular case? Whatever objective features characterize formal inference are clearly absent here. In discussing formal reasoning, Newman points to our desire for a method that may act "as a common measure between mind and mind, as a means of joint investigation, and as a recognized intellectual standard,—a standard such as to secure us against hopeless mistakes, and to emancipate us from the capricious *ipse dixit* of authority" (211). Informal reasoning is a different matter altogether: it has nothing to do with a common measure, a standard, a set of rules, or anything objective or even conventional on which to model inferences or by which to evaluate them. There is no *science* of informal inference. Informal reasoning is personal. When we infer "informally," it is extremely difficult for us to articulate our reasons; we are, after all, not very clear about what they are. Consequently, it is also extremely difficult for us—and for others—to judge our inference to be valid or invalid. Moreover, it would appear that the only classroom in which one can learn how to make valid informal inferences is the classroom of the world. So what more can Newman say about informal inference, and how can we be sure that such a process really exists?

Newman's "theory" of informal inference is, by virtue of necessity, phenomenological. It consists mainly of examples. Newman does discuss the *characteristics* of informal inference; but his examples are at the heart of his theory, and he knows that if they leave his readers unimpressed, he will not have made his case.

The distinction between formal and informal inference is foreshadowed by Newman's early distinction between implicit and explicit reason. In an 1840 sermon, he distinguishes between the "original process of reasoning" and the "process of investigating our reasonings," between "reasoning" proper and "arguing." As the prototype of formal inference, explicit reason involves "words, science, method, development, analysis, criticism, proof, system, principles, rules, laws, and others of a like nature."[11] In implicit reason

> [t]he mind ranges to and fro, and spreads out, and advances forward with a quickness which has become a proverb, and a subtlety and versatility which baffle investigation. It passes on from point to point, gaining one by some indication; another on a probability; then availing itself of an association; then falling back on some received law; next seizing on testimony; then committing itself to some popular impression, or some inward instinct, or some obscure memory; and thus it makes progress not

11 John Henry Newman, "Implicit and Explicit Reason," *University Sermons*, 258-59. This sermon was preached on St. Peter's Day, 1840.

unlike a clamberer on a steep cliff, who, by quick eye, prompt hand, and firm foot, ascends how he knows not himself, by personal endowments and by practice, rather than by rule, leaving no track behind him, and unable to teach another.[12]

Chapter 8 of the *Grammar* incorporates a theory that had long been the centrepiece of Newman's philosophical apologetic. Between 1840 and 1870, Newman only made slight modifications in his original distinction, mainly terminological ones, but although his basic vision did not change, it is only in the *Grammar* that he finally provides us with the detailed examples needed to bring his point alive.

Before giving these examples, Newman draws our attention to three characteristics of informal inference: (1) "[I]t does not supersede the logical form of inference, but is one and the same with it; only it is no longer an abstraction, but carried out into the realities of life, its premisses being instinct with the substance and the momentum of that mass of probabilities, which, acting upon each other in correction and confirmation, carry it home definitely to the individual case, which is its original scope" (232-33). (We must remember that by "probabilities" here, Newman means arguments which, though falling short of being demonstrative, "tend to induce" the reason to judge a certain proposition to be true.[13]) (2) "[S]uch a process is more or less implicit, and without the direct and full advertence of the mind exercising it. As by the use of our eyesight we recognize two brothers, yet without being able to express what it is by which we distinguish them . . . so is the mind unequal to a complete analysis of the motives which carry it on to a particular conclusion, and is swayed and determined by a body of proof, which it recognizes only as a body, and not in its constituent parts." (3) "[I]n this investigation of the method of concrete inference, we have not advanced one step towards depriving inference of its conditional character; for it is still as dependent on premisses as it is in its elementary idea" (233).

Given what Newman has already told us about formal inference, we cannot help being puzzled here. In listing these characteristics of informal inference, Newman is trying to show us that informal inference has much in common with formal inference. He is telling us that both have (or are) the same "logical form" and are conditional, dependent on premisses. However, it is hard to see how informal and formal inference can share (or be) a single logical form when only the latter involves words, rules, and the like; it is indeed the formlessness of informal inference that makes it so different from formal inference.

---

12 Ibid., 257.
13 O.Ar. A.30.11: untitled paper on faith, dated 13 May 1853. Cf. O.Ar. A.18.11: notes on opinion, belief, etc., dated 30 April 1853. See *Theological Papers*, 7, 11; Henry Tristram, "John H. Newman on the Acta of Faith," *Gregorianum* 18 (1937), 223.

True, informal and formal inference are supposedly both kinds of reasoning and seem to involve movement from the "known to the unknown." But it is not clear that the undifferentiated mass of data that results in an informal conclusion can be properly counted as a set of premises or reasons. We may even wonder whether informal "inference" is really inference or reasoning at all. If the probabilities that lead up to an informal "conclusion" are so hidden that we do not know what they are and cannot articulate them, then perhaps they are better thought of as *causes*, in which case informal "inference" is no more similar to formal inference than is, say, arriving at a belief on the basis of the latent causes of which psychoanalytical theorists speak. Moreover, if the process of informal reasoning is genuinely implicit, then is informal "inference" *conditional* in the same way as formal inference? If a person cannot explain how he has arrived at a particular "conclusion," he does not fully recognize the dependence of his "conclusion" on hidden probabilities or determinants. And if so, it may be wrong for Newman to deny that person's "conclusion" the status of *belief*. This suspicion is somewhat confirmed by Newman's willingness to compare informal inference with perception, eyesight, since in distinguishing two brothers, we do not *infer* that one is Peter and the other Paul.

Newman, of course, has an apologetical motive for comparing informal inference to formal inference: since he is trying to establish the rationality of the simple believer's faith, he has to show that the informal process going on in the simple believer's mind has enough in common with the liberal intellectual's formal reasoning to qualify as rational or reasonable. But why should the intellectual be impressed? If Newman has simply confused reasons with causes, his talk about informal "reasoning" may be empty. The rationalist need not deny, after all, that the simple Catholic's religious beliefs are *caused*, that they are the result of antecedent factors. Contemporary philosophers have had their worries about the cause/reason dichotomy, and I do not want to be simplistic here. I think it fair to observe, however, that informal inference is far less similar to formal inference than Newman's apologetical strategy requires it to be. Formal reasoning is a conscious process involving intellectual labour, respect for a standard, criticism and self-criticism, and a sort of public accountability; in contrast, informal reasoning may be a purely mechanical, irrational process. Newman does not hesitate to associate the implicit with the unconscious. Had he lived long enough to be able to read *Totem and Taboo* and *The Future of an Illusion*, which attempt to offer explanations of certain informal inferences, Newman might well have been less inclined to assign to informal reasoning as large a role as he does. To his credit, Freud at least looks for order and structure in the unconscious, while Newman does not even bother. But that is a point to which we shall have to return. Now we must start looking at some of Newman's examples.

Newman gives three sets of examples. The first consists of three general examples; the second consists of seven examples that emphasize the role of personal factors; and the third consists of three examples in which the person reasoning actually acknowledges the informal character of his inference. The typology is not too important: on the one hand, all informal inferences must share certain features in virtue of which they are informal, and it is their informality that interests us; on the other hand, informal inferences vary with the nature and circumstances of the particular case under review, so that no two are completely alike. The three examples that we shall now be considering are as close to being representative as any. We shall turn first to the two examples I cited at the beginning of this study, the Britain-is-an-island inference and the factory-girl's inference.

The island example is the first of Newman's thirteen examples (234-35) and is the one that he had given most often in previous years. Having already quoted it *in toto* in chapter 1, I shall only paraphrase it here. Britons are absolutely *certain*, beyond the shadow of a doubt, that Britain is an island. They have no more doubt about this than about the most fundamental truths of geometry. Their reasons for believing are such as these: they have been taught to believe it; maps indicate it; they have never heard it questioned; every speaker they have ever heard has taken it for granted; every book they have ever read has taken it for granted; it is implied in one way or another by routine transactions, the social and commercial system, and world affairs; numberless facts rest on it; and no evidence has as yet been marshalled against it. But all this evidence is circumstantial. What one is taught as a child often turns out to be false; maps make mistakes; one has only read a small fraction of the world's books; and so on. So if someone has not circumnavigated Britain, what right does that person have to feel *certain* that Britain is an island? Britons cannot present a demonstrative argument in support of this belief. Still, their belief is supported by a mass of data, by countless probabilities. This body of proof has led them to their conclusion, and clearly the certitude that follows upon their inference is justified.

Why is this inference informal? It cannot be put into the form of a syllogism, but it seems verbal enough. Newman earlier argued that induction and analogy are formal because they involve an appeal to a general principle or law (226); since this inference does not seem to involve such an appeal, it may not be inductive in Newman's sense. Nevertheless, when asked why we believe that Britain is an island, we can articulate our reasons, in words; the probabilities are not really "too fine to avail separately," and given time, we can list hundreds of very specific reasons for believing ("Uncle Paul told me so when I was a child") or fifteen or twenty more general reasons ("I was taught so as a child"). Not only is our giving of reasons a verbal activity, but each and every reason we give is subject to critical evaluation. If my *only* reason for believing were that Uncle Paul told me so, it would be clear to everyone that my inference is not a very strong one. Newman himself gives the example of how people long and widely entertained the belief that the earth is immovable (235). Though the people who held this belief could give reasons for holding it, their belief and reasons were not above criticism, and it was eventually possible to show those reasons inadequate. Similarly, there is nothing mysteriously ineffable about our reasons for holding that Britain is an island. We can state those reasons quite explicitly, and whoever wants to challenge our belief must state why with the same degree of explicitness. We can even point to certain rules here, such as "If every map of the world I have ever examined indicates something, and I have examined over a thousand, and maps have only misled me on less than 1 per cent of the occasions that I have relied on them, then that thing is almost certainly true." Of course, this kind of rule is very different from the kind with which formal logic is normally associated.

What interests Newman is that we feel *certain* that Britain is an island, even though our reasons are all just probabilities. However, this talk about certitude is a red herring. If Newman is right, then informal inference can no more yield an unconditional conclusion than formal inference can; all conclusions are, *qua* conclusions, conditional. The conceptual gap between an informal conclusion and a belief is as great as that between a formal conclusion and a belief. So the connection between certitude and our mode of inference is not yet clear. Moreover, as we saw earlier, when we say that we are certain that Britain is an island, we may wrongly believe that we are certain, or we may be unjustified in feeling certain, or we may simply mean that we believe the proposition very, very strongly.

The inferring that results in our concluding that Britain is an island is undoubtedly complex. Newman sees its complexity as a sign of its informality. But formal deductive arguments can be complex, too. Newman associates formal reasoning with simple syllogisms, but a formal deductive inference can have more than a hundred premises. In arriving at or confirming the conclusion that Britain is an island, we may make complex deductions as well as complex inductions, and the premises and conclusions of the deductive inferences are no less concrete than those of the inductive ones. If we are temporarily left speechless when asked why we believe Britain to be an island, it is not because we do not *know* why we believe, or cannot say, but because we consider the evidence so obvious that we cannot understand why anyone would ask such a question. We can produce dozens of arguments, many of which can even be reduced to syllogistic form, and all of which confirm and reconfirm our conclusion. One of Newman's problems is that he can only see us as having made *one* inference when we have actually made *many*—our map inference, our Uncle Paul inference, our book inference, our individual book inferences, and so on. When we were young children, our being taught to believe that Britain is an island was probably enough to make us feel certain that it is. Our reasoning then? "Whatever has been taught to me is true; I have been taught that Britain is an island; so it must be true that Britain is an island." Could any inference be more formal?

We turn now to the factory-girl's inference, Newman's ninth example (247-48). Newman includes it in his second set of examples, since it supposedly illustrates the role of personal factors. Newman begins by contrasting the poor, dying factory-girl with the sceptical philosopher Montaigne, who was endowed with "a good estate, health, leisure, and an easy temper, literary tastes and a sufficiency of books." Newman seems to be suggesting here that prosperous, easy-going people have no need to believe in God and immortality; this is an odd suggestion, but we shall let it pass here. The factory-girl has a miserable life, and reflects that "if this should be the end of all, . . . if this life is the end, and . . . there is no God to wipe away all tears from all eyes, I could go mad." Newman writes:

> Here is an argument for the immortality of the soul. As to its force, be it great or small, will it make a figure in a logical disputation, carried on *secundum artem*? Can any scientific common measure compel the intellects of Dives and Lazarus to take the same estimate of it? Is there any test of the validity of it better than the *ipse dixit* of private judgment, that is, the judgment of those who have a right to judge, and next, the agreement of many private judgments in one and the same view of it?

This is Newman at his rhetorical best; a rationalistic liberal would feel like a monster if he deprived the poor factory-girl of the little consolation left to her. Alas, Newman is not at his philosophical best, and that is what concerns us now.

What exactly is the factory-girl's inference, and how does it constitute an argument for the immortality of the soul? The factory-girl seems to be a believer, and she has not gone mad yet; but nothing that she has said suggests that she believes because she wants to or needs to, or because she does not want to go mad. As far as we know, she believes for the very same reasons that more prosperous people do, or because she uncritically accepts the word of her local priest or minister. It is Newman, and not the factory-girl herself, who is drawing the causal arrow between the misery of her life and her belief in God and immortality. Newman is being rather presumptuous. If we could interview the factory-girl, she might make the following observations: "This Newman fellow is patronizing me. He may mean well, but he seems to think that I am a fool. I do not believe simply because my life is miserable; I am not just fantasizing here. I believe in God because a world without God does not make any sense to me. There *must* be a Creator: how else could everything have come into being? And the world is too orderly not to have been designed by some superhuman being. Besides, I could not *understand* a universe in which virtue is not ultimately rewarded. As for immortality, how can anyone not believe in it? After all, a soul is not a material thing, so it cannot be destroyed. So I would be a believer even if I were as rich and as smart as Montaigne. Anyway, my situation down at the factory is bound to improve. A few of us girls have started organizing a union. Some socialist organizer is coming down here to help us next week. I wish this Newman fellow would use his influence to put pressure on the industrialists and politicians who are trying to bust our union. But these priests are so unreliable: they wring their hands a lot, but most of them are pretty conservative, and they are rarely there when you need them."

Newman is not simply reminding us of how consoling religious faith can be; he thinks that there is an *argument* here. What are its premises? Newman can hardly be blamed for refusing to say: his point here is that inferences such as the factory-girl's are informal and cannot be formalized or verbalized without having violence done to them. "Here is an argument for the immortality of the soul. As to its force, be it great or small, will it make a figure in a logical disputation, carried on *secundum artem*?" Newman's question is a hypothetical one, but maybe it deserves an affirmative answer. The following inference seems reasonably formal: "Virtue is not always rewarded in this life; goodness must ultimately be rewarded; therefore, virtue is sometimes rewarded in a future life." (The factory-girl does not actually speak of *immortality*; she simply refuses to believe that "this life is the end.") This inference does not have the emotional power of the factory-girl's remarks; the factory-girl's "argument" is advanced in a particular context, and her emotions move us. But to the extent that she has presented us with an argument, an inference, a piece of *reasoning*, she has given us something quite formal. We can check its validity and reflect on the plausibility of its component premises. Her argument must ultimately be separated from its context if we—who unlike the factory-girl have much for which to be thankful—are to be able to understand and evaluate it. Those of us who regard her argument as sound do so not because we pity her, but because we believe her argument to be valid and to have true or plausible premises.

"Can any scientific common measure compel the intellects of Dives and Lazarus to take the same estimate of it?" To some extent, yes: if Dives and Lazarus are reasonable men, and if my formal version of the argument is an adequate translation, then Dives and Lazarus will agree that the argument is valid. Dives and Lazarus may well disagree, however, about the second premise; they may have different opinions about whether goodness must ultimately be rewarded. Such a disagreement has nothing to do with the formality or informality of the argument. And if my translation of the argument is inadequate, then Dives and Lazarus will have no easy time figuring out what the argument *is* and taking *any* estimate of it.

"Is there any test of the validity of it better than the *ipse dixit* of private judgment . . . ?" Newman wants us to give a negative answer to this third question, too; he has been trying to show that there can be no impersonal evaluation of an informal inference. If what I have been arguing is true, then Newman is wrong to place the island and factory-girl's inferences *beyond criticism*: if we can understand someone's reasons, then we can evaluate them by certain standards. But Newman's latest hypothetical question creates new problems for his analysis. First, he seems to be suggesting here that not only is the factory-girl's argument valid, but only she is in the position to determine it to be so. Now, even if we were willing to go along with Newman's claim that reasons of a mysteriously intimate nature have helped to lead the factory-girl to her faith, why would we want to consider the issue of *validity* as relevant? What sense does it make to speak of her inference as "valid" if it is so personal that it has nothing to do with any common measure, standard, or rules? How can such an inference be *in*valid? And if it cannot be invalid, what point is there in characterizing it as "valid"? Her conclusion may be practically efficacious—consoling, satisfying, encouraging—but it is rather misleading to characterize such efficacy as "validity." Let me carry this criticism a step further: it may be possible for another factory-girl in essentially the same miserable situation to "infer" that there cannot be a God, for no God would allow an innocent, virtuous factory-girl to suffer as she does. Do we then have two inferences with the same premises, diametrically opposed conclusions, and equal "validity"? Newman again wants to have his cake and eat it: he wants to free informal inference from impersonal criticism and at the same time force us to admit that a personal inference can be "valid."

Newman's reference to "private judgment" creates even bigger problems for him. Here he is looking favourably on private judgment and promoting it as the best test of the validity of an informal inference. Elsewhere in his writings, however, he associates private judgment with Protestantism, as, for example, in the *Essay on Development*, where he writes, "Calvinism and Unitarianism may be called developments, that is, exhibitions, of the principle of private judgment, though they have nothing in common viewed as doctrines."[14] He even wrote a poem entitled "Private Judgment," which ends with this dramatic verse:

> Wand'rers! come home! obey the call!
> A Mother pleads, who ne'er let fall
>   One grain of Holy Truth;
> Warn you and win she shall and must,
> For now she lifts her from the dust,
>   To reign as in her youth.[15]

Newman's use of the term "private judgment" is more than just ambiguous;[16] it can be dangerous, providing a foundation for forms of subjectivism, liberalism, and relativism that Newman hates and fears.

Later in the *Grammar* Newman makes this interesting observation: "Thus, when Laud said that he did not see his way to come to terms with the Holy See, 'till Rome was other than she was,' no Catholic would admit the sentiment: but any Catholic may understand that this is just the judgment consistent with Laud's actual condition of thought and cast of opinions, his ecclesiastical position, and the existing state of England" (282). Given the variation in private judgment among the factory-girl, Montaigne, and Laud, we cannot know how much force Newman's appeal to private judgment is meant to have, for if private judgment validates or legitimates the factory-girl's informal inference, it would seem to validate the informal inferences of Montaigne and Laud, too. Had Newman attempted to show that the private judgment of Montaigne and Laud is somehow defective, his views would not now seem so relativistic. But to attack the informal inferences of a Montaigne or a Laud would be to rob them of their informality and undermine Newman's whole theory of informal inference.

However, in the factory-girl example, Newman qualifies his appeal to private judgment in two ways. He tells us that the *ipse dixit* of private judgment is to be understood as (1) "the judgment of those who have a right to judge"; and (2) "the agreement of many private judgments in one and the same view of it." These may well be more than qualifications; what began as an appeal to private judgment may be turning out to be a double appeal to authority and conventional judgment. Consider authority first. If Newman is simply thinking of the Roman Catholic hierarchy here, then he has already lost the open-minded reader. Later he speaks of the value of the reasoning faculty "as exercised by gifted, or by educated or otherwise well-

---

14 Newman, *Essay on Development*, 34, 74.
15 John Henry Newman, "Private Judgment," in *Verses on Various Occasions*, 74-75. The poem was written in 1832.
16 Kenny, *Political Thought*, 105-106.

prepared minds" (283). He is obviously not thinking of Montaigne, Laud, Hume, and Bentham. But is the factory-girl really more "gifted" or "educated" than such people? If what makes her more gifted and well-prepared is simply her Catholic faith, then Newman has not gone very far towards convincing us of the *rationality* of faith. And what about conventional judgment? Do the overwhelming majority of people really make the same inference that the factory-girl makes? No; and even if they did, that would not count for much, since as Newman well knows, the majority is not always right or rational. It not only has believed that the earth is flat and immovable, but has allowed Socrates to be poisoned and Jesus of Nazareth to be crucified. Moreover, since Newman has repeatedly insisted that informal inference involves personal factors, how can he expect a simple "agreement" of many private judgments in "one and the same view" of the factory-girl's argument? He has just warned us that even Dives and Lazarus cannot be expected to take the same estimate of it.

We turn now to an example from the third set, an example in which the reasoner himself acknowledges that his inference is informal. Here is Newman's thirteenth and last example:

[This instance] is one of a literary character, the divination of the author-ship of a certain anonymous publication, as suggested mainly by inter-nal evidence, as I find it in a critique written some twenty years ago. In the extract which I make from it, we may observe the same steady march of a proof towards a conclusion, which is (as it were) out of sight;—a reckoning, or a reasonable judgment, that the conclusion really is proved, and a personal certitude upon that judgment, joined with a confession that a logical argument could not well be made out for it, and that the various details in which the proof consisted were in no small measure implicit and impalpable.

"Rumour speaks uniformly and clearly enough in attributing it to the pen of a particular individual. Nor, although a cursory reader might well skim the book without finding in it anything to suggest, &c., ... will it appear improbable to the more attentive student of its internal evidence; and the improbability will decrease more and more, in proportion as the *reader is capable* of judging and appreciating the *delicate, and at first invisible touches*, which limit, to *those who understand them*, the indi-viduals who can have written it to a very small number indeed. The utmost scepticism as to its authorship (*which we do not feel ourselves*) cannot remove it farther from him than to that of some one among his most intimate friends; so that, leaving others to discuss antecedent probabilities," &c.

Here is a writer who professes to have no doubt at all about the authorship of a book,—which at the same time he cannot prove by mere argumentation set down in words. The reasons of his conviction are too delicate, too intricate, nay, they are in part invisible; invisible, except to those who from circumstances have an intellectual perception of what does not appear to the many. They are personal to the individual. This again is an instance, distinctly set before us, of the particular mode in which the mind progresses in concrete matter, viz. from merely probable antecedents to the sufficient proof of a fact or a truth, and, after the proof, to an act of certitude about it. (259-60)

This example looks more promising than the other two. The writer, W, professes to be certain that A is the author of the anonymous publication, but he cannot verbally articulate his reasons for so believing, and he regards those reasons as "invisible." He has made an inference, but his reasoning does not seem to have been verbal or formal.

Has W actually *inferred* or just *perceived* that A is the author? He seems to have inferred: even though he regards his reasons as invisible, too delicate and too implicit to put into words, he is sure that he *had* reasons. Besides, he had to examine the book before making a judgment, and this examination took some time, whereas perception takes only a fraction of a second. Still again, he did not come to apprehend a visual object but a *proposition*; he concluded—he "saw" —that "A is the author of this publication." But as I suggested earlier, Newman's "informal inference" may have as much in common with perception as with formal inference. I am not thinking here of "perception" in the way that physiologists or experimental psychologists do, but in the way that modern empiricist epistemologists like Price, Chisholm, and Yolton do.[17] When I say, "I see Mike in the next room," the person standing beside me is not necessarily being mischievous in asking, "Are you sure it is Mike that you see?" I then take a "closer look" at the man in the next room, and this look takes considerably longer than a fraction of a second. Finally I assert, almost in the way of concluding, "Yes; that is Mike, all right." There is a big difference, epistemologically speaking, between seeing Mike and "being appeared red to" or "sensing redly" or "having a red appearance," so much so that some empiricist epistemologists believe that the judgment "I see Mike" is founded on or derived from other propositions that are directly evident (e.g., "I am appeared red to," which is evident to me when I look in the direction of Mike's hair). Such empiricist epistemologists have been criticized for their "foundationalism," and it does seem to do violence to ordinary language to say that one must "infer" that he sees Mike.[18] This philosophical disagreement is a complicated one, and all we need to note here is that in regarding judgments like W's, as informal *inferences*, Newman may be ignoring or even begging some relevant epistemological questions. Is perception of people and material objects a kind of informal inference? Is a

17 H. H. Price, *Perception* (London: Methuen and Co., 1932); R. M. Chisholm, *Perceiving: A Philosophical Study* (Ithaca, New York: Cornell University Press, 1957); John W. Yolton, *Metaphysical Analysis* (Toronto: University of Toronto Press, 1967).

18 See, for example, John Austin, *Sense and Sensibilia* (Oxford: Clarendon Press, 1962).

judgment like *W*'s more a perception than an inference? If not, how are we to account for the fact that such a judgment seems to have so many features in common with, say, seeing Mike that a formal inference lacks altogether?

I myself am inclined to agree with Newman that *W* has made an inference. But must *W*'s inference be regarded as informal and mysterious? When we ask *W* how he knows that *A* is the author, he may initially respond, "It is too hard to say." But if we press *W*, then after some introspection and reflection he will start to enumerate the main considerations that led him to his judgment. He will point, for example, to the book's very long paragraphs, its frequent use of certain idioms, the unusual spelling of certain words, the frequent use of a certain kind of sexual symbolism, the occasional use of puns, the references to certain obscure writers like Amort and Dmowski, and so on. *W*'s reasons are not beyond criticism; we will point out to him that *B* and *C* also write very long paragraphs, that *C* and *D* use the same kind of sexual symbolism, that *D*, *E*, and *F* occasionally refer to Amort and Dmowski. We may even convince *W* that the book may not have been written by *A* after all and that it was more likely written by *D*.

I have not been attempting here to make any profound contributions to logical theory and the psychology of cognition. My aim has been rather more modest, to show that the inferences that Newman presents in his examples are unmysterious. It is important to remember what Newman is ultimately trying to show. Newman does not have a full-blown theory of informal inference, and his interest in the modes of inference is not purely intellectual. His apologetical aim is twofold, to show that the ordinary Catholic's reasoning in religious matters is both respectably rational and beyond criticism. When he speaks of "informal inference," Newman has in mind a mental act or process that is rational because it is inferential and beyond criticism because it is informal. If Newman is right, the believer's religious faith is based on reasoning, but a reasoning that is too subtle to be analyzable. Newman tries to strengthen his case by showing that religious reasoning has a relatively uncontroversial counterpart in the secular reasoning involved in such inferences as the "island" and "literary" examples. We must be careful not to overstate our criticism of Newman's "theory." We do not want to challenge Newman's claim that inference is often non-syllogistic, non-deductive, and non-demonstrative. We do not want to challenge his claim that inference need not be deductive or inductive. There is even a great interest now in something called "informal logic." Newman, however, has remarkably little to contribute to our understanding of non-demonstrative inference; he is actually trying to convince us that "informal inference" is mysteriously incomprehensible. When Newman describes informal inference as "personal," "implicit," and "non-verbal," he is almost using these adjectives as *euphemisms* for "mysterious" and "incomprehensible." By showing that the inferences in his examples are unmysterious, we do not show that they are deductive, but we do show that they are sufficiently "verbal" to be critically analyzed.

We might say, then, that Newman's "theory" of informal inference is to some extent a *refusal to theorize* about informal inference. To the savage mind, almost everything seems mysterious or even miraculous; but wonder gives birth to science, which heals ignorance. And just as scientists once showed thunder and lightning to be unmysterious, contemporary logicians and psychologists daily shed new light on processes that Newman could only look on with awe.

There is an irrationalistic tone to some of Newman's comments in this section as when he writes:

> It is this distinction between ratiocination as the exercise of a living faculty in the individual intellect, and mere skill in argumentative science, which is the true interpretation of the prejudice which exists against logic in the popular mind, and of the animadversions which are levelled against it, as that its formulas make a pedant and a *doctrinaire*, that it never makes converts, that it leads to rationalism, that Englishmen are too practical to be logical, that an ounce of common-sense goes farther than many cartloads of logic, that Laputa is the land of logicians, and the like. Such maxims mean, when analyzed, that the processes of reasoning which legitimately lead to assent, to action, to certitude, are in fact too multiform, subtle, omnigenous, too implicit, to allow of being measured by rule, that they are after all personal,—verbal argumentation being useful only in subordination to a higher logic. (240)

The charge of irrationalism was actually directed against the *Grammar* in Newman's lifetime by A. M. Fairbairn, and it so disturbed Newman that he formally replied to it.[19] Much of his reply is devoted to a discussion of the ambiguity of the term "reason." Newman could not have been so sensitive to this ambiguity—or so familiar with informal reasoning—when he wrote as a young man that "it [is not] any credit to a man to have resolved only to take up with what he considers rational,"[20] or that "Christ has so willed it, that we should get at the Truth, not by ingenious speculations, reasonings, or investigations of our own, but by teaching."[21] And he could hardly have had much respect for rationality when as a young clergyman he preached: "Confidence, then, in our own reasoning powers leads to (what St. Paul calls) foolishness, by causing in our hearts an indifference towards, or a distaste for Scripture information. But, besides thus keep-

19 The exchange took place in *The Contemporary Review* (1885). See *Theological Papers*, 140-57.
20 John Henry Newman, "Faith without Sight," in *Parochial and Plain Sermons*, vol. 2, 24.
21 John Henry Newman, "The Mind of Little Children," ibid., vol. 2, 66.

ing us from the best of guides, it also makes us fools, because it is a confidence in a *bad* guide. Our reasoning powers are very weak in all inquiries into moral and religious truth."[22] We shall never know for sure whether his subsequent talk about informal inference represented a change of heart, a change of mind, a change of terminology, or just a change of apologetical strategy.

I have not meant to suggest in anything I have said so far that one is obliged to be rational at all times; even such aggressive rationalists as Plato and Spinoza are willing to pay emotion and appetite their due and to acknowledge that people do not live by reason alone. But I do agree with the many critics of the *Grammar* who see it as undervaluing genuine reason. Consider this type of situation: we are discussing a very important matter with a friend, and he suddenly announces his commitment to some outrageous position. When we then ask him, "Why do you believe *that*?" or "How did you come to *that* conclusion?" he is evasive and answers, "I'm not sure; my reasons are too subtle to be put into words," or "I have my reasons, but they are too personal for you to understand," or "On intuition," or, simply, "I don't know." What are we to make of our friend's judgment, and what are we to make of his *rationality*? Yet, it is precisely in situations like this one that it is so very important for us to press people like our friend to work harder at articulating their reasons. We do not go about asking our friends why they believe that Britain is an island, and we may not be concerned enough to press *W* to explain why he believes that *A* wrote a certain anonymous publication. But the beliefs about which people argue are often too important to be treated as the termini of intellectual operations that are mysteriously incomprehensible and uncriticizable. When someone announces that a particular book should be censored or that certain people should lose their jobs, a great deal may be at stake, and we may well have a moral obligation to demand that he give a better defense of his position than "My reasons are too subtle to be put into words." Newman would have been the first to admit that religious beliefs are among the most important about which people argue; he was, after all, a religious *apologist* who thought that he was making an important contribution to civilization by "explicitly" and "verbally" defending the Catholic faith.

Earlier in chapter 8, Newman acknowledged our need to discover "an instrument of reasoning (that is, of gaining new truths by means of old), which may be less vague and arbitrary than the talent and experience of the few or the common-sense of the many" (210). He told us there that it is "a necessity, if it be possible, to analyze the process of reasoning, and to invent a method which may act as a common measure between mind and mind, as a means of joint inves-

---

22 John Henry Newman, "The Self-Wise Inquirer," ibid., vol. 1, 218.

tigation, and as a recognized intellectual standard,—a standard such as to secure us against hopeless mistakes, and to emancipate us from the capricious *ipse dixit* of authority" (211). "*A necessity, if it be possible*": is it possible? Newman has gone some way towards analyzing the process of reasoning, but he has also argued that it is folly to think that one can go much further; if Newman's phenomenological analysis is sound as far as it goes, then it is clear that inference in concrete matter is too complex and too subtle to be analyzed more deeply. And what about the "common measure," the "intellectual standard"? Newman will not leave us with false hopes: "Inference, considered in the sense of verbal argumentation, determines neither our principles, nor our ultimate judgments. . . . [I]t is neither the test of truth, nor the adequate basis of assent" (229). If Newman is right, then the bitter truth is that we are stuck with the vague and arbitrary talent of the few and the common sense of the many, with the hopeless mistakes and the dependence on capricious authority. Fortunately, Newman is wrong: necessity is the mother of invention. Neurophysiologists, experimental psychologists, and phenomenologists have not been intimidated by Newman's warning, and they have managed to attain deeper and deeper insight into the nature of cognitive processes. And every day verbal reasoning wins new admirers, who use it to persuade and enlighten, to resolve disputes, and to understand.

3 Natural inference

Newman closes chapter 8 with a short section on "natural" inference. "Natural" or "material" inference is "the mode in which we ordinarily reason" (261) and is inference of the most implicit, direct, and spontaneous kind. Newman does not clearly distinguish between natural and informal inference. Since natural inference is implicit and non-formal, he may regard it as a *kind* of informal inference; or he may consider it a wholly different mode of inference. He tells us that natural inference is "not from propositions to propositions, but from things to things, from concrete to concrete, from wholes to wholes" (260). This remark is somewhat perplexing. At the beginning of the *Grammar*, Newman defined "inference" as the conditional acceptance of a *proposition*, and while he is more concerned now with a process than with a propositional attitude, it is still disturbing to see propositions so dramatically stripped of their original importance. Moreover, it is not clear how a non-propositional "thing" or "whole" can be a premise or conclusion, so that one is inclined to wonder whether Newman is confusing reasoning, inference, with another process of thought. Still again, it is not clear how a non-propositional "thing" or "whole" can be an object of assent or belief.

Natural inferences are so implicit, direct, and spontaneous that they seem to us to be instances of "divination" (261, 263), "instinct" (262-64), "intuition" (262), and "perception" (262-64). In ordinary minds, natural reasoning is "biassed and degraded by prejudice, passion, and self-interest"; only rarely is it characterized by "precision, subtlety, promptitude, and truth." The purer form "belongs to all of us in a measure" (261), but it is most impressively exemplified by instances of genius in ratiocination. Most of Newman's discussion is taken up with the consideration of such instances, the insights of such men as Newton and Napoleon. As Newman believes that natural inference is the mode in which we *ordinarily* reason, it is rather unfortunate that he does not offer any examples of "ordinary" natural inference.

It is in this section of the *Grammar* that Newman first refers to the "illative faculty." He says that inferential processes in concrete matter are the action of the mind's "ratiocinative or illative faculty" (260), which "is not so much one faculty, as a collection of similar or analogous faculties under one name, there being really as many faculties as there are distinct subject-matters, though in the same person some of them may, if it so happen, be united" (267). Newton and Napoleon both had a genius for ratiocination, but that genius lay in different provinces. But as we shall see in the next chapter, Newman's idea of the illative faculty is not so simple, and what he says about it is not entirely consistent.

Having drawn our attention to the special intellectual gifts that certain individuals have in various provinces, Newman goes on to observe how important it is for us to trust authorities: "Instead of trusting logical science, we must trust persons, namely, those who by long acquaintance with their subject have a right to judge. And if we wish ourselves to share in their convictions and the grounds of them, we must follow their history, and learn as they have learned" (268-69). It is not hard to see the apologetical significance of this point, for it at least indirectly supports the influence of the Catholic hierarchy.

Newman began the second part of the *Grammar* by setting down an agenda; having completed his first two tasks, it only remained for him to solve his old "paradox," the "apparent inconsistency which is involved in holding that an unconditional acceptance of a proposition can be the result of its conditional verification" (135). Has he done this? Several passages in chapter 8 suggest that he thinks so. He introduced his examples of informal inference with the comment: "Having thus explained the view which I would take of reasoning in the concrete, viz. that, from the nature of the case, and from the constitution of the human mind, certitude is the result of arguments which, taken in the letter, and not in their full implicit sense, are but probabilities, I proceed to dwell on some instances . . ." (234). And he ended his discussion of informal inference by saying: "I trust the foregoing remarks may not deserve the blame of a needless refinement. I have thought it incumbent on me to illustrate the intellectual process by which we pass from conditional inference to unconditional assent; and I have had only the alternative of lying under the imputation of a paradox or of a subtlety" (260). These statements, along with several in chapter 9, suggest that once one understands how informal inference differs from formal inference, the solution to the old paradox is immediately obvious. What Newman now says about *natural* inference seems to contribute further to the solution. He writes:

> Whether the consequents, at which we arrive from the antecedents with which we start, lead us to assent or only towards assent, those antecedents commonly are not recognized by us as subjects for analysis; nay, often are only indirectly recognized as antecedents at all. Not only is the inference with its process ignored, but the antecedent also. To the mind itself the reasoning is a simple divination or prediction. . . . (260-61)

These comments suggest that while natural inference is *logically* conditional, it is not *psychologically* conditional, so that it is compatible with psychological certitude. He again seems to be saying then that the old paradox disappears as soon as one realizes that most inference is not formal.

And yet, the fact remains that whether it is formal, informal, or natural, inference is inference, nothing more and nothing less. In outlining the characteristics of informal inference, Newman has actually gone to the trouble of reminding us that "in this investigation of the method of concrete inference, we have not advanced one step towards depriving inference of its conditional character; for it is still as dependent on premises as it is in its elementary idea" (233). In presenting his examples of informal inference, Newman has, it is true, consistently drawn our attention to the fact that certitude *follows* upon such inferences. But Newman has not really explained yet *how* a conclusion gives way to a belief. Moreover, he well knows that while a reflective person like Locke or himself is only "indirectly" aware of the antecedents in any *particular* inference, such a person realizes, at least in his moments of reflection, that *all* inferences depend on such antecedents.

The last section of chapter 8 poses serious problems for the expositor. Since Newman has not clearly defined the relation of natural inference to informal inference, one is almost tempted to see Newman as implying that natural inference, unlike informal, is actually unconditional. But if natural inference is unconditional, then how is it "inference"? If, however, Newman is arguing here that natural inference is logically conditional but psychologically unconditional, then his solution to his paradox amounts to the claim that for all *practical* purposes, most inference is not conditional at all. Such a claim trivializes one of the basic principles on which the entire *Grammar* rests, for even the conclusion of a formal demonstration can come, *in time*, to be accepted, "held," without a concomitant psychological awareness that it was once derived from premises.

Newman comes remarkably close to saying that he neither *knows* nor *cares* how his "paradox" is to be solved. At the beginning of chapter 9, he writes, "How it comes about that we can be certain is not my business to determine; for me it is sufficient that certitude is felt" (270). Newman's "paradox" need not worry those of us who reject his views on inference, belief, and certitude; but we can hardly help being puzzled by his announcement that it is not his "business" to explain how we can be certain.

Another problem for the expositor is that Newman's discussions of natural inference in chapter 8 and illative judgment in chapter 9 cover common ground but do not quite fit together. In chapter 8, the illative faculty is seen as nothing more than the faculty that enables us to make inferences in concrete matter; here the "insights" of Newton and Napoleon are taken to be natural inferences. But in chapter 9, the picture becomes more complicated. Certain statements in chapter 9 suggest that illative judgment involves *more* than just inferring, and that "insight" is not quite the same as natural inference. One way of looking at illative judgment in chapter 9 is to see it as a bridge between inference and certitude, a solution to Newman's "paradox." Also, the range of the illative faculty is much wider in chapter 9 than in chapter 8. In any case, having already associated the illative faculty with inferences that are like "intuitive perceptions" and "instinctive apprehensions," Newman ends chapter 8 by elevating the illative faculty to the rank of a "sense": "Judgment then in all concrete matter is the architectonic faculty; and what may be called the Illative Sense, or right judgment in ratiocination, is one branch of it" (269).

Chapter Six

The Illative Sense

1 Illative judgment contrasted with inference

No other notion in the *Grammar* is as famous or infamous as the illative sense, and while Newman regards it as something quite ordinary with which we are all familiar, readers have taken rather different views of his invocation of it. To some the illative sense is Newman's greatest discovery,[1] while to others his appeal to it is clear evidence that he is ultimately committed to a dangerous intuitionism with irrationalistic and relativistic implications.[2] Undoubtedly there are many who share D'Arcy's view that the illative sense is a *deus ex machina*: "The illative sense is introduced as a newcomer without antecedents and without its proper title, and is made to do duty for all manner of acts and processes of thought because in the previous chapters thought has been deprived of some of its functions."[3] In D'Arcy's view, Newman's talk about an illative "*sense*" will "make the philosophic purist wince...."[4]

The chapter entitled "The Illative Sense" contains little in the way of polemic, and its subdued tone suggests that Newman feels that he has left his most controversial claims behind him. Chapter 9 is largely synoptic, and the *illative sense* is to some extent a synoptic concept. As Fey observes, "Newman introduced the expression, *illative sense*, to summarize and denote 'the perfection' of our complex intellectual activity when it combines real assent and notional inference, formal exhibitions and informal reflection—in coming to know what is the case."[5]

Newman had not used the term "illative sense" in any of his earlier philosophical writings. However, as far back as the *University Ser-*

---

1 E.g., Norris, *Method*, 42; Zeno, "Psychological Discovery," *passim*.
2 E.g., Arnold Lunn, *Roman Converts* (London: Chapman and Hall, 1924), 80.
3 D'Arcy, *Nature of Belief*, 148-49.
4 Ibid., 148.
5 Fey, *Faith and Doubt*, 177. Cf. Lash, "Introduction," 17.

mons, he had already attached great importance to the "reasoning faculty," and had also treated reason itself as a faculty: "Reason does not really perceive any thing; but it is a faculty of proceeding from things that are perceived to things which are not."[6] Such innocuous talk about a "reasoning faculty" or "faculty of reason" is compatible with common usage and common sense; and in the *Grammar*, Newman associates the illative sense with ratiocination or reasoning.

Some scholars feel that Newman is using the term "sense" loosely here. Horgan, for example, writes, "The word 'sense' here was unfortunate, because it seemed to suggest an irrational instinct, whereas Newman clearly intended an intellectual power, in the same way that one speaks of common sense or good sense. ... It is not a power distinct from intellect: it is simply the intellect judging."[7] Cronin adds, " 'Sense' and 'instinct' with Newman are not of necessity nonrational. He uses them to describe a function not adequately designated by existing terms."[8] Still, Newman's use of the term "sense" is deliberate: he not only includes it in the title of chapter 9 but capitalizes it at various places in the chapter.

And what about the unusual term "illative"? Some interesting background information has been provided by Pailin:

> The term "illative" appears in the *Grammar of Assent* without any explicit definition. It is an uncommon word which is defined in contemporary dictionaries [from 1864 and 1901] in terms of "inference; deduction; conclusion." Newman may have noticed the word in Locke who writes of "illation" as the intellectual faculty which "consists in nothing but the perception of the connexion there is between the ideas, in each step of the deduction." In this paragraph, the term seems to be used synonymously with "inference" and "reason." The phrase "illative conjunctions" is found in Whately's *Logic* in a passage which Newman helped to compose.[9]

Newman does not appear to have regarded his use of "illative" as technical, but the term must have seemed rather formal even to Victorian readers of the *Grammar*.[10]

While the *illative sense* is to some extent a synoptic concept, Newman may well need it in order to deal with his old "paradox." Though some of his remarks suggest otherwise, he probably realizes that he has not yet solved it. The *illative sense* is the only playing card left in his hand.

Newman's paradox is not *our* paradox; *we* need not be troubled by it. For though we may agree with Newman that inference ordinarily

6 John Henry Newman, "The Nature of Faith in Relation to Reason," *University Sermons*, 206. This sermon was preached on 13 January 1839.
7 Horgan, "Faith and Reason," 148.
8 Cronin, *Knowledge*, 79.
9 Pailin, *Way to Faith*, 144.
10 Ibid.

precedes belief, we reject most of the doctrines that get him into trouble. Newman is faced with an "apparent inconsistency" only because of his odd views on inference, belief, and certitude. He believes that inference and belief are rival propositional attitudes, that belief is unconditional, that a conditional acceptance of a proposition always precedes an unconditional one, and that inferring a proposition is a continuous activity. But while we do not have to worry about Newman's paradox, Newman does.

As we have seen, Newman has already blurred the distinction between arriving at a *conclusion* in concrete matter and arriving at *certitude* in concrete matter. If he is to hold to his original distinction between inference and belief, he must now argue that, in the process of judgment, something is *combined* with inference that enables the individual to move from conditional acceptance of a proposition to unconditional acceptance. Informal or natural inference cannot by itself lead one to certitude; it can only lead one to a conclusion. So if the illative sense is simply a faculty that enables one to reason, to make inferences, it does not lead one to certitude. Throughout chapter 9, Newman associates the illative sense with our ability to reason. However, he also suggests that the illative sense is what enables us to be *certain* in concrete matter, to recognize that probabilities have converged to a point where *certitude* is warranted. Here it is implied that illative judgment is more than just reasoning, concluding, or inferring.

Having introduced the concept of the illative sense in chapter 8, Newman now goes on in chapter 9 to associate it with certitude:

> Certitude is a mental state: certainty is a quality of propositions. Those propositions I call certain, which are such that I am certain of them. Certitude is not a passive impression made upon the mind from without, by argumentative compulsion, but in all concrete questions (nay, even in abstract, for though the reasoning is abstract, the mind which judges of it is concrete) it is an active recognition of propositions as true, such as it is the duty of each individual himself to exercise at the bidding of reason, and, when reason forbids, to withhold. And reason never bids us to be certain except on an absolute proof; and such a proof can never be furnished to us by the logic of words, for as certitude is of the mind, so is the act of inference which leads to it. Every one who reasons, is his own centre; and no expedient for attaining a common measure of minds can reverse this truth;—but then the question follows, is there any *criterion* of the accuracy of an inference, such as may be our warrant that certitude is rightly elicited in favour of the proposition inferred, since our warrant cannot, as I have said, be scientific? I have already said that the sole and final judgment on the validity of an inference in concrete matter is committed to the personal action of the ratiocinative faculty, the perfection or virtue of which I have called the Illative Sense, a use of the word "sense" parallel to our use of it in "good sense," "common sense," a "sense of beauty," &c.;—and I own I do not see any way to go farther than

this in answer to the question. However, I can at least explain my meaning more fully; and therefore I will now speak, first of the sanction of the Illative Sense, next of its nature, and then of its range. (271)

Throughout this passage, Newman associates the illative sense with reasoning and inference. But if one studies the passage carefully, one finds that Newman is not simply saying that the illative sense is the faculty that enables us to reason or infer in concrete matter. One thing Newman says here is that the illative sense *judges* whether certitude is *rightly elicited* in favour of the proposition inferred. Illative judgment, then, is not simply a matter of inferring, but also involves a judgment on the validity of the inference. This "sole and final judgment" is precisely what Newman needs to bridge the gap between inference and certitude. Another thing Newman says is that the illative sense is the "perfection or virtue" of the ratiocinative faculty. It is not simply the power of concluding but, as he says later, the power of judging and concluding *when in its perfection* (276). Finally, it is worth noting that Newman again draws our attention to his earlier view that certitude does not follow *directly* from reasoning but is exercised "at the bidding" of reason. Acquiescence to the dictates of reason is seen here not as a mechanical response but as a matter of duty.

The moves Newman makes here provide him with the device needed for solving his paradox. The way to certitude has now been marked out for us. As one infers, one determines, by the personal action of the illative sense, whether one's inference is valid, whether certitude is rightly elicited in favour of the proposition inferred. This judgment, which is not itself an inference but more akin to a perception,[11] a sensation,[12] or an intuition, enables the mind to set aside the original conditions and focus on the proposition itself. The bridge is clear: between inference and certitude comes a judgment on the validity of the inference.

I am not endorsing Newman's position here; I am simply trying to understand it, which is no easy task since much of it is obscure and ambiguous. Sometimes Newman appears to be associating the illative sense only with the judgment on the validity of an inference; at other times he seems to think that the illative sense is what enables us to perform all of the necessary intellectual operations: the basic inferring, the intermediate judging, and the final believing. This ambiguity carries over to his slightly more formal description of the "nature" of the illative sense. There Newman speaks of the illative sense in four respects: "as viewed in itself, in its subject-matter, in the process it uses, and in its function and scope" (280).

11 Cf. Pailin above on Locke's definition of "illation."
12 The activity of the illative *sense* is a kind of *sensation*.

> First, viewed in its exercise, it is one and the same in all concrete matters, though employed in them in different measures. . . . Secondly, it is in fact attached to definite subject-matters, so that a given individual may possess it in one department of thought, for instance, history, and not in another, for instance, philosophy. . . . Thirdly, in coming to its conclusion, it proceeds always in the same way, by a method of reasoning. . . . Fourthly, in no class of concrete reasonings, whether in experimental science, historical research, or theology, is there any ultimate test of truth and error in our inferences besides the trustworthiness of the Illative Sense that gives them its sanction. . . . (281)

Notice that Newman says here that the illative sense both comes to a conclusion—in which case illative judgment involves inferring—and is the "test of truth and error in our inferences." The illative sense then can be understood broadly or narrowly. Understood broadly, the term "illative sense" serves the purpose that Fey describes: it summarizes and denotes the "perfection" of the *entire complex* of intellectual activity, the sequence of activities that begins with informal inference and ends with certitude. Understood narrowly, the term refers only to the intermediate judgment that bridges the gap between inference and certitude. This ambiguity also carries over to Newman's understanding of ratiocination or reasoning. Raw reasoning, informal or natural inference, can only give us a conclusion; but the refined, "perfected" reasoning that involves a judgment on our inference can actually give us certitude.

What is involved in judging an informal or natural inference to be valid? In the domain of formal reasoning, our criterion of the validity or accuracy of an inference is something scientific and impersonal, a common measure. The inference that I have made can be assessed, tested, by an objective or conventional standard, by rules. We can evaluate it by referring to truth-tables, Venn diagrams, the mnemonic schemes of the medieval logicians ("Barbara, Celarent . . ."), and so on. But if, as Newman believes, informal and natural inference are mysteriously implicit and personal, then so must be the method by which we judge them to be valid. Is Newman justified, however, in assuming that we *do* judge them to be valid? Newman needs a bridge in order to solve his paradox; but since we do not endorse Newman's basic claims about the nature of inference, belief, and certitude, why should we accept his claim that there must be a kind of judgment that bridges inference and belief in concrete matter?

Newman will invite us to consider the *need* for a test. Formal inferences are not always valid; the study of logic is valuable because it helps us to make and recognize valid inferences. In the domain of formal reasoning, one must get into the habit of inferring carefully and precisely, for otherwise one's inferring will lead one astray. Is it not the same with informal reasoning? In the domain of informal reasoning, some inferences are better than others. What one infers informally is not necessarily valid. And some people are consistently more successful than others in making informal inferences. This is especially apparent in the case of geniuses like Newton and Napoleon, who in a particular department of thought make judgments that are remarkably astute. Inferring is one thing, inferring *well* another. Of course, ultimately there is a public test of the validity of a judgment in concrete matter. In most cases, data can *eventually* be produced that will indicate whether a certain informal inference is valid or invalid. One need not have the gifts of a Newton or Napoleon to be able to realize *in time* that the great man's judgments were astute. And yet, it can hardly be mere coincidence that the inferences of a Newton or Napoleon have so often turned out to be valid, while those of his rivals have so often turned out not to be. Is this not an indication that, in addition to inferring, a Newton or a Napoleon is able to "see" that a certain line of reasoning is fruitful and another barren? And do not all of us have this ability to "see" in other areas and on a smaller scale?

In criticizing Newman's theory of informal inference, I argued that informal inferences are not as mysterious as Newman would like us to think. We can see now why Newman is so interested in men of genius. Who can explain the genius of a Newton or Napoleon? Who among us believes that one can train oneself to make judgments of the kind that Newton and Napoleon made? Is there not something "mysterious" about the "insight" of such men, something that cannot be explained by their diligence, experience, and so forth? If we are prepared to acknowledge the mysteriousness of *their* insight, then perhaps we are forced to admit that there is a certain degree of mysteriousness in *all* insight. "[W]hat is left to us but to take things as they are, and to resign ourselves to what we find? that is, instead of devising, what cannot be, some sufficient science of reasoning which may compel certitude in concrete conclusions, to confess that there is no ultimate test of truth besides the testimony born to truth by the mind itself, and that this phenomenon, perplexing as we may find it, is a normal and inevitable characteristic of the mental constitution of a being like man on a stage such as the world" (275).

So if informal inference is not all that mysterious, perhaps illative judgment *is*. When *W* insists that *A* is the author of an anonymous publication, we can attack all of the reasons that we have forced him to articulate; we may even persuade him to abandon his belief. But what happens when *W* turns out to be right, and consistently so, in making such judgments? Are we not reduced to the level of the wise fools who produced detailed arguments to prove that Newton and Napoleon were wrong? Furthermore, if we reject Newman's claim that we possess a certain faculty that passes judgment on our inferences in concrete matter, and we argue instead that W or Newton or Napoleon "simply" infers better than other people in his field, have we shown judgment to be any less mysterious than Newman claims it is? Obviously not.

But what has Newman actually accomplished here? He has, of course, solved his "paradox"; but that "paradox" is the offspring of a conceptual framework that we have seen to be thoroughly unsatisfactory. He has also forced us to concede that a certain aspect of judgment is indeed mysterious, at least insofar as it looks like something that phenomenologists, psychologists, and physiologists will have no easy time explaining in the years to come. The concession may not be as large as it initially appears. Newman wants us "to confess that there is no ultimate test of truth besides the testimony born to truth by the mind itself." But though we are baffled and humiliated when W or Newton or Napoleon turns out to be right in spite of our careful criticisms of his judgment, the fact remains that, more often than not, rational criticism hits the mark. Few scientists are Newtons, and few military strategists are Napoleons. The "insights" of the typical scientist and military leader are normally not so profound as to outweigh the mass of verbal argumentation that is pitted against their judgments. Similarly, whenever W turns out to be wrong, which often he will, our high opinion of verbal reasoning is confirmed. When it has been proved that we were right to argue that the author of the anonymous publication is probably D and not A, then W will agree with us that what he had earlier "seen," in his moment of "insight," has turned out to be as illusory as the pink elephants that the alcoholic "sees" on the ceiling. Reason is sometimes overvalued, but people are more inclined to undervalue it, and Newman undervalued it in a way that Newton and Napoleon probably did not.

Then again, while we are reluctant to think of the insights of a Newton as anything short of mysterious, we do not experience the same sense of awe when we consider the insights of ordinary people in ordinary situations. Such insights may be qualitatively, as well as quantitatively, different from those of a Newton. Scientists who study cognition may well tremble at the very idea of having to plumb the depths of Newton's mind. But as we noted earlier, Newman was awe-struck by intellectual processes that modern philosophers and psychologists find less than mysterious, and it is not clear why we should follow him in assuming that if the insight of a Newton is hard to fathom, so must be that of a factory-girl. Moreover, we should not have too much difficulty explaining why an ordinary educated person's judgments are generally more accurate than a peasant's: it is not because of a mysterious power of insight, but because education has provided the educated person with knowledge, intellectual skills, and an appreciation of the importance of clear thinking and disciplined reasoning.

Newman, in fact, believes that it is our duty to "strengthen and perfect" the illative sense (281). If the illative sense is a sense in the same way as "good sense" and "common sense," then it is hard to see how one can go about cultivating it. Newman does not give us any specific instructions on how to carry out this duty. Perhaps he is afraid to; for as soon as he starts to enumerate the ways in which one can improve one's intellectual judgment, he not only deprives the illative sense of much of its personal character but draws our attention to the superiority of the educated person's power of judgment to the devout peasant's. This reminds us of a strange tension in Newman's thought: the author of the *Grammar* exalts the common man's judgment at the expense of that of philosophers, intellectuals, and rationalists; but as the author of *The Idea of a University*, he offered an eloquent and much admired defense of liberal education.

Newman attempts to explain the illative sense by comparing it to parallel faculties, and the one that receives most of his attention is what Aristotle calls "*phronesis*," "the faculty which guides the mind in matters of conduct" (277). Newman's interpretation of the *Nicomachean Ethics* is unusual:

> What it is to be virtuous, how we are to gain the just idea and standard of virtue, how we are to approximate in practice to our own standard, what is right and wrong in a particular case, for the answers in fulness and accuracy to these and similar questions, the philosopher refers us to no code of laws, to no moral treatise, because no science of life, applicable to the case of an individual, has been or can be written. Such is Aristotle's doctrine, and it is undoubtedly true. An ethical system may supply laws, general rules, guiding principles, a number of examples, suggestions, landmarks, limitations, cautions, distinctions, solutions of critical or anxious difficulties; but who is to apply them to a particular case? whither can we go, except to the living intellect, our own, or another's? (277)

Although Aristotle attaches great importance to *phronesis*, his general approach in the *Ethics* is scientific and prescriptive. Unlike Shaftesbury, Hume, and Newman, Aristotle believes that morality has more to do with rationality than with a "moral sense," and though he acknowledges that ethics admits of less precision than most sciences, and that its students require worldly experience, he clearly believes that the philosophical study of morality is of great value to those who are capable of undertaking it. Displaying the careful verbal argumentation that one would expect from the intellectual par excellence and author of the *Organon*, he proceeds in the *Ethics* to enumerate and analyze the virtues, explain the practical syllogism, and advocate the life of self-realization through philosophical contemplation. His model of the man of practical wisdom is not the superstitious peasant. By taking Aristotle's theory of *phronesis* out of context, Newman distorts and misuses it.

Drawing on certain passages from the first half of chapter 9, I have offered an interpretation of Newman's views on illative judgment according to which illative judgment involves more than just inferring. In this interpretation, illative judgment is seen as involving perception-like judgment *on* one's inferences. This intermediate judgment, most impressively exemplified by the judgments of men of genius in their special department of thought, is what is ordinarily called "insight." If this is what Newman has in mind, then he is a forerunner of a modern philosopher of science like Polanyi, who writes that "true discovery is not a strictly logical performance, and accordingly we may describe the obstacle to be overcome in solving a problem as a 'logical gap' and speak of the width of the logical gap as the measure of the ingenuity required for solving the problem. Illumination is then the leap by which the logical gap is crossed."[13] If such an interpretation is correct, then Newman has solved his personal paradox and supported his claim that the believer's *certitude* (and not just his conclusion) can be reasonable and justified even though it ultimately rests on mere probabilities.

Noting that Newman comes close to ignoring the logical difference between an assent and a conclusion, Pailin adds that Newman ultimately manages to distinguish between the result of the reasoning and the certitude that it evokes:

> He describes the mental process in reaching certainty as passing from "the proof to an act of certitude about it." Again, he writes that "from probabilities we may construct legitimate proof, sufficient for certitude." In all these cases he has left room even if only just, for a personal decision between the reasoning process and the acceptance of its conclusions as certain.[14]

Pailin sees the intermediate judgment as a kind of *decision*, and elaborating on this view, he writes:

> The gap between the reception of a proposition as having demonstrated probability and an unconditional assent to that proposition is one that we cannot bridge by reasoning. It is a gap which divides the logic of reasoning from the logic of personal commitment. It is bridged by our decision to move from the one logical sphere to the other.[15]

Lash is understandably sceptical: "One of the most serious weaknesses of Pailin's study is that he simply takes for granted that assent is to be 'leapt' into, and criticizes Newman for holding that the leap is

13 Michael Polanyi, *Personal Knowledge* (London: 1958), 123; cf. Norris, *Method*, 46.
14 Pailin, *Way to Faith*, 159.
15 Ibid. The term "demonstrated" is misleading here.

to be performed, the 'gap . . . bridged by an act of will,' rather than of intellect."[16] But what then *does* the intermediate judgment involve? Can anything be said about the "perception" of an implicit inference's validity other than that it occurs? Perhaps, but Newman himself has nothing further to add on the role played by the illative sense in the "final resolution of concrete questions" (283).

He does go on, however, to assign to the illative sense a role at earlier stages of inquiry. He says that the illative sense makes judgments at the "start" and "course" of the inquiry (283), and that in considering examples of such judgments we come to appreciate the full "range" of the faculty. The illative sense does not just take us from proof to certitude but actually provides us the the "starting-points" of our inquiry, the principles and assumptions with which reasoning begins:

> § Nor, lastly is an action of the mind itself less necessary in relation to those first elements of thought which in all reasoning are assumptions, the principles, tastes, and opinions, very often of a personal character, which are half the battle in the inference with which the reasoning is to terminate. It is the mind itself that detects them in their obscure recesses, illustrates them, eliminates them, resolves them into simpler ideas, as the case may be. The mind contemplates them without the use of words, by a process which cannot be analyzed. (282)

> § [An inquiry] is carried on from starting-points, and with collateral aids, not formally proved, but more or less assumed, the process of assumption lying in the action of the Illative Sense, as applied to primary elements of thought. . . . (290)

Needless to say, Newman can easily produce any number of examples of how inquiry or reasoning proceeds from assumptions, and in the remainder of chapter 9 he goes on to do so. In criticizing his treatment of formal inference in chapter 8 (216-22), I pointed to the relativistic, historicistic implications of Newman's talk about the assumptions and first principles on which reasoning rests. The last section of chapter 9 is largely a recapitulation and elaboration[17] of his earlier theme, although Newman is more explicitly and emphatically attributing the determination of "starting-points" to a faculty.

But an additional criticism is in order. In impugning formal reasoning in chapter 8, Newman observes that inference "can only conclude probabilities . . . because its premisses are assumed" (216). He treats presumption as almost arbitrary and warns that "for genuine proof in concrete matter we require an *organon* more delicate, versatile, and elastic than verbal argumentation" (217). In now associating presumption with the exercise of an illative *sense*, he sometimes seems to

16 Lash, "Introduction," 17.
17 Ibid.

be suggesting that presumption has a *cognitive* dimension. For example, near the end of chapter 9, he writes, "Facts cannot be proved by presumptions, yet it is remarkable that in cases where nothing stronger than presumption was even professed, scientific men have sometimes acted as if they thought this kind of argument, taken by itself, decisive of a fact which was in debate" (298-99). The fact remains, however, that invoking a "sense" that provides us with our "starting-points" will not save Newman from relativism. And what makes Newman's position all the more problematic is that he wants to have his cake and eat it, to both impugn formal inference for its assumptions and associate the illative sense's determination of "starting-points" with the "ultimate test of truth" (275).

As Pailin observes, "There are several passages which show that Newman recognizes the subjective bias of illation but he is sufficiently optimistic not to count it of major importance."[18] "[W]hile illative reasoning is influenced by all kinds of personal prejudice, Newman does not consider that this challenges the general validity of its conclusions";[19] and yet, "It is apparent, however, that Newman considers that the basic assumptions which each of us entertains are finally to be traced back to our individual nature."[20]

Newman's catalogue of examples is a mixed bag. Most of them seem to be nothing more than excuses for Newman to discourse on a variety of theological subjects. The tension in Newman's analysis is amply illustrated by an adjoining pair of examples.

> "[W]e often hear of the exploits of some great lawyer, judge or advocate, who is able in perplexed cases, when common minds see nothing but a hopeless heap of facts, foreign or contrary to each other, to detect the principle which rightly interprets the riddle, and, to the admiration of all hearers, converts a chaos into an orderly and luminous whole. This is what is meant by originality in thinking: it is the discovery of an aspect of a subject-matter, simpler, it may be, and more intelligible than any hitherto taken. (291)

Here we have a case of "detection," "discovery," the grasping of the "intelligible." But Newman immediately proceeds to contrast this case with a similar one:

> On the other hand, such aspects are often unreal, as being mere exhibitions of ingenuity, not of true originality of mind. This is especially the case in what are called philosophical views of history. Such seems to me the theory advocated in a work of great learning, vigour, and acuteness, Warburton's "Divine Legation of Moses." I do not call Gibbon merely ingenious; still his account of the rise of Christianity is the mere subjective view of one who could not enter into its depth and power. (291)

18 Pailin, *Way to Faith*, 152.
19 Ibid.
20 Ibid.

How are we to distinguish genuine "detection" and "discovery" from "ingenuity" and a "mere subjective view" if "there is no ultimate test of truth besides the testimony born to truth by the mind itself"? How can Newman assume that his insight is "deeper" and "more powerful" than Gibbon's if he is not prepared to produce the explicit, verbal, publicly assessable arguments that will resolve the dispute? And how can he assume that the illative sense of the devout factory-girl or peasant is in historical matters more reliable and more acute than that of a man who, for all his faults, is quite possibly the greatest historical writer in the English language?

More often than not, truth manages to rise to the surface for the edification of the public. We hear of the exploits of people like a great lawyer, judge, or advocate because they have interpreted the riddle to the admiration of all hearers. We learn in time that Newton and Napoleon had genuine insight and not a counterfeit article. Perhaps in time we shall know too whether Gibbon's insight was truly less profound than Newman's and the factory-girl's. In matters of religion, of course, truth is rather shy and often prefers to stay submerged below the surface. As an apologist, Newman believes that truth is bolder in such matters than is generally thought. Yet, he refuses to pay serious enough attention to the formal, verbal arguments of philosophers and theologians, and dogmatic though he is, he carries on a risky flirtation with epistemological relativism. For as Arnold Lunn reminds us, "Others who were not of his school have claimed that the 'illative sense' leads them to other goals, and that developments of Christian doctrine from which Newman would have shrunk in horror fulfill his tests."[21]

2 Coda: An egotist's apologetic

We finally come to the tenth and last chapter of the *Grammar*. It is the least frequently discussed chapter of the essay, and even some of Newman's most devoted admirers find it at least slightly embarrassing. Perhaps their attitude is best articulated by Benard, who in spite of his obvious admiration for Newman, observes:

> In the last chapter, Newman applies [his] theory to belief in revealed religion. This positive apologetic will strike many readers as the weakest part of the *Grammar*. But this is not surprising when we consider that Newman was not professing his apologetic to be *the* proof of Christianity, but merely that evidence from the convergence of probabilities which was personally convincing to him. He does not maintain that everyone will be convinced by it, though he naturally hopes and expects that many will be.[22]

21 Lunn, *Roman Converts*, 80.
22 Benard, *Preface*, 168.

Newman is, above all else, an apologist, a witness for his faith. Even as a young man, he already had a clear idea of his vocation and mission, and when he fell out of favour with his Anglican colleagues, he put his imposing rhetorical skills at the service of the Roman Catholic hierarchy. The first nine chapters of the *Grammar* are subtly apologetical, but the book ends with a "positive" apologetic, a list of "specimens . . . of the arguments adducible for Christianity" (379). While Ker rightly criticizes O'Donoghue for viewing the *Grammar* as an attempt to provide a *systematic* proof of Christianity,[23] the last chapter should dispel any lingering doubts we may have had about the book's being denominationally biased.[24]

For when all is said and done, the *Grammar* is not a book about how people identify the author of an anonymous publication or why we have a right to feel certain that Britain is an island; it is a work of philosophical apologetics that "belongs in the field of high, relentless, religious controversy."[25] And it is not enough for Newman to have persuaded us that the simple believer's commitment may be more reasonable than the liberals think; a work by the mature Newman can never be less than an outright defense of Roman Catholic Christianity. And so, having taken three-hundred pages to set the stage, Newman is finally ready to attempt to "prove Christianity" in the appropriate "informal" way:

> I am suspicious then of scientific demonstrations in a question of concrete fact, in a discussion between fallible men . . . . For me, it is more congenial to my own judgment to attempt to prove Christianity in the same informal way in which I can prove for certain that I have been born into this world, and that I shall die out of it. (319)

In one of the most famous passages in the entire corpus of his writings, he warns us:

> I begin with expressing a sentiment, which is habitually in my thoughts, whenever they are turned to the subject of mental or moral science, and which I am willing to apply here to the Evidences of Religion as it properly applies to Metaphysics or Ethics, viz. that in these provinces of inquiry egotism is true modesty. In religious inquiry each of us can speak only for himself, and for himself he has a right to speak. His own experiences are enough for himself, but he cannot speak for others: he cannot lay down the law; he can only bring his own experiences to the common stock of psychological facts. (300)

But Newman's egotism is true egotism too, and the reader cannot fail to notice that Newman thinks his "personal" ideas sufficiently important to warrant the reader's attention. Nor is this the least bit surprising, for the *Grammar* was written by the author of the *Apologia Pro*

23 Ker, "Newman on Truth," 67-68.
24 Contrast Pailin, *Way to Faith*, 193; Elbert, *Evolution*, 11.
25 O'Donoghue, "Privileged Access," 250.

Vita Sua and various other autobiographical studies. All of us are to some extent self-conscious, but few men have made such a parade of their self-absorption as Newman. Interestingly enough, Newman was not always convinced that egotism is true modesty, for as a young cleric he preached, "Surely it is our duty ever to look off ourselves, and to look unto Jesus, that is, to shun the contemplation of our feelings, emotions, frame and state of mind, as if that were the main business of religion, and to leave these mainly to be secured in their fruits."[26]

In any case, Newman is in trouble here, for he argues in the previous chapters that implicit reasoning is non-verbal and that it involves the cumulation of probabilities too fine to avail separately. Why, we must wonder, does Newman think it easier to verbalize in *these* "personal" matters than in others? Again Newman wants to have his cake and eat it: he wants to describe the evidence for Christianity so as to show that it is more reasonable to be a Christian than not to be; and yet, in the same work, he wants to persuade us that the evidence is too personal and too implicit to be vulnerable to critical analysis. Benard is right to emphasize that Newman is not declaring his apologetic to be *the* proof of Christianity but only the evidence that is personally convincing to Newman himself. Still, Newman would not have presented such evidence if he thought that it was flimsy and ridiculous, something for liberals and atheists to hold up as plain proof of the absurdity of the Catholic faith. Newman is fully aware of how much is at stake in chapter 10, and he observes that he is writing here "not without much anxiety, lest I should injure so large, momentous, and sacred a subject by a necessarily cursory treatment" (300).

"I have no scruple in beginning the review I shall take of Christianity by professing to consult for those only whose minds are properly prepared for it; and by being prepared, I mean to denote those who are imbued with the religious opinions and sentiments which I have identified with Natural Religion." Here Newman is not addressing himself to those whose opinions "characterize a civilized age," the liberals and intellectuals who say that all we know of God is through the laws of nature, or that miracles are impossible, or that prayer is a superstition. It is plainly absurd, he argues, "to attempt to prove a second proposition to those who do not admit the first" (323). Whom then is he endeavouring to convince? Is he simply preaching to the converted, reassuring them that their religious commitment is more reasonable than they have hitherto realized? I think not. He is also speaking to those who respect the evidences for *natural religion* but do not pay respectful attention to Christian revelation: half-hearted Christians, Jews, Moslems, and members of various cults. But

26 John Henry Newman, "Self-Contemplation," in *Parochial and Plain Sermons*, vol. 2, 163.

how "natural" can natural religion be if it does not characterize a large part of human society, including many philosophers and intellectuals? Newman cannot afford to ignore this large segment of society; he cannot afford to argue that it is made up of people who are simply "unprepared." And so he dismisses the opinions of such people as "simply false," as contradicting "the primary teachings of nature in the human race" (324). Newman anticipates an obvious criticism: "[N]o appeal will avail me, which is made to religions so notoriously immoral as those of paganism . . ." (325). Is it better to be "naturally" religious as a member of a pagan cult is than to be a civilized liberal with no interest in ecclesiastical religion? Not necessarily, Newman answers, for the pagan is immoral, and it is one thing to praise him and another to make use of his testimony. Newman insists that he is only doing the latter. "[N]o religion is from God, which contradicts our sense of right and wrong" (325). Yet, Newman has not proved that the opinions of liberals contradict "primary teachings of nature"; the most that he has shown is that over the centuries people have generally tended to be religious in some sense, and this is far from having shown that the civilized liberal is "unnatural" and holds false opinions.

Newman's next major move is to argue that Christianity is the only religion "which tends to fulfil the aspirations, needs, and foreshadowings of natural faith and devotion" (333). He begins this argument by asserting that an important effect of natural religion is the anticipation it creates that a revelation will be given (328). This empirical claim is not supported by Newman with empirical data, and many counterexamples come to mind. The fact is, as Newman well knows, many people consider themselves religious long after they have given up belief in the divine origin of the scriptures. As for members of primitive religious cults, they do not seem to be bothered by the "anticipation" of which Newman speaks; most of them seem to be quite content with their "natural" religion until sophisticated missionaries *convince* them that they *ought* to acknowledge that a revelation has been given. And history teaches us that the intelligent missionary, who refuses to use force or deception, does not always have an easy time persuading "savages" that the Bible is what they have always wanted.

But let us assume, for the sake of argument, that natural faith must somehow be fulfilled or completed. Why does Christianity do the job better than other religions? Newman insists that he is not biased, even though he has been educated in Christianity (333-34). He suggests that he is working with objective criteria in mind: "I have taken my idea of what a revelation must be, in good measure, from the actual religions of the world; and as to its ethics, the ideas with which I come to it are derived not simply from the Gospel, but prior to it from heathen moralists. . . ." These remarks imply that Newman considers himself a serious student of comparative religion. But his knowledge of non-Christian religions is remarkably limited, and even his remarks about Protestant denominations are often inaccurate.

The most important of the distinguishing features of Christianity, Newman tells us, is that "[i]t alone has a definite message addressed to all mankind. . . . Christianity [unlike Islam and the religions of the far East] . . . is in its idea an announcement, a preaching. . . ." It has actually been embraced by peoples of all races, classes, and under every degree of civilization. Though it has had reverses as well as successes, "it has had a grand history . . . and is as vigorous in its age as in its youth." It has a distinction in the world and a pre-eminence; "it has upon it *primâ facie* signs of divinity." No rival religion can "match prerogatives so special" (334). And though some oriental religions appear to be older, Christianity is the continuation of an earlier revelation, "which may be traced back into prehistoric times." And so it is based upon a "continuous and systematic" revelation in a way in which the religions of the East are not (335).

These arguments are, to say the least, sketchy. Newman's defenders will not apologize for their sketchiness; Newman, after all, regards his reasoning in this section as personal and implicit. Still, he is trying here to make the implicit somewhat explicit, and so he has given us something to criticize. Consider, then, some of the "special prerogatives" of Christianity that he thinks no rival religion can match. First, Christianity "alone has a definite message addressed to all mankind." It alone is catholic, universal. Other religions depend on "external circumstances" and reflect the race, time, place, and climate in which they arose. How seriously can such "probabilities" be taken? There are, of course, ideas and ideals in the New Testament that have universal significance and transcend the bounds of a particular culture. But similar ideas and ideals are embodied in the sacred books of other peoples, in the Torah, the Koran, the Bhagavad Gita. "When a man surrenders all desires that come to the heart and by the grace of God finds the joy of God, then his soul has indeed found peace."[27] Here is a statement that Newman can whole-heartedly endorse; yet it is from a sacred book that predates the New Testament by several centuries. It no more depends on "external circumstances" than does the Sermon on the Mount. Moreover, there is much in the Bible that does reflect the cultural background of its message.

Again, Christians are not the only religious believers who see their sacred books as having universal significance. Moslems have tradi-

27 *Bhagavad Gita*, trans. Juan Mascaró (Harmondsworth, England: Penguin Books, 1962), 53.

tionally sought expansion of their sacred community just as much as Christians have.[28] Jews can argue that their ideals are necessarily more universal than those of Christians, for while Jews reject most of the teachings of the New Testament, Christians profess their acceptance of the Jewish Bible as revelation. The Jews do not aggressively seek converts, while many Christian denominations feel obliged to vigorously disseminate their "good news." But here we have a different kind of universalism. The fact that Christians want everyone in the world to agree with them does not in itself suggest that Christianity is based on a genuine and exclusive revelation from God. On the contrary, it simply tells us something about Christians.[29] We should not be surprised that Christianity has been embraced by peoples of all races, classes, etc. Churches have sent out thousands upon thousands of missionaries to convert the heathens. Yet many of those who have been converted see their Christian belief and practice from their own personal and cultural perspective.

Newman's argument here runs perilously close to being conventionalistic. But surely there is not necessarily truth in numbers. The acceptability of slavery has been embraced by peoples of all races and classes. So has totalitarianism. The fact that a doctrine is widely accepted does not establish its truth. And in any case, a solitary figure can, with the help of a handful of disciples, educate the majority and successfully transform or overturn a society's values.

As for the "grand" history of Christianity, it involves reverses as well as successes. Feudalism, the Crusades, and the Inquisition are surely not *prima facie* signs of divinity. Many people who have condemned Newman's church have done so on the basis of Newman's criterion that no religion is from God that contradicts our sense of right and wrong. Finally, even Newman admits that in an important sense Christianity is not as vigorous in its age as it was in its youth. For Newman himself is continually attacking many modern tendencies in religion and is trying to *revive* the spirit of the early Christians.

Having dismissed Islam and the Eastern religions, Newman next directs his attention to the Jews. "What nation," he asks, "has so grand, so romantic, so terrible a history?" (337). The Jews are known as a people of progress, and their country may be called the classical home of the religious principle. Their dedication to theism is "a phenomenon singular and solitary in history, and must have a meaning." Clearly God and providence are at work here. We cannot dismiss Jewish talk about a divine mission as one more of many "pretences to a divine mission." For when all other peoples lapsed into polytheism,

28 C. Warren Hollister, *Medieval Europe: A Short History* (New York: John Wiley & Sons, 1964), 94.
29 Cf. Jay Newman, *Foundations of Religious Tolerance* (Toronto: University of Toronto Press, 1982), ch. 6.

this one people, the Jews, continued to profess, "as their distinguish-ing doctrine, the Divine Unity and Government of the world. . . ." And they are its witnesses, "even to torture and death." But the "last age of their history is as strange as their first." For when the time of destined blessing came, instead of favour coming on them from above, "they fell under the power of their enemies, and were overthrown, their holy city razed to the ground, their polity destroyed, and the remnant of their people cast off to wander far and away through every land except their own, as we find them at this day . . ." (335-36).

Why, Newman asks, when they were looking out for a deliverer, was all reversed for once and for all? Why is it that these people who were "the favoured servants of God" now have a peculiar reproach and note of infamy affixed to their name? Newman answers, "I have said they were in God's favour under a covenant,—perhaps they did not fulfil the conditions of it." That they sinned is corroborated by the chapter of Deuteronomy that "strikingly anticipates the nature of their punishment" (being "scattered throughout all the kingdoms of the earth," "having a fearful heart and languishing eyes and a soul consumed with heaviness," being destined to "suffer wrong," and so forth). Now contrast the condition of the Jews with that of the Chris-tians:

> It is an historical fact, that, at the very time that the Jews committed their unpardonable sin, whatever it was, and were driven out from their home to wander over the earth, their Christian brethren, born of the same stock . . . undertook the very work which, according to the promise, their nation actually was ordained to execute . . . . And since that time the two children of the promise have ever been found together—of the promise forfeited and the promise fulfilled; and whereas the Christian has been in high place, so the Jew has been degraded and despised . . . . Further, Christianity clears up the mystery which hangs over Judaism, account-ing fully for the punishment of the people, by specifying their sin, their heinous sin. If, instead of hailing their own Messiah, they crucified Him, then the strange scourge which has pursued them after the deed, and the energetic wording of the curse before it, are explained by the very strangeness of their guilt. (339-40)

And so we have here, according to Newman, a phenomenon of "cumulative marvels." But what we really have here is some terrible reasoning combined with a classic statement of what has come to be known as "theological anti-Semitism." Newman begins his argument by asserting that the country of the Jews is the classical home of the religious principle, and that the Jews' dedication to theism is a singu-lar and solitary phenomenon that must have a meaning. However, Judaism did not emerge from a vacuum; it incorporated many doc-trines and practices of other ancient religions. The Jewish world-view underwent considerable development in ancient times, and in more recent times it has continued to undergo development. (Newman does not acknowledge the latter fact, for he regards Judaism as a dead religion.) As for Jewish dedication to theism, it is not as remarkable as Newman claims. The Torah itself portrays the children of Israel as a "stiff-necked" people who, even after having been taken out of bondage in Egypt, still lapsed into idol-worship. It is not so obvious that Jewish civilization necessarily involves providence. Still, it is only when Newman discusses the tragic "fate" of the Jewish people that his argument actually turns ugly. Here Newman argues that the suffering of the Jews is an indication that they are an accursed people who have been punished for having crucified their own Messiah instead of hailing him and fulfilling the conditions of the covenant. And since the Christian has been in high place while the Jew has been degraded and despised, we may "informally" infer that Christianity is the true religion.

It is passages like these, so often neglected by Newman's admirers, that led Kingsley to compare Newman to the sophists of old. Let us begin by observing that the modern history of the Jews has not been an uninterrupted string of disasters. In some societies, like our own, the Jews have flourished—spiritually, culturally, economically—in spite of the obstacles placed in their path. It was only after the advent of Christianity that the Jews had the written Talmud, the writings of Ibn Ezra and Maimonides, the Chasidic movement, and so forth. We no longer find them wandering "far and away through every land except their own." And I dare say that the Jews, having produced some of our greatest modern leaders—intellectual, artistic, political—are in educated circles much less despised than the superstitious and bigoted Catholic peasants that Newman regards so highly. But consider Newman's question: Why have these people who were the favoured servants of God so often been condemned and persecuted? The only answer that Newman can think of is that they are being punished by God. But Edward Synan provides a more reasonable answer.

> Europe dominated by the papacy, it can be argued, knew neither equality nor justice; medieval legislation was as savage in its intentions as in its penalties, and the brunt of these fell upon the helpless Jewish population. The medieval Jew went in fear of mob violence, a threat often tolerated and, at times, incited by the authorities responsible for public order.... The Church was not ashamed to make use of disinguous devices to allure converts; she was ready to reward the apostate from the faith of Israel, to threaten the steadfast, to force the attendance of simple Jewish believers at conversionist sermons.[30]

Is it God or the gentiles that have persecuted the Jews? Even those who see the church as an instrument of God's will do occasionally complain about its traditional conception, portrayal, and treatment of the

---

30 Edward A. Synan, *The Popes and the Jews in the Middle Ages* (New York: Macmillan, 1965), 1.

Jews. And modern anti-Semitism is largely a legacy that has been passed on from St. Paul to the medievals to the Newmans and on to the many people who, as Synan observes, do not "reach the standard set by Pope John XXIII," as even "in some rectories, kinship according to the flesh with the Nazarene all Christians call their Lord does not count necessarily as a patent of nobility."[31]

But Newman is not consistent, and in the *Grammar* we find the bizarre juxtaposition of his "Jew" argument with his "martyrs" argument. In the "Jew" argument, Newman counts as an evidence of Christianity the "fact" that the Christian has been in high place while the Jew has been degraded. Yet Newman is obsessed with the suffering and sacrifices of Christian martyrs. He gives us numerous examples of the "ardent spirit" and "of the living faith on which it was founded." He tells us about Barulas, a child of seven, who was "scourged to blood for repeating his catechism before the heathen judge." He describes a girl under eighteen who, after asking the prayers of some Christian prisoners, "was seized at once, and her sides torn upon with the iron rakes" (373). He tells us of the "memorable persecution" of Blandina, who was "placed in the notorious red-hot chair" and "exposed in a net to a wild bull" (371-72). And so on (361-75). The suffering that these Christian martyrs underwent— and were willing to undergo—must be regarded, Newman feels, as one of the "probabilities" that, when combined with others, points to the truth of Christianity. The Jews, who only a few pages earlier Newman described as witnesses "even to torture and death," are simply being *punished*. What about Barulas and Blandina? Are *they* being punished? No, Newman assures us; *they* will get their *reward*, later. Newman was so interested in Jews and martyrs that he even wrote poems about them. In his 1833 poem "Judaism" (a "Tragic Chorus"), Newman talks about the piteous race, fearful to look upon, unvenerable, polluted in its kin. Newman's advice to the Jews is straightforward: "Come to our fonts, your lustre to regain."[32] Contrast the miserable Jews with the martyr convert he describes in an 1856 hymn:

> Forth from the heathen ranks she stept,
> The forfeit crown to claim
> Of Christian souls who had not kept
> Their birthright and their name.

....

31 Ibid., 3. Cf. Paul E. Grosser and Edwin G. Halperin, *Anti-Semitism: The Causes and Effects of a Prejudice* (Secaucus, New Jersey: Citadel Press, 1979 [1976]); Raul Hilberg, *The Destruction of the European Jews* (Chicago: Quadrangle Books, 1961), 1-17.
32 John Henry Newman, "Judaism (*A Tragic Chorus*)," in *Verses on Various Occasions*, 192-94.

And running, in a little hour,
Of life the course complete,
She reach'd the Throne of endless power,
And sits at Jesu' feet.[33]

Is it not possible that when she reached "the Throne of endless power," she encountered non-Catholics and maybe even Jews?[34] Whenever I read this particular section of the *Grammar*, I think of Spinoza's letter to another convert to Catholicism, Albert Burgh. "[N]ot only have you become a member of the Roman Church," Spinoza writes, but "you are a very keen champion of it and have already learned to curse and rage petulantly against your opponents." After refusing to recount the vices of priests and popes, he writes:

> But you who presume that you have at last found the best religion, or rather the best men, to whom you have given over your credulity, *how do you know that they are the best among all those who have taught other religions, or are teaching them now, or will teach them in the future? Have you examined all those religions, both ancient and modern, which are taught here and in India and everywhere throughout the world?* For you can give no reason for your faith. But you will say that you assent to the inward testimony of the Spirit of God, while the others are cheated and misled by the Prince of evil Spirits. But all those outside the Roman Church make the same claims with the same right for their Churches as you do for yours.
>
> As to what you add about the common consent of myriads of men, and of the uninterrupted succession of the Church, etc., this is the same old song of the Pharisees. For these also, with no less confidence than the adherents of the Roman Church, produce their myriads of witnesses . . . . They trace their lineage to Adam. They boast with equal arrogance that their Church maintains its growth, stability, and solidity to this very day, in spite of the hostility of the Heathen and the Christians. . . . But what they chiefly pride themselves on is that they number far more martyrs than any other nation and daily increase the number of those who with extraordinary constancy of mind have suffered for the faith which they profess.[35]

Newman's arguments may seem dated; but many people still believe that these and similar arguments are sound and justify the believer's certitude regarding Christianity. Such arguments have been refuted over and over again, but since people refuse to let them die once and for all, it is necessary to reconsider them in every generation.

The key question in evaluating the last sections of chapter 10 is whether what Newman counts here as "probabilities" are respectable arguments. Sometimes Newman wants to hide behind his claim that the reasons that support the Catholic's religious conviction are too

33 John Henry Newman, "A Martyr Convert," ibid., 307-309.
34 Cf. Hollis, *World*, 171.
35 Letter, Spinoza to Burgh, December 1675, trans. A. Wolf, in *The Correspondence of Spinoza* (London: George Allen and Unwin, 1928), 350-55.

delicate, intricate, fine, and subtle to be stated. But he sees that one cannot keep hiding behind this claim and at the same time be a convincing apologist. So he takes a stab at putting his personal, implicit reasons on paper. Still, even at the end he hedges: "Here I end my specimens, among the many which might be given, of the arguments adducible for Christianity." And he hedges further, telling us that Christianity is addressed to "minds which are in the normal condition of human nature" (379). It is hard to believe that Newman gives us a random selection of "specimens"; he must be giving the strongest of the "probabilities" that are personally convincing to him. And many people will conclude, after reading the last sections of the *Grammar*, that no matter how reasonable Newman thinks it is, his own personal commitment to Christianity, resting as it does on the unsatisfactory "probabilities" discussed in chapter 10, is *not* a reasonable commitment. Consider the irony: all along Newman has been trying to convince us that the faith of the simple Catholic believer may be more rational than the liberals contend, but he ends up drawing our attention to the fact that even the Catholic faith of a former Oxford don may rest on a shaky foundation.

There is method in Newman's madness. Newman believes that history is as legitimate an instrument as science is for deciding on the truth of a religion,[36] and the "probabilities" presented in chapter 10 are historical in character. Newman was no Hegelian, but he was a practising historian who had a great interest in the philosophy of history.[37] In chapter 10 of the *Grammar*, as in the *Essay on Development*, Newman is clearly moving in the direction of an "historical apologetics," an alternative to the traditional apologetics of the Thomists. Newman's interest in an historical apologetics reflects the nineteenth-century preoccupation with history as a form of experience and knowledge. And while Newman's preference for an historical apologetics has its roots in his personal fascination with historical writing and his distaste for philosophical rationalism, it puts him in the company of such secular thinkers as Droysen, Dilthey, Ortega y Gasset, Croce, and Collingwood, philosophers of culture and civilization. Preoccupation with historical experience and knowledge often deteriorates into historicistic relativism; but it also leads thinkers to look for pattern and meaning in history.[38] Like the historicists, Newman alternately moves in both directions: he embraces a relativistic position in discussing the assumptions of historians in chapter 9 (284-90), but he is interested in pattern and meaning in history in

36 Cf. Lash, *Newman on Development*, 23-27.
37 See Thomas Bokenkotter, *Cardinal Newman as an Historian* (Louvain: Publications Universitaires de Louvain, 1959).
38 Cf. Jay Newman, "Historicism and Perennialism," *Revue de l'Université d'Ottawa* 43 (1973), 264-70.

chapter 10. However, the analysis in chapter 10 is so heavy-handed, and so glaringly based on gratuitous assumptions, that it undermines rather than supports Newman's apologetical interests.

3 Models of illative judgment

Nevertheless, Gilson is right in observing that years after its first publication, the *Grammar* has "preserved intact its power of sugges-tion, its actuality and its fecundity as a method of investigation whose potentialities are far from being exhausted."[39] The *illative sense* is an interesting device, one worthy of philosophical and psychological investigation. Phenomenological investigation will no longer help here, since we are called upon to move beyond the analysis of con-sciousness. Newman had neither the tools nor the vision nor the interest needed for moving to the next stage of investigation. He lacked the tools because modern scientific psychology was only in its infancy. He lacked the vision both because there are limits to any one man's genius and because he was hampered by theological blinders. And he lacked the interest because he had an ax to grind, a vested interest in making illative judgment a mysterious and awe-inspiring phenomenon. Newman is clearly right in acknowledging that non-inferential, non-rational factors at some point enter into the reasoning process and combine with reasons in the ultimate determination of our beliefs. But instead of leaving the issue where Newman does, let us briefly consider some models of illative judgment.

A *A Gestalt model: D'Arcy*

The English Roman Catholic epistemologist, M. C. D'Arcy, has at-tempted to translate Newman's talk into a "different idiom." Accord-ing to D'Arcy, "[I]t is difficult to find a place for an illative sense or instinct in any convincing philosophical system, whereas there is a heap of evidence to be drawn from modern psychology, from observa-tion of the methods employed in the sciences, in historical investiga-tion, in the fine arts and from everyday experiences, which fits in with what I have called interpretation. . . ."[40] "Interpretation" involves the discernment of unity: "We always . . . behold an object, and an object which is more or less determinate. The detail may have ragged edges, but it never lacks some kind of unity; and this unity is reached not by inference, but by some interpretation, of the manifold in terms of its

39 Etienne Gilson, "Introduction" to John Henry Newman, *An Essay in Aid of a Grammar of Assent* (Garden City, New York: Image Books, Doubleday, 1955), 21.
40 D'Arcy, *Nature of Belief*, 201.

unity or a unity."[41] For example, in the case of a book, "while we have scamped the detail, we have understood the book, because we have understood the story as a whole and seen it in its unity";[42] and in being certain that Britain is an island, "we have a texture of infinite fineness, a unity, that is, of infinite complexity which explains our certitude."[43] So it is in the case of religious belief, where there is "an interpretation of the whole of experience":[44] "we perceive evidence of an infinite complex consistency by means of indirect reference in terms of unity."[45] "[A]ll our thoughts and efforts contain hidden in them an aspiration for the infinite. What is more, the defence of faith is based on its infinite consistency, and this brings us back to the argument given for natural beliefs which depended on an infinitely complex consistent whole of evidence given to us by indirect reference."[46]

Some Newman scholars approve of D'Arcy's "translation" and others do not.[47] It is worth noting, however, that D'Arcy is wrong to believe that his analysis is superior to Newman's in having helped to "restore the primacy of the intellect" and to dispense with a "*deus ex machina*, a strange faculty which is as authoritative and as unreal as Mrs. Harris."[48] The real value of D'Arcy's analysis is in its having drawn our attention to the relevance of the data of Gestalt psychology.[49]

B A pragmatic model: Schiller

A more interesting model is that of the humanistic pragmatists, William James and F. C. S. Schiller, who were familiar with Newman's work and whose philosophy of religion is occasionally compared with Newman's. This is a complex model, and we shall confine ourselves to a consideration of some of Schiller's views on the nature of religious belief. Schiller writes:

> "God," that is, if we really and honestly mean something by the term, must stand for something which has a real influence on human life. And in the ordinary religious consciousness "God" does in point of fact stand for something vital and valuable in this pragmatic way. In its most generalised form "God" probably stands for two connected principles. It

41 Ibid., 167-68.
42 Ibid., 170-71.
43 Ibid., 193-94.
44 Ibid., 296.
45 Ibid., 314.
46 Ibid., 310-11.
47 Contrast Flanagan, *Newman, Faith and the Believer*, 116-19, and Boekraad, *Conquest*, 143-44.
48 D'Arcy, *Nature of Belief*, 151.
49 Cf. Wolfgang Köhler, *Gestalt Psychology* (New York: Liveright, 1947).

means (a) a human *moral* principle of Help and Justice; and (b) an aid to the *intellectual* comprehension of the universe, sometimes supposed to amount to a complete solution of the world-problem. In the ordinary religious consciousness, however, these two (rightly) run together, and coalesce into the postulate of a Supreme Being, because no *intellectual* explanation of the world would seem satisfactory, if it did not also provide a *moral* explanation, and a response to human appeals.[50]

For Schiller, the personality of God is just one of many "theoretic truths," like identity and causation, that are "the children of postulation"; it is indispensable to a "satisfying" or "harmonious" account of mental organization because the world or experience is not satisfactorily explained in mechanical terms.[51] Schiller's view is to some extent voluntaristic: "The organism cannot help postulating, because it cannot help trying . . . , because it must act or die. . . . It therefore needs assumptions it can act on and live by, which will serve as means to the attainment of its ends. These assumptions it obtains by postulating them in the hope that they may prove tenable, and the axioms are thus the outcome of a Will-to-believe which has had its way, which has dared to postulate, and, as William James has so superbly shown, has been rewarded for its audacity by finding that the world granted what was demanded."[52] The "indispensable" postulate of the personality of God helps to free us from "the worst and most paralysing horror of the naturalistic view of life, the nightmare of an *indifferent* universe."[53] But in spite of his talk about a "Will-to-believe," Schiller's view is ultimately no more voluntaristic than Newman's, for according to Schiller, postulates arise from practical *needs*, not just *wants*. In defiance of any irrationalism, Schiller insists that the mechanistic view of the world is irrational and must be rejected for this reason. Belief in God is no more a matter of wishful thinking than believing in identity or causation.

Schiller follows James in going a step further. According to James, "If theological ideas prove to have a value for concrete life, they will be true, for pragmatism, in the sense of being good for so much."[54] James and Schiller see the process of verification as a matter of justification by appeal to value or use. For Schiller, pragmatism "awards to the ethical conception of *Good* supreme authority over the logical conception of *True* and the metaphysical conception of *Real*. The Good becomes a determinant both of the True and of the Real, and

50 F. C. S. Schiller, "Absolutism and Religion," in *Studies in Humanism* (London: Macmillan, 1907), 285-86.
51 F. C. S. Schiller, "Axioms as Postulates," in *Personal Idealism*, ed. Henry Sturt (London: Macmillan, 1902), 121.
52 Ibid., 91.
53 F. C. S. Schiller, "The Ethical Basis of Metaphysics," in *Humanism* (London: Macmillan, 1903), 13.
54 William James, *Pragmatism* (New York: Longmans, Green, 1907), 46.

their secret inspiration."[55] In this way, Schiller is able to put religious beliefs and ordinary empirical beliefs on the same epistemological level.

Newman cannot endorse all of these radical epistemological claims, and he cannot accept Schiller's conception of "faith" as "a belief in a 'verification' yet to come."[56] Schiller feels, however, that Newman's *illative sense* has important explanatory value, and he correctly observes that much in humanistic pragmatism is a wider application of principles that Newman has already applied in the philosophy of religion.[57] You will recall how Lash criticizes Pailin for arguing that Newman bridges the gap between inference and certitude with an act of the will rather than an act of the intellect. While this criticism is fair up to a point, two considerations should be kept in mind. First, Newman does attach great importance to "moral causes" or "moral motives" as factors in the ultimate determination of belief. "[S]ometimes our mind changes so quickly, so unaccountably, so disproportionately to any tangible arguments to which the change can be referred, and with such abiding recognition of the force of the old arguments, as to suggest the suspicion that moral causes, arising out of our condition, age, company, occupations, fortunes, are at the bottom" (142). Newman sees at least some of these moral causes as related to the will: "A man convinced against his will / Is of the same opinion still" (143). I suggested earlier that this position has deterministic implications that Newman did not fully realize; but in any case, the notion of the "will" with which Newman is working here has much in common with the pragmatist's "Will-to-believe," and not the least because it is associated with *implicit needs* more than conscious desires. And this brings us to the second consideration that should be kept in mind. Like the pragmatists, Newman sees the will and intellect as *cooperating* to provide us with the beliefs necessary for a life of action. Neither Newman nor Schiller is a pure voluntarist; both philosophers acknowledge the importance of inference and reasoning. But for both, intellectual needs are to be seen as partly determined by moral, emotional, and spiritual needs. Newman and Schiller both believe that somewhere in the process of judgment, "moral" considerations must be weighed, consciously or unconsciously; and the reconciliation of them with "impersonal" factors may be the psychological mechanism by which the mind is enabled to move from a conclusion to a belief, or from weak belief to strong belief. In this model, the illative sense can be seen as either reconciling the factors, or recognizing that they have been sufficiently reconciled, or both.

---

55 Schiller, "The Ethical Basis of Metaphysics," 8-9.
56 F. C. S. Schiller, "Faith, Reason, and Religion," in *Studies in Humanism*, 357.
57 Ibid., 352-53.

C A fictionalist model: Vaihinger

A model that Newman would have found even less congenial is the fictionalism or "philosophy of 'As if'" of Hans Vaihinger. Fictionalism is often seen as a variety of pragmatism, but as Vaihinger points out, it differs from pragmatism in a fundamental way:

> Fictionalism does not admit the principle of Pragmatism which runs: "An idea which is found to be useful in practice proves thereby that it is also true in theory, and the fruitful is thus always true." The principle of Fictionalism, on the other hand, or rather the outcome of Fictionalism, is as follows: "An ideal whose theoretical untruth or incorrectness, and therewith its falsity, is admitted, is not for that reason practically value-less and useless; for such an idea, in spite of its theoretical nullity may have great practical importance.[58]

Newman, of course, would not have accepted Vaihinger's view that religious beliefs, though useful enough to be "accepted" in some sense, are false. However, what interests us here is the extent to which Vaihinger has offered a model of illative judgment; and most interesting is his view that coming to believe involves a blending of rational and "voluntary" elements:

> § Philosophical analysis leads eventually, from an epistemological standpoint, to sensational contents, and from a psychological to sensations, feelings and strivings or actions.

> § Ideas, judgements and conclusions, that is to say thought, act as a means in the service of the Will to Live and dominate. Thought is originally only a means in the struggle for existence and to this extent only a biological function.

> § [The] Preponderance of the Means over the End has also taken place in thought, which in the course of time has gradually lost sight of its original practical purpose and is finally practised for its own sake as theoretical thought.

> § [A]ll thought-processes and thought constructs appear a priori to be not essentially rationalistic, but biological phenomena.

> § In this light many thought-processes and thought-constructs appear to be consciously false assumptions, which either contradict reality or are even contradictory in themselves, but which are intentionally thus formed in order to overcome difficulties of thought by this artificial deviation and reach the goal of thought by roundabout ways and by-paths. These artificial thought-constructs are called Scientific Fictions, and distinguished as conscious creations by their "As if" character.

58 Hans Vaihinger, The Philosophy of "As if," trans. C. K. Ogden (from the 6th German ed.) 2nd ed. (London: Routledge & Kegan Paul, 1935), viii. This translation contains special material that does not appear in the original German edition.

§ The "As if" world, which is formed in this manner, the world of the "unreal" is just as important as the world of the so-called real or actual (in the ordinary sense of the word); indeed it is far more important for ethics and aesthetics.[59]

This complicated model of how people come to believe is noteworthy here for two reasons. First, while Vaihinger follows Newman and Schiller in attaching great importance to the role of the "will" or non-rational factors in the determination of belief, he regards coming to believe as a biological phenomenon that can be understood and analyzed in purely scientific terms. Second, Vaihinger limits the process's epistemological significance: he insists that to a great extent we have to believe what is *false*. While Vaihinger seems to be as antipathetic to rationalism as Newman and Schiller are, he does not give non-rational factors any role in the determination of *truth* or *knowledge*. In this model, illative judgment is a matter of *weighing* narrow epistemological or theoretical demands *against* more basic practical or biological ones in the determination of our beliefs.

D *A psychoanalytical model: Freud*

We come now to the most interesting model, one that would have deeply disturbed Newman. Newman feels it is safe to emphasize the "implicit" or "unconscious" dimension of judgment only because he naïvely assumes that the unconscious is wholly incomprehensible and unanalyzable. When he says, for example, that the illative sense detects first principles in their "obscure recesses" (282), he does so in order to convince us that judgment is ultimately too mysterious to be subject to the impersonal criticism of the tough-minded scientific rationalist. Little does Newman realize that his talk about the unconscious opens up a pandora's box of troubles for the apologist.

Thirty years after the publication of the *Grammar*, Sigmund Freud announced to the world: "The interpretation of dreams is the royal road to a knowledge of the unconscious activities of the mind."[60] We can hardly underestimate the influence that Freud's vision has had on twentieth-century thought; but what we sometimes forget is that scientific exploration of the unconscious was already quite advanced by the time Freud wrote *The Interpretation of Dreams*. An excellent survey of pre-Freudian contributions can be found in *The Discovery of the Unconscious* by Henri Ellenberger, who attaches special importance to intellectual developments in the final decades of the

59 Ibid., xlv-xlvii.
60 Sigmund Freud, *The Interpretation of Dreams*, trans. James Strachey, in *The Standard Edition of the Complete Psychological Works of Sigmund Freud*, vol. 5 (London: Hogarth Press, 1953 [1900]), 608.

nineteenth century, to the work of such thinkers as Nietzsche, Von Hartmann, Fechner, Chevreul, Richet, Janet, and Flournoy.[61]

Freud, however, is of special interest to us here, not so much because of his fame and influence, but because of his radical approach to religious belief in such works as *Totem and Taboo*, *The Future of an Illusion*, and *Moses and Monotheism*. The spirit of his reflections is made clear in this brief summary by Ellenberger:

> In 1907, Freud compared obsessive compulsive symptoms of neurotics with religious rituals and creeds, and concluded that religion was a universal obsessional neurosis, and obsession an individualized religion. Twenty years later, in *The Future of an Illusion*, Freud defined religion as an illusion inspired by infantile belief in the omnipotence of thought, a universal neurosis, a kind of narcotic that hampers the free exercise of intelligence, and something man will have to give up. Religiously minded psychoanalysts objected that Freud had overstepped the boundaries of psychoanalysis and was expressing his personal philosophical opinion; but Freud no doubt believed that psychoanalysis could unmask religion as it could any neurotic symptom.[62]

I find these views as strange, uncongenial, and unsatisfactory as Newman would have found them, and I have grave doubts about the whole enterprise of depth psychology. Nevertheless, I recognize that it is intellectually dishonest to ignore the importance of such work, both as research and as theory. And more to the point, I see a psychologist like Freud as offering us a model of illative judgment that is, if provocative and speculative, as worthy of being taken seriously as whatever Newman offers us. For as mysterious as Freud's view of religious belief may be, it is certainly no more mysterious than Newman's.

I suspect that if Newman had lived long enough to appreciate the implications of the work of the Nietzsches, the Freuds, and even the religiously minded depth psychologists (such as Adler and Jung), he would have had second thoughts about the role assigned to the "implicit" in the *Grammar*. He might even have ended up seeing explicit reason as the most powerful of religion's friends in a time of need.

E *A religious-mystical model: Newman?*

Throughout this analysis, I have repeatedly drawn your attention to Newman's view that illative judgment, particularly in religious matters, is *mysterious*. For a Roman Catholic believer like Newman, certain mysteries have a religious significance (cf. 55-60, 110-31),[63]

61 Henri Ellenberger, *The Discovery of the Unconscious* (New York: Basic Books, 1970), esp. ch. 5.

62 Ibid., 525.

63 Cf. Gabriel Marcel, "On the Ontological Mystery," in *The Philosophy of Existentialism*, trans. Manya Harari (New York: Philosophical Library, 1956 [1933]), 18-22.

and faith is one of them. For Newman, faith involves *grace*. In an early sermon, he writes, "For only reflect, what is faith itself but an acceptance of things unseen from the love of them, *beyond* the determinations of calculation and experience? Faith outstrips argument."[64] And in another, "*This*, then, is the plain reason why able, or again why learned men are so often defective Christians, because there is no necessary connexion between faith and ability; because faith is one thing and ability is another; because ability of mind is a *gift*, and faith is a *grace*."[65] In the *Grammar*, Newman carefully avoids emphasizing the relation of faith to grace, and with good reason: his main theme in this work is that faith is not necessarily irrational, and references to grace are only apt to divert the reader's attention. Still, even in the *Grammar*, Newman must leave room in his model for the role of grace. And this is all the more reason for him to make the illative sense seem mysterious. He reminds us again and again that the illative faculty is a "gift"; and implied in this talk may be the idea that in leading people to respond affirmatively to Christian revelation and the teachings of the Catholic church, illative judgment is a matter of grace. Newman is not too specific about this, and we can hardly blame him, for grace is genuinely mysterious, even if illative judgment is not.

As Schiller rightly observes, the religious person sees God as the ultimate explanatory principle. We must be careful, however, not to explain too many things by *direct* reference to God's agency, for when things once so explained have been shown to admit of a less mysterious explanation, God is diminished in the eyes of his people.[66]

---

64 John Henry Newman, "Subjection of the Reason and Feelings to the Revealed Word," in *Parochial and Plain Sermons*, vol. 6, 259.
65 John Henry Newman, "Truth hidden when not sought after," ibid., vol. 8, 188.
66 Cf. Numbers 20:12.

Chapter Seven

Mens ad Cor Loquitur

1 Why there is so little analytical criticism
of the *Grammar*

Much of the analysis in this study has been rather tedious, and all I can offer in the way of an apology is the observation that the analytical criticism of Newman's philosophical work is almost a thankless task. As we saw earlier, no less eminent a scholar than Frederick Copleston has declared that detailed criticism of particular points in Newman's philosophy "necessarily seems pedantic, and appears, to those who value Newman's general approach, as more or less irrelevant."[1] What joy can there be in exposing oneself as a pedant?

This is just the beginning of the philosophical critic's woes. Many of Newman's admirers cannot tolerate the slightest criticism of the master. Academics and ecclesiastics fall victim to idol-worship as easily as the devotees of charismatic politicians and show business personalities. Consider, for example, some of the cults that have sprung up in recent years around Wittgenstein, Heidegger, Popper, and Lonergan. But the Newmanists are in a class of their own. New-manists see their master as more than just a great thinker: they regard him as a spiritual giant, a saintly figure. They also see him as one of intellectual history's great victims, a tragic figure despised not only by ignorant, ruthless adversaries but by some of the very people whose cause he pleaded. To such enthusiasts, the modern philosoph-ical critic, no matter how sincere in his intentions, is upholding the ignoble tradition of Kingsley and Achilli, Manning and Talbot, Fair-bairn and Harper, Carlyle and the Stephens.

Most of the commentary on the *Grammar* has been written by enthusiasts, who have found it too painful to examine the *Grammar* critically and have generally regarded analytical criticism as "irrele-

1 Copleston, *History*, vol. 8, pt. 2, 288.

vant." But the book will not be fully appreciated until a substantial body of critical literature has developed.

And what about the non-enthusiasts? The *Grammar* is certainly a famous book, a classic. But while well known, it has rarely been known well. There have been numerous references to it in the philosophical literature. Here and there one finds a passing reference to this or that idea in the *Grammar*, and some passages in the book are frequently quoted. Occasionally one even finds a non-enthusiast commenting on the *Grammar*'s "interesting," "unusual," or "suggestive" approach. But Newman's philosophical critic cannot expect much of a hearing from most non-enthusiasts; interest in the *Grammar* is not that great. Newman is not one of the great philosophers, and his philosophical works neither deserve nor receive the same degree of attention as those of Plato, Spinoza, Hume, and Nietzsche. The *Grammar* probably deserves more attention than it gets, but the same can be said for many philosophical works.

The neglect of the *Grammar* is probably partly a result of the mild anti-Catholic sentiment that pervades much of the non-Catholic philosophical community. And given Newman's many rude remarks about liberals and other non-Catholics, we can understand why most non-Catholic readers find the *Grammar* a particularly uncongenial work. Moreover, the modern philosophical reader is apt to be easily discouraged by the book's peculiar style. A writer of Newman's age observes that "Newman gives us colossal fragments, but he does not usually construct a finished edifice."[2] Though the *Grammar* is perhaps Newman's most systematic work, its organization is not always apparent on a first reading. With its host of examples, its theological asides, and its rhetoric and preaching, it can scare away the philosopher who is accustomed to studying the texts of an Aquinas, Hume, Husserl, or Wittgenstein.

Even most Catholic philosophers have little interest in Newman's mental philosophy. Many of them admire Newman as a defender of the faith, a great Catholic writer, an innovative theologian, and a defender of liberal education. But few of them see any point in examining the *Grammar* closely. In spite of Gilson's generous appraisal of the book, few neo-Thomists consider it a serious philosophical work, and some regard it as an outright embarrassment. An earlier group of Catholic philosophers, the semi-apostate modernist school of Loisy and Tyrrell, whole-heartedly embraced the *Grammar*, and by doing so, almost bestowed the kiss of death upon it. Even after all these years, conservative Catholic philosophers have the lingering suspicion that the *Grammar* is not quite orthodox; and as we have seen, their suspicion is not wholly unjustified. No wonder then that

---

2 Richard Simpson in *The Rambler* (December 1858). Cf. Norris, *Method*, 23.

many a modern philosopher-priest would simply rather not know what doctrines the book contains. As for more adventurous Catholic thinkers, they prefer to find their inspiration in the works of such alien sages as Whitehead and Heidegger, perhaps partly because they do not want to appear narrow and provincial to their non-Catholic colleagues.[3]

There has always been *some* serious philosophical criticism of the *Grammar*, from Harper and Fairbairn in Newman's day, to H. H. Price, John Hick, and David Pailin in our own. Such critics have recognized that while Newman is not a full-fledged philosopher, the *Grammar* has genuine philosophical content; and it is precisely because the book has such content that it merits genuine philosophical criticism. Here the *Grammar* has not been served well by the most zealous of its self-proclaimed "defenders": in their negative response to philosophical criticisms of the book, they have forgotten that if philosophical ideas are worth considering at all, then they are worth considering critically and analytically. Copleston may well be right when he says that those who value Newman's general approach are apt to regard detailed criticism of the *Grammar*'s particular points as "irrelevant." Nevertheless, there are also open-minded readers of the *Grammar* who are waiting to be convinced, one way or the other, with regard to both the value of the book's general approach and the plausibility of its particular points. Furthermore, valuing Newman's general approach does not require one to ignore his philosophical mistakes.

If my analysis in the foregoing chapters has been a reasonably accurate one, then most of the major theses in the *Grammar* are false, and most of its major arguments are unsound. But Newman's philosophical mistakes, like those of greater philosophical minds, can often be quite illuminating. Few contemporary philosophers can endorse the principal claims of a Descartes, Leibniz, Hegel, or Nietzsche; yet they keep returning to the work of such philosophers, for it is food for thought, an impetus to reflection. The *Grammar* too gives us a great deal to reflect upon, and that alone would justify its fame.

So there is no good reason why we should not treat the *Grammar* as we would treat any other well-known work of philosophy; if we read it carefully and critically, we should be able to attain the same kind of insight that we get when we examine a more conventional philosophical work. We shall not always find insight *in* the text; but insight should follow upon our studious examination of the text. So it is with philosophical inquiry in general: what is at stake is primarily intellectual, a matter of understanding. If one refuses to take the *Grammar* seriously as a contribution to philosophy, if one refuses to reflect

---

3 Cf. Jay Newman, "The Teaching of Philosophy in Catholic Colleges," *Teaching Philosophy* 3 (1980), 271-81.

critically on the philosophical issues it raises, then whether one's view of Newman's personality is positive or negative, one will miss out on new insights into whether belief is unconditional or some inference is non-verbal or most certitude is warranted.

However, philosophical inquiry is not only an intellectual activity but a practical one too. We read books of philosophy partly because we want better ideas about how to *live*. One of the virtues of the *Grammar* is that it constantly reminds us of the relation of belief to action. The controversy into which the *Grammar* enters is a practical one as well as an intellectual one, and so it is to practical considerations that we now turn.

2 What is at stake here?

The author of the *Grammar* clearly has more on his mind than "theoretical puzzles"[4]; his aim is to promote virtue as well as wisdom, and he associates both with religion. All of Newman's works—historical, theological, poetical, philosophical, and educational—have the words "Christian apologetics" written all over them in capital letters. Newman is first and foremost a religious apologist, and the religion that he is defending in his mature works is his own brand of traditional Catholicism. All of his works aim at inspiring in us a more positive view of religious belief and practice, and he sees his mission as an urgent one. We have to remember that Newman wrote at a time when recent intellectual developments had left conservative Christian theologians in a state of shock and dismay. Newman's era is that of Comte, Darwin, Marx, Bentham, and the Tübingen school of biblical criticism. Many Christian intellectuals of that time saw ecclesiastical Christianity as fighting for its life. If Newman could have shown in the *Grammar* that religious commitment is "personal" without being irrational, he would have made it invulnerable to "impersonal," scientific criticism. At an earlier stage in the history of Christianity, apologists found it prudent to appeal to the authority of reason, logic, and science: the medieval Schoolmen were the greatest scientific thinkers of their era. But by Newman's time, things had changed dramatically; reason, logic, and science had come to be seen more and more as threats to traditional religion. Newman was one of many nineteenth-century religionists who recognized the need for a fresh, new type of apologetics. He saw clearly that old-fashioned apologetics could no longer cope with the furious onslaught of positivism, materialism, and liberalism.

4 Copleston, *History*, vol. 8, pt. 2, 270.

On the surface, at least, it would seem then that what is ultimately at stake in the Grammar is whether traditional religion is reasonable and justifiable in the modern world. There are many different apologetical maneuvers in the book, appeals to conscience, to history, to ordinary language, to testimony. Behind them lies a grand design, the invocation of *personal reason*. We have seen, however, that most of the apologetical moves fail, and that some even backfire. Of greater importance, the grand apologetical strategy is itself a double-edged sword. Newman is short-sighted, for whatever value radical subjectivism has as a temporary shield against scientific criticism of traditional religion, it is hardly compatible with the absolutism that distinguishes traditional religion from the watered-down varieties of religion against which Newman is constantly railing. If the *illative sense* protects the pious Catholic factory-girl from the tough-minded liberal, why should it not also protect the tolerant, progressive liberal from the bigoted Catholic reactionary?

The Grammar as a whole is denominationally biased, but the same cannot be said of the theory of illative judgment. The illative sense is gloriously impartial, leading people equally to Christianity and Islam, positivism and humanism, liberalism and conservatism, wisdom and ignorance. The theory of illative judgment no more *supports* Christianity—or religion—than it does any other system of beliefs or practices. Newman himself argues that the illative sense (or the group of faculties that it represents) operates in many secular domains. Most of the examples in the Grammar are secular: Newman wants us to see how similar religious reasoning is to less controversial kinds of reasoning. Whatever its apologetical value, the *illative sense* is a device that has unlimited applicability. It justifies everything and nothing.

And so in the last analysis, much more is at stake in the Grammar than the reasonableness of religion, Christian or otherwise: what is ultimately at stake here is the reasonableness of *reason itself*. I am reminded of Schiller's memorable comment that pragmatism "vindicates the rationality of Irrationalism, without itself becoming irrational."[5] And I am also reminded once again of Kingsley's comparison of Newman with the most radical of all subjectivists: "Like the sophists of old, he has used reason to destroy reason."

Nor is Newman's "rational irrationalism" all that unusual. The most vigorous defenders of irrationalism and subjectivism have always been reflective men, philosophers, "thinkers." The history of ideas is strewn with their names: Protagoras, Peter Damiani, Pascal, Rousseau, Unamuno, for example. With Kierkegaard and Nietzsche, Newman is one of the *epigoni* of romanticism and one of the forerunners of existentialism. "Quarry the granite rock with razors, or moor

5 Schiller, "The Ethical Basis of Metaphysics," 6.

the vessel with a thread of silk; then may you hope with such keen and delicate instruments as human knowledge and human reason to contend against those giants, the passion and the pride of man."[6] "After all, man is *not* a reasoning animal; he is a seeing, feeling, contemplating, acting animal" (90). Has any writer in any language sounded this note more clearly or more poignantly?

And yet, not all detractors of reason have shared Newman's predilection for Roman Catholicism. Kierkegaard began and ended up with some sort of Protestant outlook. Nietzsche was an enemy of all religion. More than a handful of existentialists have flirted with fascism, Nazism, and similar forms of barbarism. (Indeed, many a detractor of reason has associated Catholicism with dry Scholastic rationalism.) The same variation can be observed among less reflective irrationalists, a class that includes kindly peasants, vicious peasants, saints, sinners, lovers, haters, Grand Inquisitors, and Nazi storm troopers who "think" with their "blood."

We can agree with Newman that some forms of rationalism are sterile, artificial, or dangerous. Man is not *just* a reasoning animal. Nor are our passions, desires, dreams, and sentiments always to be despised. Often the flight from reason is wholly appropriate; and it is a good thing that we all have at least a touch of mysticism in us. The greatest of philosophical rationalists, such as Plato and Spinoza, have hardly underestimated the importance of the non-rational elements of personality. On the contrary, they constantly remind us of how hard it is to be rational, and how easy it is to succumb to domination by our emotions. It is precisely because rationality is hard-earned and no mere "gift" that people must be helped and encouraged to cultivate it. Newman, however, gives aid and comfort to those who refuse to do the demanding work of thinking in an orderly and intelligent way: he deprives true reason of its importance, and puts in its place a counterfeit article, an ostensibly mysterious and "personal" process. In Newman's model, the lazy, superstitious peasant may be more "rational" than the disciplined, dedicated scholar.

To what extent is the plight of peasants and factory-girls at stake here? Newman seems to see himself as the protector of the downtrodden. But is he? Let me say first that I myself have not the slightest desire to see the oppressed people of the world deprived of their peace of mind, of whatever little consolation is left open to them. And if my understanding of nineteenth-century liberalism is reasonably correct, then it was not the intention of Brougham, Peel, Bentham, and Mill to make peasants and factory-girls more miserable than they already were. Far from it: classical liberalism was largely an effort to ameliorate the living conditions of the poor; and it also promoted *freedom of*

6 Cf. Newman, *The Idea of a University*, 111.

thought, religious and otherwise. The classical liberals were not enemies of religion per se but of a certain kind of religion—intolerant, authoritarian, superstitious, callous, and reactionary. They wanted to see the peasants and factory-girls get their fair share of the fruits of civilization: material prosperity, leisure time, aesthetic experience, and above all, education and knowledge. And yet, at the same time, they vigorously defended freedom of religion, and insisted that people should not be prevented by force from believing what they wish, regardless of how absurd it is, as long as they do not harm others.[7]

Unlike the liberals—and unlike his fellow cardinal, Manning— Newman had little interest in the economic and educational advancement of the poor and oppressed. Newman always patronizes the peasants and factory-girls: he considers them quaint, charming, romantic specimens. How can we expect someone like Newman to be able to identify with the simple Catholic believer? We get a good insight into his social outlook when we consider his talk about the need to turn Roman Catholics into English "gentlemen."[8] Such talk betrays Newman's deep-rooted class-consciousness. Moreover, Newman's commitment to freedom of religion is only a shadow of the liberal's. However eager he is to protect the Catholic peasant's right to believe, he is just as eager to see non-Catholics deprived of their "illusions." As we have seen, Newman is very much a bigot, even by his own admission.

How can such a radical subjectivist end up as a bigot? Should not a belief in the "personal" nature of judgment incline one to tolerance? Newman, in fact, is no exception to the historical rule. The closer one moves towards subjectivism, the less confidence one has in the power of reason to resolve disagreements. The classic example of this is the sophistry of Thrasymachus and Callicles.[9] Having abandoned absolutism—metaphysical, epistemological, and ethical—such early sophists as Protagoras and Gorgias relied heavily on the power of rhetoric. Since reason cannot lead one to objective truth, they thought, the best way to get on in the world is to use slick rhetoric to persuade others to adopt one's personal views. But by the time of Thrasymachus and Callicles, the loss of confidence in reason had led sophists to believe that might makes right, that one should strive to attain the raw social power necessary for promoting one's personal interests, beliefs, and values. Subjectivism and relativism can lead to a dangerous form of dogmatism. Not only do they lead one to believe that one's judgments are invulnerable to criticism, but they can also

---

7 Cf. John Stuart Mill, On Liberty (London: Parker, 1859), ch. 2.
8 See A. Dwight Culler, The Imperial Intellect: A Study of Newman's Educational Ideal (New Haven: Yale University Press, 1955), 189-90, 228-29, 238-43.
9 Plato Republic 336-47; Gorgias 482-527.

lead one to accept the inevitability of force as a substitute for rational discourse in the resolution of disagreements. Of course, absolutists can be dogmatic too, as can rationalists. But that is another story; my only point here is that we should not expect the radical subjectivist to be any more tolerant than anyone else.

We see, then, that much of what the *Grammar* teaches is harmful as well as false. Still, many people have spoken of it, with deep affection, as a book that has brought considerable consolation to their lives. It is not hard to see why. For one thing, people are often too lazy to be rational, and Newman gives us an excuse for our idleness. Logic, he tells us, leaves people "jaded and wearied"; minds are "gorged and surfeited by the logical operation" (90). "Resolve to believe nothing, and you must prove your proofs and analyze your elements, sinking farther and farther, and finding 'in the lowest depth a lower deep,' till you come to the broad bosom of scepticism" (91). We all know what Newman means. Even the most rational of people often find themselves in the position of not wanting to explain why they believe what they do. Indeed, even the most rational of people want to hold on to certain beliefs that they do not have good grounds for holding. The *Grammar* is reassuring: it tells us that even in our intellectual torpor, we may be more rational than we realize. An analogy with morality is apposite. Even the kindest, saintliest people occasionally treat their fellow human beings shabbily and inconsiderately; and what a consolation it is for them to be reminded that they are only human, and to hear that their mischievous behaviour was not really so bad anyway.

Moreover, the tone of the *Grammar* is spiritual and uplifting. What a pleasant change it can be from the countless philosophy books that are cynical, pessimistic, materialistic, dehumanizing, and depressing. And it has an existential dimension as well. Newman is certainly no pedant. He never forgets how hard our lives can be and how great our psychic needs are. The author of the *Grammar* seems to take a detailed, active, and cordial interest in his reader's existential situation.[10] The *Grammar* is quintessential Newman: *cor ad cor loquitur*. Alas, the heart cannot always be allowed to have its way.

3 A final illustration

Though Newman misuses it, the idea of illative judgment is an interesting one. Indeed, as we have already observed, it is rather more interesting than Newman realizes. If illative judgment is not as mysterious as Newman thinks, it is mysterious enough in its own way, at least insofar as we have a long way to go before we shall fully under-

10 Bremond, *Mystery*, 323.

stand it. The same holds true for belief itself. There are aspects of belief that we do not yet understand, and perhaps there are some that we shall never be able to understand. Still, unlike Newman, we keep trying, and sometimes we are rewarded for our effort.

I have not offered a systematic theory of belief in this study. My aim here has been comparatively narrow, to provide an analytical philosophical criticism of the mental philosophy of John Henry Newman. In examining the *Grammar*, of course, I have contributed to the philosophical literature on belief; but I am not pretending to have provided anything in the way of a systematic, comprehensive approach to belief. Newman never intended to provide such a theory either. And perhaps he would have been surprised to learn that the *Grammar* is still one of the most famous of all works on the philosophy of belief.

I have briefly described some of the different kinds of data that give us a fuller understanding of illative judgment, data from Gestalt psychology, pragmatism, fictionalism, and psychoanalytic theory. I have only scratched the surface, partly because my own knowledge in this area is very limited. My knowledge in most areas is very limited, just as Newman's was, but no one has the right to assume that whatever lies beyond the limits of his own understanding is mysterious. The concept of mystery is too profound to be taken so lightly. Still, I am prepared to allow that belief is mysterious enough in its own way, and that philosophical and religious beliefs are more mysterious than most.

I want to tell a story now, part of which is fictional and most of which is not. (Which part is which is not important here.) The story begins with my arrival at a party on a humid summer evening. I have had a long and tiring day, much of which has been taken up with worrying about some financial, professional, and domestic problems. I am looking forward to a quiet, relaxing evening. But no sooner have I started sipping my pineapple juice when a belligerent young stranger engages me in conversation. "I hear that you're interested in religion," he says, "and frankly, I can't see how an intelligent person can take religion seriously any more." My spirits sag as I think to myself, "This is just what I didn't need tonight." After unsuccessfully trying to convert the conversation into light-weight chit-chat, I am subjected to a barrage of quotations from Feuerbach, Marx, Nietzsche, and Freud. After mumbling a few words about how religion is a matter of personal faith, I am met with the fair observation that people have had faith in everything from astrology to Nazism. And when I point out how religion seems to have had a generally positive influence on moral development, I am quickly reminded of how much misery religious intolerance has created.

Seeing no exit, and consoled by the knowledge that some of the best philosophizing has taken place at parties,[11] I rise to the challenge. With a confidence and eloquence that would bring joy to the hearts of my fellow academic philosophers, I produce a wide assortment of traditional arguments used to defend religious belief. I talk about the necessity of a first cause, design in nature, and religious experience; I confront the belligerent stranger with moral, pragmatic, historical, and anthropological considerations. The stranger is not impressed by the individual arguments, but he realizes now that the issues here are too complex to be resolved in a short conversation on a humid summer evening. He backs away, but before leaving takes one parting shot. "Tell me," he asks, "do you really find all of these silly arguments convincing?" I answer cautiously, *too* cautiously: "I suppose so . . . some of them, anyway . . . I think . . ." Suddenly realizing that I may have just blown the whole game, I cheat a bit. I start telling the stranger the kinds of things Newman tells us in the *Grammar* about informal inference and illative judgment. The stranger is puzzled, even somewhat impressed. "I'll have to think about all that," he says, and moves on.

Having returned to my pineapple juice, I am now joined by an attractive young woman. I think to myself that things are already getting better. She tells me that she is active in church work, and I speak briefly about my previous conversation. "Some people are so narrow-minded," she observes. She then immediately proceeds to proselytize, to urge me to join her religious sect, which, from the sound of it, is rather strange indeed. She subjects me to a barrage of quotations from scripture, from the leaders of her sect, and from books by "scientists" of whom I have never heard. I try to reason with her, but to no avail. She keeps talking, preaching, and gesturing; and she refuses to listen to a word that I say. The humidity is becoming unbearable, and I already have a splitting headache. I start telling this young woman about informal inference and illative judgment. Sizing up the situation, she concludes that I am too shrewd and too sinister to be saved.

I take a seat on a comfortable-looking sofa, and next to me is a quiet but sociable fellow, who exchanges small talk with me about the weather, the carpeting, and our hosts at the party. After about ten minutes, he tells me that he is going to take me into his confidence: he is a member of a neo-fascist terrorist organization that plans to take radical action against the communists, homosexuals, and atheists who control the government, the mass media, and the labour unions. "Ah," I think, "finally some comic relief." But this man is *serious*; he really believes these things about communists, the media, and so

11 Cf. Plato *Republic*; *Symposium*.

forth. He even presents me with "evidence." Not knowing what else to do, I try to reason with him, to show him how flimsy his arguments are. But he is not impressed and tells me that I am tragically naïve. Angry and disturbed, I complain to him that he is not making an effort to be rational. His response is unsettling; he tells me that I have a very narrow view of what being rational involves and that rationality is actually far more subtle and more "personal" than I realize. He then goes on to talk about something that sounds awfully similar to Newman's *illative judgment*. Distressed, I ask, "Have you been reading the *Grammar of Assent* lately?" But what does it matter? Nothing I say here will induce him to abandon his insane beliefs. The man is irrational, is he not? And yet it is a sobering thought that many perceptive minds have also been considered irrational.

So much for my story, which I hope serves to illustrate the use and abuse of the theory of illative judgment. The story presents us with a variety of beliefs: religious, political, epistemological, and phenomenological. All these beliefs, and the processes by which they are arrived at, are subject to a greater degree of analysis and evaluation than they have been given at the party. Of greater importance to us, they are subject to far more analysis and evaluation than Newman would have us believe. Such analysis can be purely rational, or logical, involving the presentation and assessment of *reasons*; or it can also include explanations like those of the pragmatist, fictionalist, psychoanalytical theorist, and so on. In either case, it could go far towards making the beliefs and processes in question seem considerably less mysterious to us. Nevertheless, any particular analysis would itself be subject to analysis and evaluation, and perhaps no "common measure" could compel the intellects of Newman, Mill, Schiller, and Freud to take the same estimate of it. It is precisely at the point when the most sophisticated analyses fail to elicit the endorsement of a broad spectrum of serious, hard-working inquirers that we are forced to concede to Newman that belief is, for the time being anyway, mysterious in its own way.

Index